NOOK HD

2nd Edition

the missing manual®

The book that should have been in the box·

Preston Gralla

O'REILLY®

Beijing | Cambridge | Farnham | Köln | Sebastopol | Tokyo

NOOK HD: The Missing Manual, Second Edition
By Preston Gralla

Copyright © 2013 Preston Gralla. All rights reserved.
Printed in the United States of America.

Published by O'Reilly Media, Inc., 1005 Gravenstein Highway North, Sebastopol, CA 95472.

O'Reilly books may be purchased for educational, business, or sales promotional use. Online editions are also available for most titles (safari.oreilly.com). For more information, contact our corporate/institutional sales department: 800.998.9938 or corporate@oreilly.com.

Executive Editor: Brian Sawyer	**Indexer:** Julie Hawks
Editor: Nan Barber	**Cover Designers:** Randy Comer, Karen
Production Editor: Kristen Borg	Montgomery, and Suzy Wiviott
Copyeditor: Carla Spoon	**Interior Designer:** Monica Kamsvaag,
Illustrations: Rob Romano and	Ron Bilodeau, and Peter Amirault
Rebecca Demarest	

March 2012:   First Edition (*NOOK Tablet: The Missing Manual*).
February 2013:   Second Edition.

Revision History for the 2nd Edition:

2013-02-01   First release
2013-03-22   Second release

See *http://oreilly.com/catalog/errata.csp?isbn=0636920028666* for release details.

The O'Reilly logo is a registered trademark of O'Reilly Media, Inc.
NOOK HD: The Missing Manual and related trade dress are trademarks of O'Reilly Media, Inc.

Many of the designations used by manufacturers and sellers to distinguish their products are claimed as trademarks. Where those designations appear in this book, and O'Reilly Media, Inc. was aware of a trademark claim, the designations have been printed in caps or initial caps. Adobe Photoshop™ is a registered trademark of Adobe Systems, Inc. in the United States and other countries. O'Reilly Media, Inc. is independent of Adobe Systems, Inc.

While every precaution has been taken in the preparation of this book, the publisher and author assume no responsibility for errors or omissions, or for damages resulting from the use of the information contained herein.

ISBN: 978-1-449-35953-9
[LSI]

Contents

The Missing Credits

About the Author

Preston Gralla (author) is the author of more than 40 books that have been translated into 20 languages, including *Samsung Galaxy SII: The Missing Manual*, *Droid X2: The Missing Manual*, *Droid 2: The Missing Manual*, *Big Book of Windows Hacks*, *Windows Vista in a Nutshell*, *How the Internet Works*, and *How Wireless Works*. He is a contributing editor to *Computerworld*, a founder and editor-in-chief of Case Study Forum, and was a founding editor and then editorial director of *PC/Computing*, executive editor for *CNet/ZDNet*, and the founding managing editor of *PC Week*.

He has written about technology for many national newspapers and magazines, including *USA Today*, *Los Angeles Times*, *Dallas Morning News* (for whom he wrote a technology column), *PC World*, and numerous others. As a widely recognized technology expert, he has made many television and radio appearances, including on the CBS Early Show, MSNBC, ABC World News Now, and National Public Radio. Under his editorship, *PC/Computing* was a finalist for General Excellence in the National Magazine Awards. He has also won the "Best Feature in a Computing Publication" award from the Computer Press Association.

Gralla is also the recipient of a 2010–2011 Fiction Fellowship from the Massachusetts Cultural Council. He lives in Cambridge, Massachusetts, with his wife (his two children have flown the coop). He welcomes feedback about his books by email at *preston@gralla.com*.

About the Creative Team

Nan Barber (editor) has worked with the Missing Manual series since its inception—long enough to remember booting up her computer from a floppy disk. Email: *nanbarber@oreilly.com*.

Kristen Borg (production editor) is happily planning her summer wedding. Now living in Boston, she hails from Arizona and considers New England winters a fair trade for no longer finding scorpions in her hairdryer. Email: *kristen@oreilly.com*.

Julie Hawks (indexer) is an indexer for the Missing Manual series. She is currently pursuing a masters degree in Religious Studies while discovering the joys of warm winters in the Carolinas. Email: *juliehawks@gmail.com*.

Carla Spoon (proofreader) is a freelance writer and copy editor. An avid runner, she works and feeds her tech gadget addiction from her home office in the shadow of Mount Rainier. Email: *carla_spoon@comcast.net*.

Acknowledgements

Many thanks go to my editor Nan Barber, who not only patiently shepherded this book through the lengthy writing and publishing process, but provided valuable feedback and sharpened my prose. Thanks also go to Brian Sawyer, for making the introduction that ultimately led to this book.

I'd also like to thank all the other folks at O'Reilly who worked on this book, especially Kristen Borg and Peter Amirault for bringing the beautiful finished product to fruition, Matt Jorgenson and Carla Spoon for excising errors, and Julie Hawks for writing the index.

—Preston Gralla

The Missing Manual Series

Missing Manuals are witty, superbly written guides to computer products that don't come with printed manuals (which is just about all of them). Each book features a handcrafted index and cross-references to specific pages (not just chapters). Recent and upcoming titles include:

Access 2010: The Missing Manual by Matthew MacDonald

Access 2013: The Missing Manual by Matthew MacDonald

Adobe Edge Animate: The Missing Manual by Chris Grover

Buying a Home: The Missing Manual by Nancy Conner

Creating a Website: The Missing Manual, Third Edition by Matthew MacDonald

CSS3: The Missing Manual by David Sawyer McFarland

David Pogue's Digital Photography: The Missing Manual by David Pogue

Dreamweaver CS6: The Missing Manual by David Sawyer McFarland

Droid 2: The Missing Manual by Preston Gralla

Droid X2: The Missing Manual by Preston Gralla

Excel 2010: The Missing Manual by Matthew MacDonald

Excel 2013: The Missing Manual by Matthew MacDonald

FileMaker Pro 12: The Missing Manual by Susan Prosser and Stuart Gripman

Flash CS6: The Missing Manual by Chris Grover

Galaxy S II: The Missing Manual by Preston Gralla

Galaxy Tab: The Missing Manual by Preston Gralla

Google+: The Missing Manual by Kevin Purdy

HTML5: The Missing Manual by Matthew MacDonald

iMovie '11 & iDVD: The Missing Manual by David Pogue and Aaron Miller

iPad: The Missing Manual, Fifth Edition by J.D. Biersdorfer

iPhone: The Missing Manual, Fifth Edition by David Pogue

iPhone App Development: The Missing Manual by Craig Hockenberry

iPhoto '11: The Missing Manual by David Pogue and Lesa Snider

iPod: The Missing Manual, Tenth Edition by J.D. Biersdorfer and David Pogue

JavaScript & jQuery: The Missing Manual, Second Edition by David Sawyer McFarland

Kindle Fire HD: The Missing Manual by Peter Meyers

Living Green: The Missing Manual by Nancy Conner

Mac OS X Lion: The Missing Manual by David Pogue

Microsoft Project 2010: The Missing Manual by Bonnie Biafore

Microsoft Project 2013: The Missing Manual by Bonnie Biafore

Motorola Xoom: The Missing Manual by Preston Gralla

Netbooks: The Missing Manual by J.D. Biersdorfer

NOOK HD: The Missing Manual by Preston Gralla

Office 2010: The Missing Manual by Nancy Conner and Matthew MacDonald

Office 2011 for Macintosh: The Missing Manual by Chris Grover

Office 2013: The Missing Manual by Nancy Conner and Matthew MacDonald

OS X Mountain Lion: The Missing Manual by David Pogue

Personal Investing: The Missing Manual by Bonnie Biafore

Photoshop CS6: The Missing Manual by Lesa Snider

Photoshop Elements 11: The Missing Manual by Barbara Brundage

PHP & MySQL: The Missing Manual, Second Edition by Brett McLaughlin

QuickBooks 2012: The Missing Manual by Bonnie Biafore

QuickBooks 2013: The Missing Manual by Bonnie Biafore

Switching to the Mac: The Missing Manual, Lion Edition by David Pogue

Switching to the Mac: The Missing Manual, Mountain Lion Edition by David Pogue

Windows 7: The Missing Manual by David Pogue

Windows 8: The Missing Manual by David Pogue

WordPress: The Missing Manual by Matthew MacDonald

Your Body: The Missing Manual by Matthew MacDonald

Your Brain: The Missing Manual by Matthew MacDonald

Your Money: The Missing Manual by J.D. Roth

For a full list of all Missing Manuals in print, go to *www.missingmanuals.com/library.html*.

Introduction

WHAT GIVES YOU ACCESS to the world's greatest literature, today's best-sellers, tomorrow's up-and-coming authors, the world's top newspapers and magazines, TV shows and movies, great games, email, and more?

It's the NOOK HD and its larger cousin, the NOOK HD+—the two new models of combo ereader and Android tablet from bookseller Barnes & Noble.

This book will help you get the most out of your NOOK HD or HD+, and there's a lot you can get out of it, as you'll see. Whether you're looking just to get started or want to dig deep into the tablet's capabilities, this book's got you covered.

> **NOTE** This book covers the features available on the NOOK HD+ as well as the NOOK HD. When the HD+ differs in any significant way from the NOOK HD, we'll let you know.

About the NOOK HD and NOOK HD+

You likely already know that the NOOK HD and NOOK HD+ let you read thousands of books, magazines, and newspapers, as well as Microsoft Office documents and PDF files—and do all that in an elegant, easy-to-carry piece of hardware.

But that's just the beginning of what these amazing devices can do. Even though they pack plenty of power and have spectacular screens, they're smaller, more portable, and less expensive than many other tablets. They do just about everything that bulkier, costlier tablets can do.

Want to stream the latest movies and TV shows to it? You'll find the screen well suited for TV and movie watching, because it's crisp and clear with a high resolution. Movies and TV shows are often clearer and sharper on the NOOK's high-resolution screen even than on larger tablets.

There's a lot more to the NOOK HD and NOOK HD+ than reading and watching TV and movies. Want to browse to any website? Read and compose email? Keep track of all your contacts? It does all that as well.

How about playing Internet radio stations, playing games, sharing books with your friends, discussing books with others, borrowing books from the library?

Yep, it does all that and more. You can also download thousands of apps that do pretty much anything you want. The NOOK HD and NOOK HD+ are much more than just ereaders; they're also powerful, portable tablets. You don't want to wait to make use of all their amazing capabilities, though. That's where this book comes in—it will put you on the fast track to all the NOOK's magic.

Buying a NOOK

Before you can start using a NOOK HD or NOOK HD+, you (naturally) need to buy one. If you've got a Barnes & Noble store near you (and you probably do, considering how many there are), head for the NOOK section—pretty much all the stores have one, and the salespeople are more than happy to help you find it. You can hold NOOKs in your hands, try them out, and ask for advice about them. And once you do that, you'll most likely want to buy one.

As this book goes to press, the NOOK HD costs $199 or $229, depending on the amount of storage. The $199 version comes with 8 GB and the $229 version comes with 16 GB. The NOOK HD+ costs either $269 or $299. The $269 version comes with 16 GB of memory and the $299 version has 32 GB. Why the price difference? It's all about size. The HD+ comes with a 9-inch screen instead of the 7-incher on the HD. And to power that larger screen, it's got a faster processor—1.5 GHz versus the 1.3 GHz with the NOOK HD.

Those prices may change, though, so be on the lookout for the special deals that Barnes & Noble occasionally runs. Barnes & Noble is pushing the NOOK HD and NOOK HD+ heavily, so there's a chance you'll be able to find some kind of deal. Do a web search for terms like "NOOK deals" to see if any are available. Also make sure to head to *www.barnesandnoble.com* or *www.bn.com* on the Web, and then click the NOOK icon to see if there are any specials in effect.

TIP Barnes & Noble stores aren't the only retail outlets where you can buy a NOOK HD or a NOOK HD+—other stores have them as well. For example, many Best Buy stores also stock them.

If you're not near a Barnes & Noble store or other retail outlet that stocks NOOKs, or if you just prefer buying over the Internet, the *www.bn.com* website is a great place to buy. Shipping is typically free, so you won't pay extra for the convenience of buying online. And you can also buy at some other online outlets, such as *www.bestbuy.com*.

Finally, if you plan to use the NOOK outside your home, strongly consider buying a cover or case. A cover protects your NOOK and its screen from damage, so they're well worth the small investment. They typically range in price from $15 all the way up to $90 for designer-name leather ones. Some covers are great for commuters, because you can just flip open the top, start reading, and then flip the top down when you're done. You'll find a good selection at Barnes & Noble and other retailers.

What's New in the NOOK HD and NOOK HD+

With the NOOK HD and HD+, Barnes and Noble significantly improved the NOOK tablet, including hardware, software, and new services. Following are the most important highlights of what's new.

Better Hardware

The NOOK HD and HD+'s hardware marks an improvement over the NOOK Tablet's. The NOOK HD's 7-incher is clearer and brighter than the NOOK Tablet's, with a resolution of 1440 by 600 pixels, with 243 pixels per inch. It displays video at 720p. The NOOK HD+'s larger 9-inch screen is even more impressive: a 1920 by 1280 pixel resolution at 256 pixels per inch, and displays video at a full 1080 HD. Not sure what all this means? A better screen for reading, using apps, and watching video.

Under the hood there have been improvements as well. The NOOK HD now has a faster processor, a dual core 1.3 GHz (gigahertz), while the HD+ has a dual core 1.5 Ghz processor to power its larger screen. If you're not a spec maven, what all this means is that both devices are super-fast.

There have been a number of other minor hardware changes as well, including a 30-pin-to-USB cable that connects the NOOK HD and HD+ to PCs and to power outlets. The microSD slot has been relocated, and can now accept microSD card with more storage, up to 64 GB now.

Oh, and there's one cosmetic change as well. The NOOK HD, unlike the NOOK Tablet, doesn't have the small distinctive circular notch on its lower-left corner, although the HD+ still has it.

For more details about the new hardware, see Chapter 1.

Cleaner Home Screen and Overall Interface

The NOOK's home screen and interface have been cleaned-up and simplified, making it easier to use and find content to read, run, and play. The home screen, for example, is much less cluttered. No longer are there multiple layers of content and navigation. In the new NOOK interface, there are fewer navigation buttons and content layers, with notifications moved to the top of the screen. Overall, it's easier to find and use content. At the top of the screen is the Active Shelf—a scrolling list of books, publications, and apps, like a carousel. There's also a Recent Drawer with a list of books, apps, and other items you've recently opened. A row of icons at the bottom of the screen gives you instant access to your Library, apps, the Web, email, and the NOOK Shop. For more details, see Chapter 3.

You'll find other changes throughout the interface. The Library, for example, has been simplified, making it much easier to find books, videos and movies, apps, and other content. (For details, see Chapter 5.) And there's a revamped Quick Settings screen that makes it easier to make the NOOK work exactly the way you want it to.

Profiles

The new Profiles feature is a significant addition. You can create up to six differ-ent profiles for family members, including children's profiles. Each profile can be customized for a person's interests. A children's profile is controlled by a parent, who can limit access to the Web, apps, files, and so on. Each profile has its own its own content library, home screen of recently viewed content, and prefer-ences. There's a single payment source for all profiles, and so content from any profile can be shared with any other profile or all profiles. For more details about Profiles, see Chapter 4.

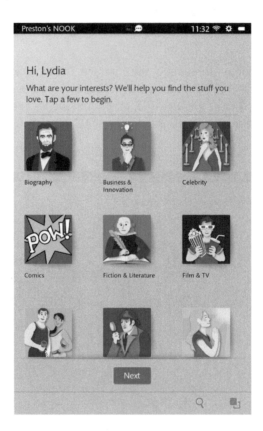

New Video Services

There's a reason the NOOK HD and HD+ both feature clear, vivid, high-resolution screens—there are now new video services your device can use. The new NOOK Video service lets you buy or rent videos from the NOOK Shop. You'll be able to stream them or download them straight to your device. In addition, the HD and HD+ also work with the cloud-based UltraViolet video service. With UltraViolet, if you buy a movie disc (in a retail store or online) that's part of UltraViolet, not only will you be able to play the movie with the disc, but you can also stream it from the UltraViolet cloud to any UltraViolet-compatible device, which means the NOOK or NOOK HD+. For details about the NOOK's new video services, see Chapter 9.

Better Web Browsing

Browsing the Web is much improved over the previous version of the NOOK. The NOOK HD and HD+ are built on top of version 4.0 of the Android operating system, known as Ice Cream Sandwich, and so the NOOK's browser is based on that. The NOOK now includes a tabbed interface for its web browsers, so you can easily browse to multiple sites simultaneously and switch between them. And you can now save entire web pages to your NOOK, in order to revisit them. For details, see Chapter 13.

Better Email

The email client has also been improved. It's now much easier to navigate among your mail folders (Inbox, Drafts, Sent, and so on). Reading messages is visually more appealing because of a cleaner layout, although the basic functionality remains the same. For details, see Chapter 14.

Scrapbooks

This new feature lets you save pages from books, magazines, and catalogs so you can later easily find and browse through them. See Chapter 5 for details.

About This Book

There's an entire world to explore in the NOOK HD and NOOK HD+, and the little leaflet that comes in the box doesn't begin to give you all the help, advice, and guidance you need. So this book is the manual that should have accompanied the NOOK HD and NOOK HD+. This book refers to the NOOK HD, or the NOOK generally, but that information also applies to the NOOK HD+. The book indicates those few instances in which the NOOK HD and NOOK HD+ work differently.

The brain running the NOOK HD and NOOK HD+ is a piece of software from Google called Android. Barnes & Noble then tweaked Android quite dramatically to turn it into an ereader and tablet. So the NOOK doesn't look like or work like other Android tablets you may have seen—but underneath it all, it's an Android.

There's a chance that since this book was written, there have been some changes to the NOOK HD and NOOK HD+. To help keep yourself up to date about them, head to this book's Errata/Changes page, at *http://oreil.ly/V6ZMAU.*

About the Outline

NOOK HD: The Missing Manual is divided into eight parts, each of which has several chapters:

- **Part One, The Basics,** covers everything you need to know about using the NOOK as an ereader and tablet. It gives you a guided tour of the hardware, shows you how to set up the NOOK so it works just the way you like, and then shows you how to use it for the first time. By the time you finish you'll be a pro.

- **Part Two, Reading Books and Periodicals,** shows you everything you need to know about reading using your NOOK. You'll become an instant expert at using all of its remarkable reading tools, including using bookmarks and notes, changing font and text size, and searching inside books and publications. And it also has an entire chapter devoted to kids' books, including how you can record your voice reading a book to your children.

- **Part Three, Managing Your Library,** covers how to buy books, newspapers, and magazines, and then track them in your own personal library. You'll learn how to find what you want to buy fast and get the lowdown about it, and then keep track of everything in a customizable library. And you'll also see how you can borrow books from friends, and lend to them as well—and how you can borrow books for free from the library.

- **Part Four, Apps, Media, and Files,** lets you take advantage of many of the NOOK's most remarkable features. You'll see how to find, download, install, and use thousands of apps, and get recommendations for some of the best ones on the planet. You'll also see how you can watch movies and TV shows, as well as listen to streaming Internet radio stations—or play your own music collection. Also included is how to transfer files to your NOOK, and how to use the NOOK's built-in music player.

- **Part Five, The Web and Email,** covers the NOOK as a great Internet device. You'll find out how to browse the Web and send and receive email using any email account.

- **Part Six, Getting Social,** shows you how to use the NOOK's many social features—sharing books, reviews, and recommendations with friends—and using the NOOK in concert with Facebook and Twitter. It shows how to use the NOOK to keep track of your contacts as well.

- **Part Seven, Advanced Topics,** shows you how to tweak the NOOK's features. It also reveals how to *root* your NOOK, which means changing its software to run like a standard Android tablet.

- **Part Eight, Appendixes,** has three reference chapters. *Appendix A, Maintenance and Troubleshooting,* offers plenty of help troubleshooting issues with the NOOK's operation, and a rundown of accessories you can use with it. *Appendix B, File Formats,* lists the file formats your NOOK can handle. *Appendix C, Visiting B&N with Your NOOK HD,* covers some nifty things you can do with your NOOK when you visit a Barnes & Noble store, like read books free for an hour.

About→These→Arrows

In this book and the entire Missing Manual series, you'll find instructions like this one: Tap Settings→Sounds→Mute. That's a shorthand way of giving longer instructions like this: "Tap the Settings button. On the screen that opens, tap Sounds. And from the screen that opens after that, tap the Mute option."

It's also used to make it easier to understand instructions you'll need to follow on your PC or Mac, such as File→Print.

About the Online Resources

As the owner of a Missing Manual, you've got more than just a book to read. Online, you'll find example files so you can get some hands-on experience, as well as tips, articles, and maybe even a video or two. You can also communicate with the Missing Manual team and tell us what you love (or hate) about the book. Head over to *www.missingmanuals.com*, or go directly to one of the following sections.

Missing CD

So you don't wear down your fingers typing long web addresses, the Missing CD page offers a list of clickable links to the websites mentioned in this book. Go to *http://missingmanuals.com/cds/nookHDmm* to see them all neatly listed in one place.

Registration

If you register this book at *www.oreilly.com*, you'll be eligible for special offers—like discounts on future editions of *NOOK HD: The Missing Manual*. Registering takes only a few clicks. To get started, type *www.oreilly.com/register* into your browser to hop directly to the Registration page.

Feedback

Got questions? Need more information? Fancy yourself a book reviewer? On our Feedback page, you can get expert answers to questions that come to you while reading, share your thoughts on this Missing Manual, and find groups for folks who share your interest in the NOOK. To have your say, go to *www.missingmanuals.com/feedback*.

Errata

In an effort to keep this book as up to date and accurate as possible, each time we print more copies, we'll make any confirmed corrections you've suggested. We also note such changes on the book's website, so you can mark important corrections into your own copy of the book, if you like. Go to *http://oreil.ly/V6ZMAU* to report an error and to view existing corrections.

Safari® Books Online

Safari® Books Online (*www.safaribooksonline.com*) is an on-demand digital library that delivers expert content in both book and video form from the world's leading authors in technology and business. Technology professionals, software developers, web designers, and business and creative professionals use Safari Books Online as their primary resource for research, problem solving, learning, and certification training.

Safari Books Online offers a range of product mixes and pricing programs for organizations, government agencies, and individuals. Subscribers have access to thousands of books, training videos, and prepublication manuscripts in one fully searchable database with publishers like O'Reilly Media, Prentice Hall Professional, Addison-Wesley Professional, Microsoft Press, Sams, Que, Peachpit Press, Focal Press, Cisco Press, John Wiley & Sons, Syngress, Morgan Kaufmann, IBM Redbooks, Packt, Adobe Press, FT Press, Apress, Manning, New Riders, McGraw-Hill, Jones and Bartlett, Course Technology, and dozens more. For more information about Safari Books Online, please visit us online.

With a subscription, you can read any page and watch any video from our library online. Read books on your cellphone and mobile devices. Access new titles before they're available for print, and get exclusive access to manuscripts in development and post feedback for the authors. Copy and paste code samples, organize your favorites, download chapters, bookmark key sections, create notes, print out pages, and benefit from tons of other time-saving features.

O'Reilly Media has uploaded this book to the Safari Books Online service. To have full digital access to this book and others on similar topics from O'Reilly and other publishers, sign up for free at *http://my.safaribooksonline.com*.

The Basics

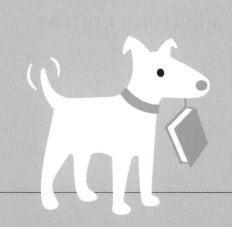

CHAPTER 1

Getting to Know Your NOOK HD

WELCOME TO THE NOOK HD, the easy-to-carry, do-everything device that lets you read books, newspapers, and magazines; watch TV and movies; listen to music; browse the Web; check your email; run countless apps...and that's just for starters. In this chapter, you'll find out everything it can do, and get a guided tour of the NOOK HD (and NOOK HD+) so you can get up and running quickly.

> **NOTE** This book covers the NOOK HD+ as well as the NOOK HD. When the NOOK HD+ differs in any significant way from the NOOK HD, we'll let you know.

What Your NOOK HD Can Do

To say that the NOOK HD is a do-everything device is not hyperbole. Take a gander at this list:

- **Read ebooks.** The NOOK HD has been designed from the ground up to be a great ereader. It's easy on the eyes, lets you carry thousands of books in its thin frame, and adds many reading extras, such as bookmarking, note taking, and more. It lets you get NOOK books from the world's largest bookstore—2.5 million titles and counting—with most under $10.

- **View multimedia inside books.** With a NOOK HD, books really come alive, because music and video can be embedded right in the book. (Try that with a paperback!) See a recipe you like, and want details about how to make it? A NOOK cookbook can contain videos showing you exactly what to do.

The Good H Buy Now Cookbook

CHOCOLATE GARNISHES

00:09/01:29

CHOCOLATE CURLS

Use these curls to garnish ice cream, cakes, and pies.

Prep: 15 minutes plus chilling

1 package (6 ounces) semisweet chocolate chips
2 tablespoons vegetable shortening

1. In heavy 1-quart saucepan, combine chocolate chips and shortening; heat over low heat, stirring frequently, until melted and smooth.

2. Pour chocolate mixture into foil-lined or disposable 5¾" by 3¼" loaf pan. Refrigerate until chocolate is set, about 2 hours.

3 of 8

NOTE Books with additional content like this are called *enhanced* books. You'll see that label when you shop for books, so you'll know when you're getting multimedia goodies.

- **Read interactive kids' books.** Interactive kids' books can include video and music, and the NOOK HD can read them aloud to kids. In fact, you can record your own voice doing the reading. For details, see Chapter 6.

- **Borrow and lend books.** Just like you can borrow and lend books with your friends, you can do that same thing with many books on your NOOK HD, using the LendMe feature. You'll even be able to borrow library books on it.

NOTE There are some restrictions on borrowing and lending books. For details, see page 191.

- **Read newspapers, catalogs, and magazines.** You can read countless newspapers, catalogs, and magazines on your NOOK HD, usually by springing for either a subscription or a single copy (if, for example, the swimsuit issue is all you want).

- **Create scrapbooks of pages clipped from catalogs and magazines.** The NOOK has a very nifty Scrapbook feature for doing just that.

- **Watch TV, movies, and other videos.** The NOOK HD's spectacular screen lets you watch TV and movies on the built-in NOOK Video service, and on the built-in Hulu Plus app. You can also download and use the Netflix app for watching movies and TV shows. (The apps are free; you have to pay for the services.) There's also a player you can use for other videos.

- **Play music, audiobooks, podcasts, and other audio content.** The built-in music player and reader apps do all the work for you, and the NOOK HD makes it easy to find all the audio content your ears desire.

- **View photos and pictures.** There's a nifty Gallery app built into the NOOK that lets you see photos and pictures in bright, vivid color.

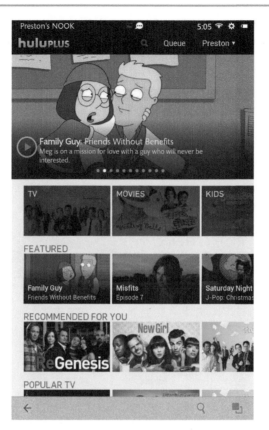

- **Browse the Web.** The NOOK HD has a web browser built right in, so you can visit any website on the Internet and view all of its contents, including videos.

- **Download and use apps.** Dying to play the latest game (Angry Birds, anyone?) or run the latest cool app? The NOOK HD lets you do that, with its built-in Apps store. Many are free, and even for-pay apps are often quite, er...cheap.

NOTE Techies may want to know that the NOOK HD is based on Google's Android operating system, which also runs many smartphones and tablets. Many of the apps written for smartphones and tablets also run on the NOOK HD.

- **Keep track of your contacts.** With the NOOK HD's Contacts app, you can keep track of friends, family, and business acquaintances, and even sync contacts with your Google account.

A Quickie Look at the Hardware

If you're the kind of guy or gal who loves specs, read on, because here's where you'll learn what's under the hood. (Don't care about hardware? Skip to the next section.)

The NOOK HD is powered by a dual core 1.3 GHz (gigahertz) processor and comes with plenty of RAM to run the tablet and all its apps. Not sure what that means? Simple: The NOOK HD is super-fast.

NOTE The NOOK HD+ has a slightly faster processor than the NOOK HD—a 1.5 GHz dual-core speed demon. The extra oomph is needed to power the HD+'s larger screen.

You can get two versions of the NOOK HD. One, which costs $199, comes with 8 GB of memory, of which approximately 5 GB is available for your stuff (the other memory is used by the operating system). You can also buy a microSD card with up to an additional 64 GB of memory.

The $229 NOOK HD comes with 16 GB of memory, of which approximately 13 GB is available for your stuff. You can buy a microSD card with an additional 64 GB of memory. Both versions measure about 7-1/2 by 5 inches, and weigh a mere 11.1 ounces at less than half an inch thick. They've got great battery life: Up to 10.5 hours for reading, or 9 hours for video.

As for the larger HD+ (it's got a 9–inch screen instead of the 7-inch screen on the NOOK HD), there's a $269 model that comes with 16 GB of memory, of which approximately 13 GB is available for your stuff.

The $299 NOOK HD+ comes with 32 GB of memory, of which approximately 28 GB is available for your stuff. As with the less-expensive NOOK HD, you can buy a microSD card with an additional 64 GB of memory with either version. Both versions measure about 9-1/2 by 6-1/2 inches and weigh 18.2 ounces. They've got great battery life—up to 10 hours for reading, or 9 hours for video.

The NOOK HD and HD+ both come with a built-in WiFi radio for connecting to hotspots and WiFi networks, a Bluetooth radio for connecting to other Bluetooth devices, as well as all the hardware you'll read about in the next section.

Power
Button

Headphone   Volume
Jack   Controls

MicroSD Slot   NOOK   30-pin
(on back of NOOK)   Button   Port

The NOOK Button

Down at the bottom of the NOOK HD, you'll find the NOOK button, which just happens to be in the horseshoe shape of the NOOK symbol. If the tablet is sleeping (see page 13), pressing the NOOK button wakes it up. If the tablet is already awake, pressing the button brings you to the Home screen (about which you'll learn more on page 18).

Speaker and Volume Buttons

Turn over your NOOK HD, and you'll see the stereo speakers near the bottom. Many apps have built-in volume controls, but the NOOK HD has physical volume buttons as well. Find them on the righthand side of the tablet, up near the top. Pressing the top button increases the volume; pressing the bottom button turns it down.

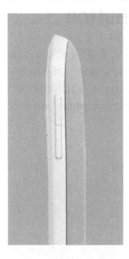

TIP At times—especially when watching certain TV shows or movies—you may find that even at maximum volume, the speakers' sounds are too low. Plugging earphones into the headphone jack, as described next, should help you hear better, and connecting external speakers to the headphone jack usually gives you more sound, too.

Headphone Jack

Near the upper-right corner of the NOOK HD, you'll see a headphone jack. There's no magic to how it works—plug in headphones or an external speaker, and you're ready to go.

Power Button

In the NOOK HD's upper-left corner lives the power button. Hold it for a second or two to turn off your NOOK HD; hold it again for a second or two to turn it back on.

TIP If your NOOK HD is sleeping, pressing the power button will wake it up. For details about sleep, see the next section.

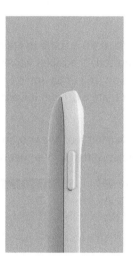

Sleeping, Locking, and Waking from Sleep

If your NOOK HD's screen stayed on all the time, it'd burn up battery life pretty quickly. So if the tablet detects that you haven't used it in a while, it blacks out the screen and locks it. In other words, the NOOK HD goes to sleep.

Normally, if you're not using your tablet for 2 minutes, the screen blacks out. But if you'd like, you can increase that interval. Press the NOOK button to get to the Home screen. Then, in the upper-right portion of the NOOK's screen, tap the small icon that looks like a gear; from the screen that appears, select All Settings→General→"Screen timeout," and from the next screen, select the interval you'd like, anywhere from 2 minutes to 1 hour.

When the screen blacks out, to make it come to life again, press either the NOOK button or the power button. The tablet wakes from its slumber. Slide the onscreen button (which is an icon of an apple or animal or something—you choose this image when you create a profile) toward the lock at the center of the screen to unlock it.

Anyone can wake your tablet like this, not just you, so if you're worried about security, you can lock your tablet so that only someone with a password can use it:

1. **Press the NOOK button to get to the Home screen.** Then, in the upper-right portion of the NOOK's screen, press the small icon that looks like a gear. A settings screen appears.

2. **Select All Settings→ General→Security and then tap the "Screen lock" listing.** A screen appears asking if you want to set up a passcode.

3. **Tap "Set Passcode," type the password you want to use, and then select Continue.**

From then on, the only way to unlock the NOOK HD is to enter the passcode after waking it from sleep.

USB Port, Connector, and Charger

At its bottom, the NOOK HD has a 30-pin port, and it serves double duty. The tablet comes with a special cable that has a 30-pin connector at one end and a USB connector on the other end. Plug the cable's 30-pin connector to the port, plug the USB connector into a special power adapter that comes with your NOOK, and then plug the power adapter into a wall outlet. That's how you charge your NOOK HD.

But the 30-pin port and USB cable do more than just drink in power. If you plug the other end of the cable into your PC or Mac instead of a wall, it lets you transfer files between your computer (either PC or Mac) and the NOOK HD. As you'll see in Chapter 12, it's a great way to transfer music or other media files from your computer to your NOOK HD.

To transfer files, open up Windows Explorer on your PC, or Finder on your Mac. The NOOK HD looks like any other USB drive, so move files just as you would normally between a USB drive and your computer.

NOTE   In order for your PC to transfer files between the NOOK HD and your PC, your PC may need to install a small piece of software called a *driver*. The installation should happen automatically when you plug in your NOOK.

Microphone

At the top edge of the NOOK HD, to the left of the headphone jack, you'll see a tiny hole. That's the microphone. Yes, it's small, but it does the job very well.

High-Resolution Color Touchscreen

Use your NOOK HD for more than a few moments, and you'll notice that the 7-inch screen is nice and bright, and fully laminated to help reduce glare. If you're a techie, you'll like to know that it's got a resolution of 1440 by 600 pixels, with 243 pixels per inch. That's a lot of pixels packed into a small space. That's why it's great not just for reading books, but watching movies and TV. It gives you a full 720p display.

As for the HD+, its 9-inch screen is even more impressive: a 1920 by 1280 pixel resolution at 256 pixels per inch. And it displays video at a full 1080 HD.

TIP Your NOOK's touchscreen will end up with fingerprints and dirt on it, because you're going to be touching it a lot. It's best to use a microfiber cloth to clean it, like the ones for cleaning eyeglasses. Find them in eyeglass stores and in many pharmacies.

SD Slot

Unlike other ereaders, the NOOK HD comes with a slot where you can add plenty of extra storage—up to a whopping 64 GB. All you need to do is buy a microSD card, available in pretty much any electronics store as well as online. Prices vary, of course, but if you shop around you should be able to find one for under $50. As you'll see on page 277, it's easy to install.

On your NOOK HD, just to the left of the 30-pin port, there's a small plastic lid. Pull it, and you'll expose the slot for the SD card. Insert the card, close the lid, and you're ready to go.

Home Screen

On the NOOK HD, just like in *The Wizard of Oz*, there's no place like home. Get used to the Home screen because you'll be spending plenty of time there, finding books to read, navigating your tablet and checking its status, and much more. Press the NOOK button to get there.

You'll explore the Home screen in much more detail in Chapter 3, but here's a brief rundown of what you'll find:

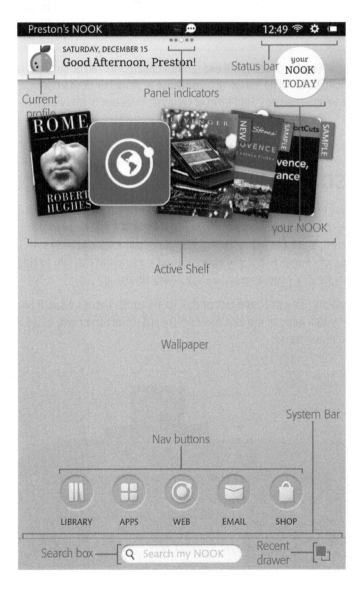

- **Status bar.** As the name says, this area tells you what's going on with your NOOK HD—whether you're connected to a WiFi network, the current time, and your battery life. Any notifications you get appear in the middle of the Status bar. Tap there, and a screen drops down showing all of your notifications. Tap a notification for more details. For example, if you tap a file that's been downloaded, tapping it will open it in an app—like a photo in the Gallery.

NOTE The Status bar is now-you-see-it-now-you-don't. It's visible most of the time, like when you're using the email app or browsing the Web. But sometimes it goes away—for example, when you're reading books or watching videos.

- **Your NOOK Today.** Tap this button to check for recent information, such as the weather and recommendations for reading and videos based on your most recent library activity. When you tap the button, its name changes to "your NOOK." Tap that button to return to the normal main screen.

- **Current Profile.** As you'll see in Chapter 4, the NOOK lets you create separate profiles for the people who use it. This button identifies the current
  profile. Tap it to switch to a different profile or create a new one.

- **Active Shelf.** At the top of the Home screen is the Active Shelf, which holds
  the books, apps, magazines, and newspapers that you've recently bought
  (or borrowed or downloaded). The shelf is a carousel. Swipe it, and you
  reveal more content. Tap any book, newspaper, or magazine you want to
  read or app you want to run.

- **Recent Drawer.** Tap here and you'll see a list of books, apps, and other
  items you've recently opened. Swipe to the right to see more than are
  displayed.

- **Search box.** Tapping here lets you launch a search. You can search your
  entire NOOK and its apps, as well as the NOOK Shop and the Web.

NOTE The Recent Drawer and the Search box are part of an area called the System bar. The System bar changes at times, depending on what you're doing on the NOOK. In the Library, for example, you'll also find an icon for opening the Library menu and in the Shop you'll find a heart icon that, when tapped, displays your Wish List.

- **Panel indicators.** With the NOOK HD, you get five different Home panels, not just one. Why more than one panel? You get more room to put books, apps, and icons on the screen. The white button indicates which of the three Home screens you're currently viewing. Swipe to the left or right to get to another one.

- **Nav buttons.** Tap on the appropriate button to jump to the Library, Apps, the web browser, the E-mail app, and the NOOK Shop.

- **Wallpaper.** Your NOOK's Home screen has wallpaper on it, just like a computer does. And just as on a computer, you can change the wallpaper. See page 53 for details.

Preston's NOOK   1:41

WEDNESDAY, NOVEMBER 14
Good Afternoon, Preston!

your
NOOK

Today in Cambridge

PARTLY SUNNY

36°F High: 46°F
Low: 33°F

AccuWeather.com*
Updated 11/14/12 7:16 am

Picked for you based
on recent library
activity

The
eBOOK
eBOOK

More choices based
on your interests

LIBRARY   APPS   WEB   EMAIL   SHOP

Q Search my NOOK

CHAPTER 2

Setting Up Your NOOK HD

NOW THAT YOU'VE TAKEN the guided tour of your NOOK HD, it's time to get started. In this chapter, you'll charge your tablet, connect to a network, register with Barnes & Noble, and then be on your merry way.

Charging Your NOOK HD

First things first—before doing anything else, charge your NOOK HD. It may already have a bit of charge, but that's not good enough; you want it to be charged completely so your reading (and watching and playing) won't be interrupted.

Get out your 30-pin USB cable and power adapter. Plug the USB end of the cable into the power adapter; plug the power adapter into a wall outlet. Then connect the 30-pin end of the cable to the 30-pin port at the bottom of your NOOK HD. Your NOOK starts charging immediately. The charging light indicator at the bottom of the NOOK, right next to the 30-pin port, will turn orange, showing that your NOOK is charging. When it's fully charged, it turns green. It takes about 3 hours to fully charge a NOOK HD, assuming the battery was completely empty to begin with.

NOTE As you'll see in Chapter 12, you can use the 30-pin USB cable to connect your NOOK HD to your computer and then transfer files between them. Unlike some smartphones and Android tablets, though, your NOOK HD doesn't charge when it's connected to a computer.

By the way, you don't need to wait for your NOOK to charge while you're going through setup. You can set it up while it's charging. So plug it in and keep this book open while you get it set up.

Initial Setup and Connecting to a Network

When you turn on your NOOK HD for the first time, you'll be welcomed with a simple message ("Hi, welcome to your NOOK") and a Next button. (You may also be asked whether you want to use U.K. or U.S. English.) You know what to do: Tap the button. Now the fun begins. Your NOOK looks around in search of a WiFi network. It lists any that it finds. If you're at home, you see your home WiFi network listed; if you're at a B&N, that network is what you see. If any public WiFi hotspots are nearby, or if you have neighbors with WiFi networks, you'll see them in the list as well.

Tap the network to which you want to connect—your home network, or whatever network you're near—and on the screen that appears, enter your password and tap Connect. If you want to see your password as you type, so that you don't make any typos, check the box next to "Show password" by tapping it. After a moment, you're connected, and a button appears at the bottom of the screen—"Continue with Setup." Tap it.

On the next screen, select your time zone, and then tap Next. Your NOOK checks for any important updates. If it finds any, it downloads them. Depending on the size of the download, it may take only a few minutes or up to 20 minutes to download and install. A small blue indicator shows the progress of the download. After the NOOK downloads the update, it installs it. (Typically, the NOOK automatically restarts after the download, and then installs the update.)

Finally, you'll come to a Terms of Service page. Tap the Agree button to accept the terms of service. If you're a lawyer with the time and inclination to actually read the terms, you can tap to display them. (If you've installed an update during the setup process, after the NOOK reboots, you'll have to tap through the screens you saw earlier in the setup process before getting to the Terms of Service page.)

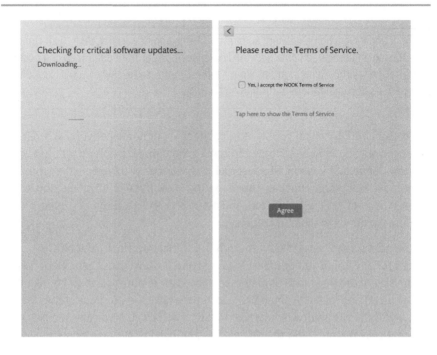

Checking for critical software updates...
Downloading...

Please read the Terms of Service.

Yes, I accept the NOOK Terms of Service

Tap here to show the Terms of Service

Agree

Your NOOK has a number assigned to it called a *MAC address*—a unique identifi-er, like an ID, that identifies your NOOK HD to the Internet. No two devices have the same MAC address, so what you see is unique in the world. You'll probably never need to know your MAC address, but if you ever need it—for instance, if you're asking for tech support—you can easily find it. After you've registered your NOOK HD, press the NOOK button, tap the Settings icon at upper right, and select All Settings→"Device Information." You'll find the MAC address there, along with other information.

Registering Your NOOK HD

Before you go any further, you have to register your NOOK HD and log in with a Barnes & Noble account. If you've ever ordered anything from *www. barnesandnoble.com* (or, to save your fingers, *www.bn.com*) or if you have a Barnes & Noble Member card, you already have an account. Tap "Yes, I have an account." From the screen that appears, enter the email address and password for your account. (Hint: Try the address that Barnes & Noble is sending you email to.) If you don't already have an account, create one now by tapping the appropriate button on the screen.

TIP If you like, you can set up a Barnes & Noble account on the Web using your PC or Mac at BN.com.

If you're registering for the first time, you also have to provide a credit card and billing address for your Barnes & Noble account. That's so you can pay for all the goodies you're about to buy. If you already have an account with a credit card on it, you're set and won't have to re-enter it.

Once you've logged in or set up your account, you come to a page that asks you to list your interests. Tap any, and based on that information, your NOOK will make suggestions for books you might want to read.

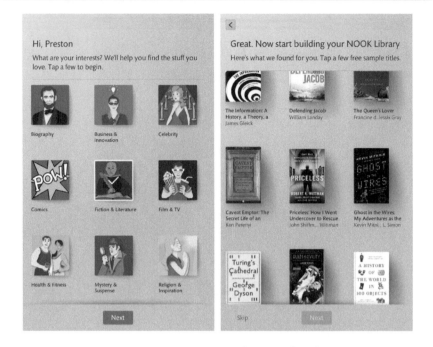

On the next page, the NOOK displays some sample titles that you might want to download. They're free, but keep in mind that they're only samples, not the full books. (You'll learn in Chapter 7 how to buy them.) Tap any you'd like to try.

After a moment or two, you'll be sent to the NOOK main screen. Enjoy! From here you can start shopping for books, movies, and music; or simply explore your NOOK. (As for what to do next, turn to Chapter 3.)

Using and Troubleshooting WiFi

You'll probably use your NOOK HD in more than one place—your home, a public WiFi hotspot in a café or airport, or at a Barnes & Noble location, to name just a few. In those cases, you need to connect to a WiFi network other than the initial one you used when you set up your tablet.

It's simple. Just follow these steps:

1. **If you're not at the Home screen, press the NOOK button.**

2. **Tap the Settings icon at the top right of the screen.** From the screen that appears, make sure that the button in the WiFi area is turned on.

3. **Tap the WiFi hotspot you want to connect to.**

4. **Type the password, if the hotspot requires one, and then tap Connect.**

That's all it takes; you're connected.

Troubleshooting WiFi

The vast majority of the time, you should have no problems making a WiFi connection. But wireless technology can be finicky sometimes, and when that happens, you might need some help. The technology is confusing enough that you may feel the need to consult a local witch doctor for help, but this book is really all you need. Don't go looking for your wizard hat yet.

One problem you may come across when connecting to your home network is that your network name doesn't show up on the NOOK HD's WiFi list. If that's the case, the likely hitch is that your home network is set up to be a *hidden* network; that is, it doesn't broadcast its presence to the world.

TIP Are you the techie type who has a burning desire to know all there is to know about the WiFi network to which you're connected? It's easy: On the wireless connection screen, tap the network's name. A screen appears with details that will warm the cockles of any geek's heart, including signal strength, exact speed of connection, type of security being used, and even the IP address your NOOK HD is currently using.

One way to solve the problem is to unhide your network; check your router's documentation for details. But there's another way to solve it as well. On the main settings screen that you get to by tapping the Settings icon, tap All Settings→Wireless & Bluetooth. In the WiFi section, tap "Find other networks"→Add Network. On the screen that appears, type the network name (called a *service set identifier* or SSID) and tap Save. (You of course need to know the name of the hidden network to do this.) If the network requires security, tap the down arrow in the Security box, and choose the type of security the network uses. (If you're at a hotspot, ask for the security type and password; if you're at home, check your router or its manual for details.) From then on, that network will show up on your network list.

You may come across other WiFi problems that need solving as well. Here's a quick rundown on how to fix some of them:

- **If a WiFi network shows up but you can't connect to it,** try turning off your NOOK HD, and then turning it back on. That often solves the problem.

- **If you keep having problems connecting to a WiFi network,** on the Wireless connection screen, tap the network name, and then tap Forget from the screen that appears. Back on the Wireless connection screen, try connecting to it again.

- **If all else fails,** call the NOOK technical support line at 1-800-THE-BOOK. You'll be able to get help from a technical wizard who can help troubleshoot whatever ails your NOOK HD.

Using Your NOOK HD at a Barnes & Noble Store

You can use your NOOK HD at any WiFi hot spot, but it really shows off its stuff when you use it at a Barnes & Noble store. When you go into the store, your NOOK HD automatically connects to its WiFi hotspot (if you've got the tablet and WiFi turned on, of course).

Tap Shop, and let the fun begin. You come to a special page with a "More in Store" section at the top. It offers you free extra content you won't find anywhere else, like articles by popular authors, review roundups, and more.

Better yet, you can spend an hour reading any ebook for free—that's right, any book that B&N sells as an ebook, you can read for up to an hour, and you won't have to pay a penny—a great way to find out whether you like a book before you commit to buying it.

If you have any questions about the NOOK HD, or need help of any kind, you'll find that you have a friend as well, because stores offer free in-person technical support and advice.

CHAPTER 3

Using Your NOOK HD for the First Time

YOU'VE FIRED UP THE NOOK HD, you've got it charged and set up, and you've registered it. Now the real fun begins. In this chapter, you'll get down to brass tacks, using the NOOK HD for the first time. You'll find out how to control it using gestures and the keyboard, and learn the ins and outs of the Home screen and all its nooks and crannies, including how to customize it.

Using Gestures to Control the NOOK HD

You control the NOOK with nothing more than your fingers, whether you're reading a book, watching a movie, downloading an app, or navigating around the screen. Here are the gestures you need to master:

- **Tap.** Tap something on your screen with your fingertip. Don't push, don't press—just a light tap will do. It performs the most basic of actions, like selecting an app to run or switching to your Library.

- **Double-tap.** Tap not once but twice on your screen in quick succession to perform a wide variety of shortcuts. Double-tap in Shop (page 151) or Library (page 169) on a book or periodical cover, and a new window opens that provides details about it.

With all the tapping, pressing, swiping, and sliding you'll do on your NOOK, the screen tends to get fingerprints on it. Your best bet for cleaning it is to use a soft cloth, like the kind used to clean eyeglasses.

- **Press and hold.** Press your finger on something and hold it there for a couple of seconds to perform a variety of functions. Most often, you'll get a pop-up menu that offers a number of choices about the image you've got your finger on. So, for example, press and hold a book cover, and a menu pops up with choices like opening the book to read it, recommending it, deleting it, archiving it, and so on. Press and hold your finger on a word in a book, then lift your finger, and the Text Selection toolbar appears, giving you a variety of choices about what to do with the text.

- **Swipe.** Slide your finger across the screen to the left or right, and you'll accomplish any one of similar tasks—like moving forward or backward in a book or scrolling through a list or collection. For example, swiping is how you scroll through a row of book covers on your Active Shelf (page 48).

- **Scroll.** Slide your finger up or down on the screen to scroll through any list that displays a scrollbar. Think of it as a vertical swipe.

NOTE The scroll gesture is useful when browsing web pages—use it to scroll up and down a page.

- **Drag.** Place your finger on an object and drag it to another location; it's like using your mouse to drag an object on a computer. Once you've dragged the object to its new location, lift your finger to let it go.

- **Pinching in and spreading out.** Pinch two fingers together—your thumb and forefinger are the best bet—and you'll get to see more of the image; in other words, you zoom out. Move your two fingers away from each other and you zoom in.

NOTE Double-tapping on a picture of magazine page often zooms in on it. Double-tap again to zoom back out.

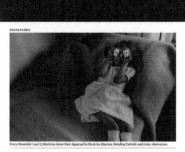

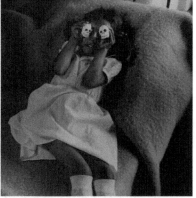

departed in Día de los Muertos, blending Catholic and Aztec observances.

bot and I decided that the most disbing aspect of the corpses was the prisingly robust tufts of pubic hair, ible where the clothes had disinterted.

Near the end of the exhibit was a v of mummy babies, the *angelitos*, their hand-sewn clothes and little ities, many dressed up as angels nts for their ascent to heaven. One

For my part, walking through th *museo*, I experienced that same inn conflict I feel whenever I hear a sto about Mexican drug traffickers wh roll severed heads onto a dance floo in Oaxaca or scatter them in ice ches along the highway in Jalisco, makir the same statement that the Spanis did 200 years ago: *Do not fuck wit us. Our brutality is epic.* I have a ha

The Keyboard

Most of the time you'll be tapping, swiping, scrolling, and pinching while using your NOOK, but sometimes you'll be using a keyboard as well—a virtual, onscreen keyboard rather than a physical one.

You don't need to do anything special to make the keyboard appear. Tap anywhere you need to enter text—in a search box on a website or in the body of an email message, say—and it automatically appears.

Use the keyboard as you would a physical one, except tap instead of type. To switch from the letter keyboard to the number and symbol one, tap the ?123 icon. You'll find plenty of numbers and symbols—but there's even more. Tap the Alt key when you're on the number and symbol keyboard to find them.

When you're in the number and symbol keyboard, tap the ABC icon to switch back.

NOTE Depending on what you're doing on your NOOK, the keyboard may change slightly. For example, when you're typing a web address into your browser, the key to the left of the space bar will be the @ sign, and the key to the right of the space bar will insert the text *.com*.

Your fingers may get a bit cramped tapping on the small screen, so if you want to feel more expansive and get a bit more room as you tap away, turn the NOOK sideways, and the keyboard expands to fill the extra space.

To make the keyboard disappear, tap the keyboard icon in the lower-left corner of the screen.

TIP Here's a quick way to insert many punctuation marks: Hold your finger on the period/comma key on the letter keyboard, and you'll get a pop-up menu of 14 common ones. Then drag your finger to highlight the character you want, and release your finger to enter it.

Accented and Special Characters

What? You say you're not satisfied with those symbols and want even more? Well, you're in luck. If you want to enter accented or special characters, such as those used in foreign languages (é, for example), it's simple to do. Press and hold your finger on a key such as the letter "a." A palette of accented characters appears. Tap the one you want to insert. The following chart shows which keys let you enter special characters.

KEY	ACCENTED AND SPECIAL CHARACTERS
A	á, à, â, ã, ä, å, æ
C	ç
E	3, è, é, ê, ë, ē
I	ì, í, î, ï, ī, 8
N	Ñ
O	ò, ó, ô, õ, ö, ō, œ, ø, 9
S	§, ß
U	ù, ú, û, ü, ū, 7
Y	´y, ÿ, 6
0	ⁿ, ø
%	‰
-	-, —
+	±
(	[, {, <
)	], }, >
"	", ", ', ',
?	¿

TIP When you hold your finger on certain letters, among the choices of characters are normal numbers, such as the number 3. They generally match the location of the numbers on the number keyboard. It's a quick way of inserting a number without having to switch back and forth between the numeric and letter keyboards.

The Status Bar

At the very top of the NOOK screen, you'll find the Status bar, which keeps you up to date with the state of your NOOK and any alerts and notifications. For example, if you're having a problem with your WiFi connection, the Status bar warns you. When you download files, the Status bar tells you about it. Let's just say it's a pretty chatty feature. The Status bar is visible most of the time but not always. It vamooses when you're reading a book, for example.

Preston's NOOK   1:45 📶 ⚙ ▬

The Status bar is divided into three sections. On the left, it identifies you, the owner of the NOOK. If you've set up Profiles (see Chapter 4), it shows the current Profile. Tap the icon to switch to another profile, or create a new one.

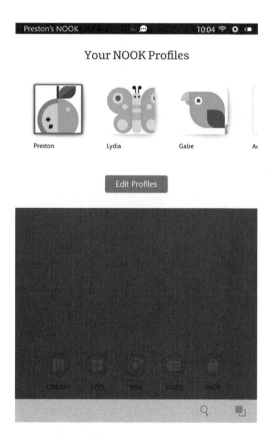

In the middle, the Status bar sends you alerts and notifications about all kinds of things—files you've downloaded, apps you're using, actions NOOK Friends have taken, a problem with your SD card, LendMe notifications, software updatesand more. Each action has a specific icon associated with it. For example, if you're using the Pandora music-streaming app, a P appears; when you're downloading a file, a down arrow appears. If things get too crowded up there, some notifications simply won't appear. Instead, you'll see a small icon of a bubble with three dots. No matter what's up there, though, tap the Status bar in the center and a drop-down menu appears listing each notification. Tap a notification to either get more details, or to launch an action, like opening a file you've downloaded, or switching to a running app.

Way over on the right, you see details about the state of your NOOK, such as its battery level, WiFi connection, and so on. Here's what you'll see:

- An icon that tells you whether you've got a WiFi connection.

The WiFi icon tells you not just that you're connected, but also indicates how strong the connection is. The more concentric partial circles you see, the greater the signal strength.

- A battery life indicator.

- The time, displayed on a 12-hour clock. If you prefer having it displayed on a 24-hour clock, change it via the Time Settings screen (page 392).

- A gear icon that, when tapped, opens the Quick Settings screen.

Quick Settings

The Status bar does one more thing for you: It launches the Quick Settings screen, which lets you fiddle with the NOOK's most important settings. Tap the gear icon on the righthand side of the Status bar, and the Quick Settings screen launches. The screen has six options:

- **Home Settings.** Tap to change a bunch of things about the Home Screen, including what appears there and more. (See "Customizing Your Home Screen" on page 49 for details.)

TIP The Home Settings may change depending on where you are on the NOOK. If you're in the NOOK Shop, for example, it changes to Shop Settings. In the Library, meanwhile, it vanishes altogether.

- **Brightness.** Move the slider to the left or right to adjust the screen's brightness.

- **Wi-Fi.** This toggle switch tells you whether WiFi is turned on or off. Tap the switch to turn it on—or off if it's already on. If you're connected to a WiFi network, its name appears here as well. Tap the Change button, and the Quick Settings screen expands to show other WiFi networks within reach. Tap any to connect to it.

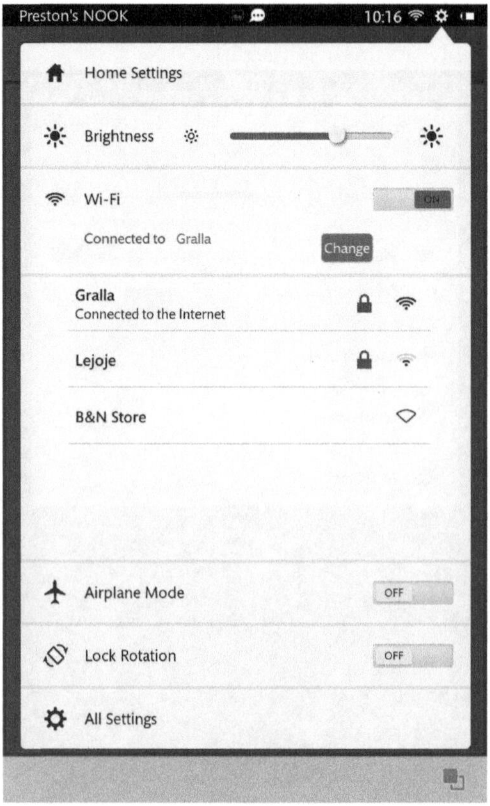

- **Airplane Mode.** Turns on (or off) Airplane Mode, in which all of your NOOK's radios (WiFi and Bluetooth) are turned off. This mode is how you can use your NOOK in the air, when the crew says you can turn on electronic devices but not their radios.

- **Lock Rotation.** When this option is turned on, the NOOK's screen orientation locks to your current orientation, either horizontal (landscape) or vertical (portrait). By default, rotation isn't locked, so your NOOK can change its screen orientation whenever you change the orientation of the NOOK itself.

- **All Settings.** Tap here to travel to central control for your NOOK's settings. How many? So many that an entire chapter is devoted to them. Turn to Chapter 17 for details.

To make the Quick Settings screen go away, tap anywhere outside it. And if you want to change even more settings—literally every single one on your NOOK—tap the All Settings button at the bottom of the Quick Settings screen.

The System Bar

Down at the bottom of the screen is the System bar. The System bar changes at times, depending on what you're doing on the NOOK. On the Home Screen, for example, you'll find the Search box and the Recent Drawer, which lists the recent books, apps, and other items you've used. (You can replace the Recent Drawer with a feature called My Recent Read. See the next page for details.) But in the Library, for example, you'll also find an icon for opening the Library menu; in the NOOK Shop, you'll find a heart icon that displays your Wish List, and a shopping bag icon that shows you the items in the Shop you've recently viewed.

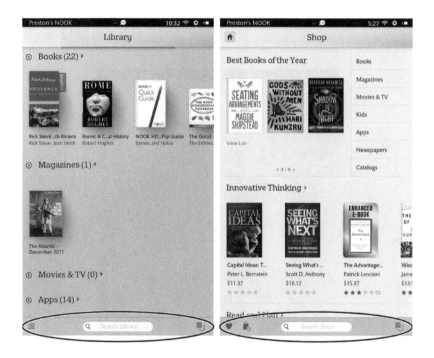

Recent Drawer

Tap here and you'll see a list of books, apps, and other items you've recently opened. Swipe to the right to see more. Tap any to open it.

My Recent Read

You can replace the Recent Drawer with a feature called My Recent Read. When you do that, the Recent Drawer icon vanishes and is replaced with the My Recent Read icon. Tap that icon, and you jump to the last thing you were reading, such as a book, magazine, or catalog. For details about how to switch back and forth between Recent Drawer and My Recent Read, see page 46.

The Active Shelf

The NOOK is a smart little companion. It keeps track of all the things you've been doing on it—what books or magazines you've been reading, what apps you've recently launched, things you've just bought, and so on. You find them on the Active Shelf—a scrolling list of books, publications, and apps running toward the top of the Home screen, like a carousel. It's like a virtual version of the little table beside your favorite chair where you keep all the things you like to use every day. There are more items than you can see on a single screen—flick your finger to the left or right to see more. Tap any to read it or run it.

The Active Shelf can't hold an infinite number of items. So after a while some time out and vanish. Don't worry, though—they haven't actually disappeared from the NOOK HD itself. They're still alive somewhere.

All items in your Active Shelf are also in your Library, so if you're looking for an item that seems to have fallen off the shelf, tap the Library button in the Status bar.

Customizing Your Home Screen

Don't like the way your Home screen looks and works? No problem. You can change it according to your heart's whim. You may want to have some items always within easy reach: for example, the books and magazines you're currently reading; Netflix so you can quickly jump to watching your favorite movies; and so on. Fortunately, you can easily move items on and off your Home screen, anchor them at specific locations, and if things get too messy, arrange them in a neat grid.

You can change its background color to a different one, or use a picture instead—that's called changing its wallpaper. You can use only certain kinds of images as wallpaper—not TV show screens, for example. You can replace the Active Shelf with the NOOK's Inbox, which shows you things you've recently bought or subscribed to.

Adding Items to Your Home Screen

To add an item to your Home screen:

1. **Press and hold an empty area of the Home screen or a panel.** At the bottom of the screen, four tabs appear: Library, Apps, Wallpapers, and Bookmarks.

2. **Tap the tab of the type of item you want to add to the Home screen.** What you'll see next varies according to what tab you've chosen. Choose Library, for example, and you'll see library categories, including Books, Magazines,

and Newspapers. Choose Apps, and you'll see your list of apps. Choose Bookmarks, and you'll see your Web bookmarks (page 300). There may be more than you can see on the screen; flick through them to see more.

NOTE For details about how to change your Home screen image, see page 53.

3. **Choose the category of item you want to add.** For example, in the Library choose Books, and you'll see individual books that you can add. You can flick through them to see more than are on the screen. (If there are no categories in the item you to add, such as Apps, skip to the next step.)

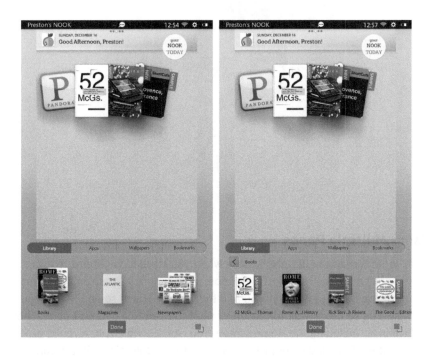

4. **With your finger, drag the item where you want it to be on the Home screen.**

5. **Keep adding items this way until you've added everything you want.**

6. **Tap Done.** That's all it takes. Welcome to your new Home screen.

Using Multiple Panes

Your Home screen can get pretty busy when you start adding items to it this way. That's where the NOOK HD's multiple panes come in. You can add items to any of the panes the same way you add them to the Home screen. When you're on the Home screen, swipe to the left or right to head to a different pane. There are five in all, including the Home screen. You can see which pane you're on by looking at the Pane Indicator just underneath the middle of the Status bar. You may want to devote one pane to books, another to news, another to Home, and so on.

Removing Items from the Home Screen

Not happy with what you've added to the Home screen? You can easily remove any item. Press and hold your finger on it, and you'll get a variety of choices. Tap "Do not show on home," and it will be gone.

When you remove an item from the Home screen, you're not actually deleting the item. It's still on your NOOK and accessible from elsewhere—the Library or the Apps menu, for example.

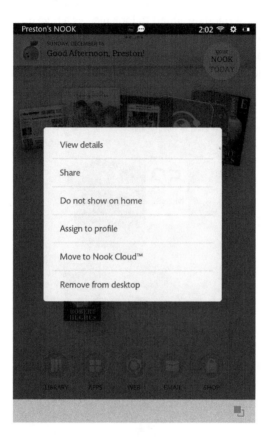

Selecting "Remove from desktop" also removes the item from the Home screen. In some instances (for example, websites you've put on your Home screen), that's the only choice you get when you press and hold your finger on it.

Changing Your Wallpaper

There are times in life when you want a change in the way things look—a new paint job on your house, a new set of furniture, a different haircut. You may feel that way sometimes about your NOOK. You can't give the NOOK a new hairdo, but you can change its *wallpaper*—the background picture on your Home screen and its panels.

To start, follow the first two steps outlined on page 50. Then:

1. **Tap Wallpapers.** At the bottom of the screen, you'll have three choices to find wallpapers: Gallery, Wallpapers, and Live Wallpapers. Wallpapers are pictures that have been designed to look nice as a background screen. The Gallery contains all the photos and pictures on your NOOK, any of which you can also use as wallpaper. Live Wallpapers are backgrounds that are active in some way. They may be animated, interactive, or automatically updated.

2. **To use one of your own pictures as wallpaper, tap the Gallery.** You'll head to the Gallery (page 268). Choose the picture you want to use. Because the pictures in the gallery haven't been optimized for the NOOK, you'll be able to crop them so that they're the right size. Choose the cropping you want, tap Crop, and it gets set as your wallpaper.

3. **To use one of the NOOK's Wallpapers or Live Wallpapers, tap either of these items.** You'll see a list of wallpapers you can use. There may be more than you see at first, so swipe through them. You see a small thumbnail of the wallpaper at the bottom of the screen, and a preview of it at the top. Select the wallpaper you want to use, tap "Set wallpaper," and then tap Done.

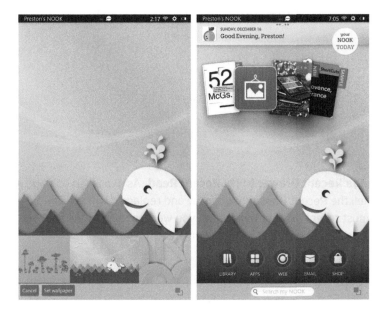

NOTE When you select a live wallpaper, you may be able to tweak how it works, like choosing its colors.

Customizing the Home Screen Using Quick Settings

There's plenty more you can change about your Home screen by using Quick Settings. Tap the settings icon in the System bar, and select Home Settings from the menu. Here's what you can do:

- **Change Recent Drawer to My Recent Read.** As explained on page 47, you can tell the Recent Drawer to go away and replace it with an icon that opens the most recent book or publication you were reading to the spot you left off. Turn off the box next to "Show my Recent Drawer."

- **Change the Active Shelf to a daily Inbox.** If you don't find the Active Shelf useful, you can change it to the NOOK's Inbox, which lists items that you've recently bought, and subscriptions to newspapers and magazines that have just arrived. In the "Select Shelf Behavior" section, select Inbox.

- **Customize what appears on the Recent Drawer and Active Shelf.** Both the Recent Drawer and Active Shelf show books, apps, TV shows, and documents. If you want, though, you can customize which show up and which don't—for example, not showing any TV shows. In the "Customize by Showing Only these Content Types" section, uncheck the boxes next to the types of content you don't want to appear.

- **Change how subscriptions appear.** When you subscribe to a newspaper, magazine, or catalog, the most recent version or most recently opened issue appears on the Recent Drawer and Active Shelf. Out of the box, only one displays. However, if you'd like, you can see up to three, or none—or every issue. At the bottom of the screen, tap Newspapers, Magazines, or Catalogs, depending on which you want to customize, and then make your choice.

Returning Home

No matter where you are or what you're doing on your NOOK, there's an easy way to return to the Home screen—and you don't even need to click your ruby slippers to get there. Press the NOOK button. You're there.

Searching Your NOOK

Here's another of the many great things about your NOOK: Even though it's chock full of books, magazines, newspaper, apps, and more, finding what you want is a breeze. That's because the NOOK has a great built-in search tool. Just type your search into the search box at the bottom of your screen, and start typing your search terms. The NOOK immediately displays results, and as you type more letters, it narrows down the search.

The keyboard at the bottom of the screen hides some of the search results, so when you want to see all the results, tap the icon on the keyboard that makes it go away (page 39). You see all the results of your search by category, such as Library or Apps. Tap any item to go to it—a book, a newspaper, or magazine, an app, results from the Web, and so on.

Here are the categories you'll search when you do a search from the Quick Nav bar:

- **Library.** Your books, magazines, and newspapers.

- **Apps.** The apps whose name or first letter combination in the name matches your search.

- **Music.** The artists, albums, and tracks in your Music app.

- **Shop.** Books, magazines, and newspapers available in the B&N store, not on your NOOK.

- **Web.** Your browser's bookmarks and history.

- **Contacts.** The people stored on your NOOK (page 373).

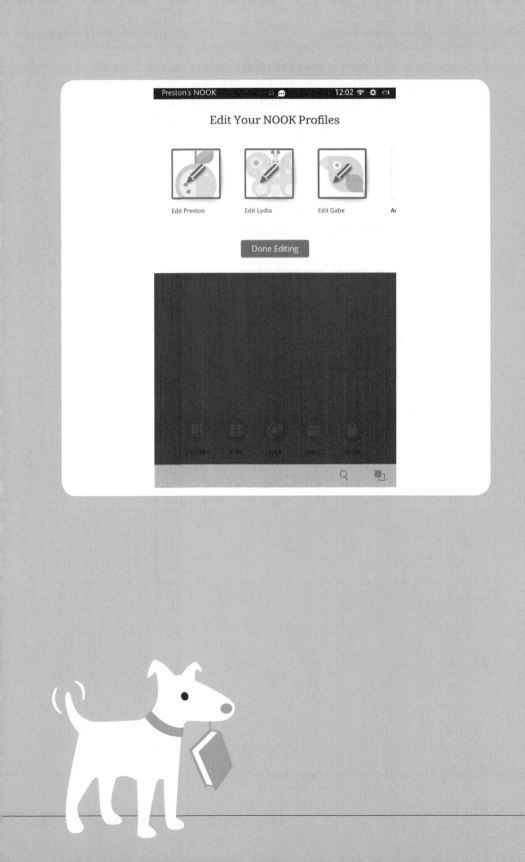

CHAPTER 4

Creating and Using Profiles

ONE OF THE NIFTIEST things about the NOOK HD is its ability to have multiple people use it, each with his or her own account, preferences, books and media, and more. No other ereader or tablet offers these family-friendly capabilities, so read on to learn how to share your NOOK with the whole gang.

Understanding Profiles

People are different. Some like detective novels, while others like literary fiction. Some prefer romantic comedies, while others can't get enough action-hero movies. Some say tomato, and others tom-ah-to. For whatever reason, whether it's hard-wiring, upbringing, age, or some combination people have different tastes and needs in a tablet.

The NOOK recognizes this fact of life and lets you create different profiles for different family members. That way, if you're a lover of literary fiction and foreign-language dramas, you don't have to wade through the young adult fiction, thrillers, buddy movies, and romantic comedies that near and dear ones have put on the NOOK. And they don't have to wade through yours, either.

In addition, if you've got kids sharing the NOOK, you can make sure that they won't have access to books, movies, and Internet content that aren't suitable for them, because you can create a kids' profile with full parental controls that limit what they can do.

NOOK profiles are delightfully flexible. So, for example, if there are books and movies that *everyone* wants to enjoy, you can give everyone access without buying multiple copies. Or, you can block access as well.

NOTE Even though the NOOK can have multiple profiles, all of the payments for all content come from a single profile. So when anyone with a profile makes a purchase, it's charged to the same account (probably yours).

Profiles have one small limitation: You can have a maximum of six of them on a single NOOK. But then again, if you were to have more than six people share a NOOK, no one would get much reading time or screen time.

The Three Types of Profiles

The NOOK lets you create three types of profiles:

- **Primary profile.** This profile is created for you automatically when you first use your NOOK—it's your profile. It can see all the content on the NOOK, including all the content viewed by other profiles. It can also create and edit other profiles. And all payments for all profiles are made through this primary profile.

- **Adult profile.** Someone with this type of profile can buy, view, and use any kind of content. The profile can control what content it sees, and can view any content on any child profile on that NOOK HD. This profile can also set parental controls for a child profile. It can't, however, make changes to the content visible to the primary profile, or edit the primary profile in any way.

- **Child profile.** Someone with a kid's profile can only buy, view, and use content that was authorized by an adult profile (including the primary profile). Children can't create or edit other profiles. Child profiles are also subject to parental controls and can never override them.

Setting Up Profiles

With that as a background, you're ready to create profiles. First, you must be connected to a WiFi network, because without a WiFi connection, you can't create or edit a profile.

Setting Up an Adult Profile

Here's how to set up an adult profile:

1. **On the Home screen, tap the icon in the upper-left corner.** That icon represents the current profile. When you tap it, a screen opens, showing all of your existing profiles.

2. **Tap the icon for creating an adult profile.** Tap the icon at the top of the screen to give the new profile its own unique icon. Below that, type the person's first name and choose a gender. If you'd like all the existing content on the NOOK to be available in the new profile's Library, turn on the "Add all content in this account to this new Profile's Library" checkbox. Otherwise, the person will start out with an empty Library. Tap Next.

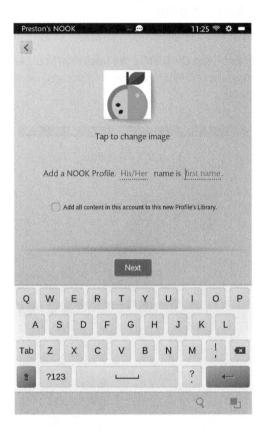

NOTE   When you tap to select an icon for the profile, you'll be sent to the Gallery. In the Gallery, tap the Avatar folder, and browse through it to choose an icon for the new profile.

3. **On the screen that appears, choose the types of content that would inter-est the owner of the new profile.** Tap Next.

4. **On the next screen, select sample content that might interest the owner of the profile.** Then tap Next.

That's all it takes. After a moment, the NOOK returns to the Home screen, with the new profile logged in. The profile will include any sample content you just selected.

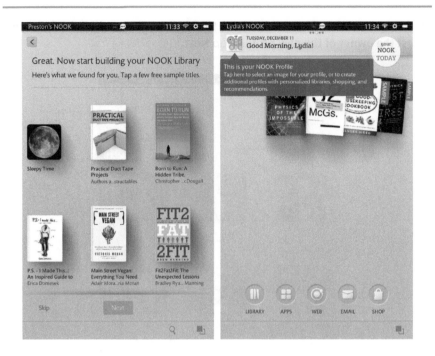

Setting Up a Child Profile

Setting up a child profile is quite similar to setting up an adult profile, with only a few changes:

1. **On the Home screen, tap the icon in the upper-left corner.** That icon represents the current profile. When you tap it, a screen opens, showing all of your existing profiles.

2. **Tap the icon for creating a child profile.** Tap the icon at the top of the screen to give the new profile its own unique icon. Below that, choose whether the profile is for a boy or for a girl, and fill in the child's name and age. Tap the box to accept the terms and conditions. Then tap Next.

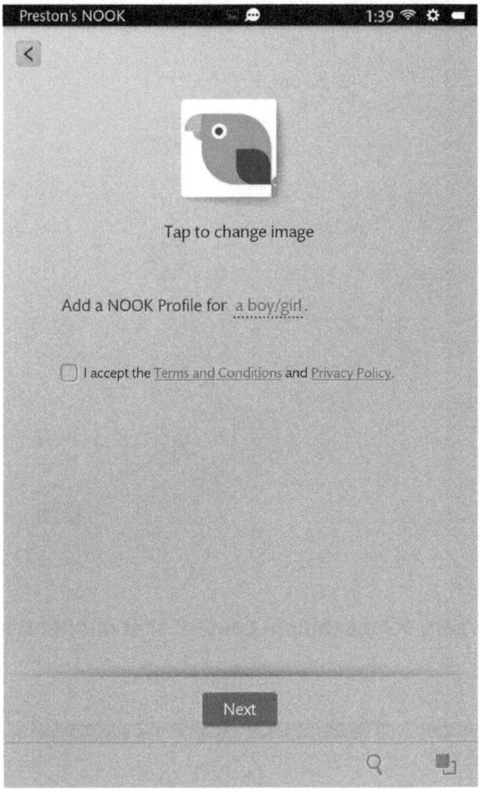

Tap to change image

Add a NOOK Profile for a boy/girl.

☐ I accept the Terms and Conditions and Privacy Policy.

Next

TIP If you don't want to select whether the profile is for a boy or girl, select "a child" from the drop-down list that appears when you tap "a boy/girl."

---

3. **Make your selections on the parental controls screen.** You can choose a variety of settings, such as whether to allow the child to browse the NOOK Shop, use video for kids, apps for kids, games for kids, and so on. In some instances there are subchoices—for example, if you check "Browse Shop," you'll have subchoices for whether to allow the child to shop only for kids content. Make sure that you scroll to the bottom of the screen and make all the choices. Especially important is the section that lets you choose what kinds of ratings to apply when filtering viewing movies and TV shows. When you're done, tap Next.

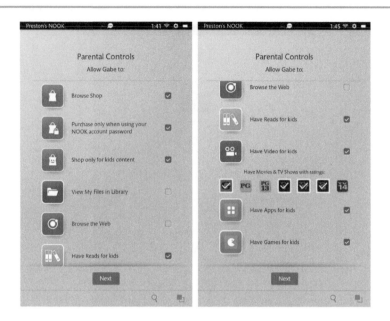

4. **On the next screen, select sample content that might interest the child.** Then tap Next.

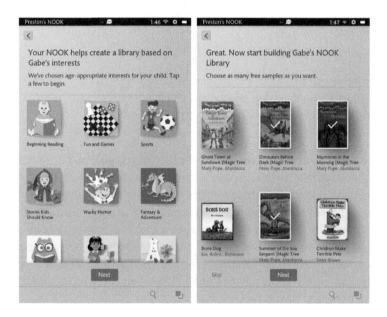

After a moment, the NOOK returns to the Home screen. You're asked whether you want to create a password for your other profiles. That way, the child won't be able to log into any other profiles (which is, after all, the whole point of having different profiles).

When you're done creating the password (or if you decided to bypass it) the NOOK shows a Home screen with the child profile logged in. The profile will include any sample content you just selected.

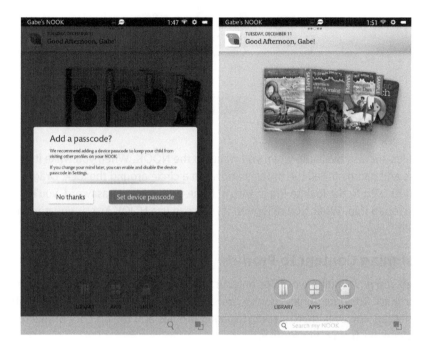

Using Profiles

Once you've got your profiles set up, you'll find it easy to switch between them. Tap the Profile button at the upper left of the Home screen, and a screen appears with icons for all of the profiles on the NOOK. Tap any to log in with that profile. If you've set a password for the profile (only adult or primary profiles can have them), you'll need to first type the password.

NOTE Profiles have separate email accounts. So an email account set up for one profile will not be visible in another profile's email account.

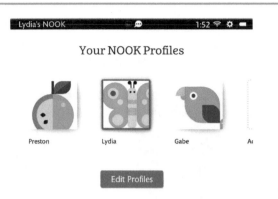

Your NOOK Profiles

Preston   Lydia   Gabe   A

Edit Profiles

Profiles are also available when you wake up the NOOK. When you wake it up, icons and names for all the profiles appear in a circle around the lock. Drag a profile's icon to the lock to log in with it. If the profile has a password, you'll have to tap it in. When you're logged in, you can use NOOK just as you normally would.

Assigning Content to Profiles

When you have multiple profiles on your NOOK, not all of its content is visible to all profiles. So some books, movies, and apps for one profile might not be visible in another. However, there's a way for adult profiles and the primary profile to view content from other profiles.

First open the Library or the listing of Apps, depending on whether you want to view content from the library or get apps for your profile from another profile's content. The procedure is the same technique whether you're sharing books, apps, or movies.

In the Library, for example, hold your finger on the book you want to add to your profile or another profile. From the screen that pops up, select "Assign to Profiles." Then tap all the profiles that you want to share the content and tap Save. That content will now be available to all of those profiles.

That works quite well on a onesy-twosy basis. But if you want to assign *lots* of content, there's a much less tedious way.

In the Library, tap the Contents icon at lower-left (it's a stack of horizontal lines). A menu pops up. Tap Manage Content for Profiles. A screen appears with various categories of content—Books, Magazines, Newspapers, Catalogs, Movies & TV, Apps, and so on. Next to each category, you see how much content is in that category and how much of that content is available to the current profile, for example, "20 of 27 books." If all the content in any category is in the current profile, there's a checkbox next to that category.

To add all the content from any category to your profile, simply tap the box next to the category, and then tap Save.

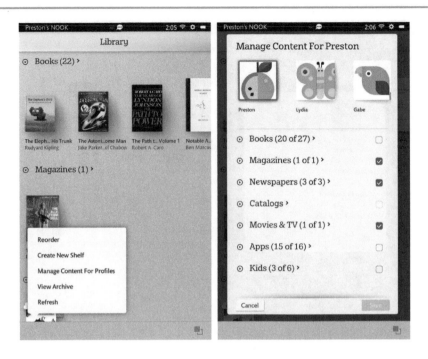

If you prefer to have only some of the content visible, tap the small arrow next to any category, and you'll see a list of everything that's available. Checkmarks appear next to the content visible in your profile. Turn on the checkboxes next to any content you want available in your profile, and then tap Save.

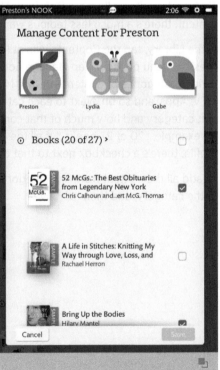

Editing Profiles

Once you create a profile, it's easy to edit or even delete it. On the Home screen, tap the Profile icon. On the screen showing all of the NOOK's profiles, tap the Edit Profiles button.

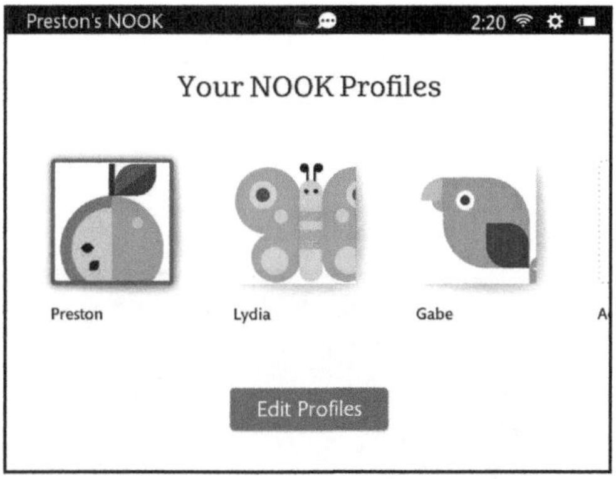

A pencil icon appears next to each profile. Tap the icon of the profile you want to edit.

A menu pops up with between three to five choices, depending on what profile you're using. Here's what each does:

Your NOOK Profiles

Preston   Lydia   Gabe

Edit Profiles

- **Change Interests.** Tap here to change the interests associated with the profile. The current interests have checkmarks next to them. Tap all the interests you want to add, just as you did when setting up the profile (page 63). To take away an interest, tap it so the checkmark disappears. When you're finished, tap Done.

- **Change Image.** Tap here to choose a new icon for the profile. Follow the same steps you took when you first created a profile to choose an image for it.

- **Manage Content.** This section lets you add or take away content visible to the profile. The screen that appears is the same as the one that lets you add entire categories of content, or choose individual content from categories, as described on page 70. Follow those same instructions. When you're done, tap Save.

- **Remove this Profile.** Removes the profile from the NOOK. Don't worry about losing its content, though, because the content will still be available to other profiles. Note that you can't delete the profile you're currently using. If you want to delete it, log into a different profile, and delete it from there. (Note: Only the Primary Profile can remove other adult profiles.)

- **Change Parental Controls.** Lets you change the parental controls for a child profile. For details, see page 67.

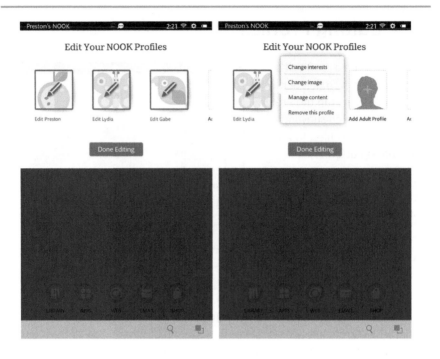

NOTE You can't delete the NOOK's primary profile.

Reading Books and Periodicals

Photo Insert   533 of 596

Go to Page

ⓘ ☰ Aa 💬 🔍   🗐

CHAPTER 5

Reading Books, Newspapers, Catalogs, and Magazines

YOUR NOOK HD DOES many things, but above all it's a great ereader for books, newspapers, and magazines. You'll find countless tools that make your reading experience efficient and enjoyable—and you'll learn all about them in this chapter.

Opening a Book

To open a book, simply tap its cover. Here are the main places you'll find a book cover to tap:

- On your Home screen, if you've placed one there

- On the Active Shelf

- In your Library

- In the Recent Drawer

TIP When browsing or searching the NOOK Shop, when you come across a book that you already have on your NOOK, its button displays "Read" rather than a price. Tap it to read the book.

A Tour of the Book Reader

Tap a book cover, and you get sent to the first page of the book, or if you've been reading it, you go to the last page you read. You'll get a simple, uninterrupted view of the book page—text along with any illustrations, photos, and so on. At the very bottom of the page, you see the page number you're on and the total number of pages in the book. You may also see icons that look like yellow notepads along the right side of the page—these indicate notes that you or another reader has added to the book. Tap a note to read it. (For the full story on notes, see page 100.)

Rome: A Cultural, Visual, and Personal History

1

Foundation

Although nobody can say when Rome began, at least there is reasonable certainty of where it did. It was in Italy, on the bank of the river Tiber, about twenty-two kilometers inland from its mouth, a delta which was to become the seaport of Ostia.

The reason no one can pinpoint when the foundation took place is that it never ascertainably did. There was no primal moment when a loose scatter of Iron and Bronze Age villages perched on hills agreed to coalesce and call itself a city. The older a city is, the more doubt about its origins, and Rome is certainly old. This did not prevent the Romans from the second century B.C.E. onward coming up with implausibly exact-looking dates for its origins: Rome, it used to be asserted, began not just in the eighth century but precisely in 753 B.C.E., and its founder was Romulus, twin brother of Remus. Here a tangled story begins, with many variants, which

24 of 596

NOTE The page numbers at the bottom of the page are for the NOOK version of the book, not the print version.

To move ahead one page, tap any spot along the right edge of the screen, or swipe your finger to the left. To move back one page, tap any spot along the left edge of the screen, or swipe your finger to the right.

TIP When you buy a book and download it to your NOOK, it's protected with a technology called *digital rights management* (DRM). DRM is there to prevent illegal copying, selling, or distribution of books. The NOOK's built-in technology ensures that you can read any book you've legitimately purchased. However, due to a DRM-related hiccup, you may need to unlock a book after you've downloaded it. If that happens to you, you'll be prompted to enter your name and the credit card number you used to buy the book. After that the book unlocks, and it's clear reading ahead.

That's just the basics, though. To unleash the full power of the NOOK's reader, tap anywhere in the center of the page or at the bottom of the page to bring up the Reading Tools menu. This menu does all kinds of nifty things—hops to the interactive table of contents, searches the book, changes the font size and brightness, and more.

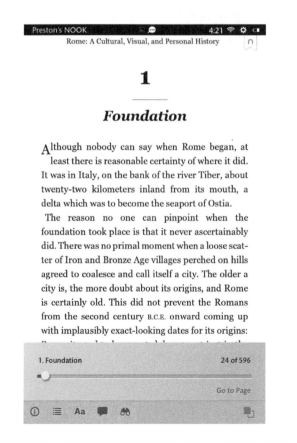

You may need a bit of practice bringing up the Reading Tools menu. If you tap too far to the right, you'll go forward one page; and too much to the left, you'll go back a page. Aim for square in the middle.

Here are the four reading tools:

- **Contents.** Jumps you back to the book's table of contents, with the current chapter highlighted. It's interactive—tap a listing in the table and you'll jump to that location in the book. Separate tabs show notes, highlights, and bookmarks and let you jump to them as well.

Preston's NOOK 4:21

Rome: A Cultural, Visual, and Personal History

1

Foundation

| Table of Contents | Highlights and Notes | Bookmarks |

1. Foundation

2. Augustus

3. Later Empire

4. Pagans Versus Christians

5. Medieval Rome and Avignon

6. Renaissance

7. Rome in the Seventeenth Century

8. High Baroque (Bernini, Borromini, Etc.)

- **Text and display.** Lets you make the text just right—not too large, not too small, with just the right font and just the right background color. You can also change the line spacing, margins, and more. See page 95 for details.

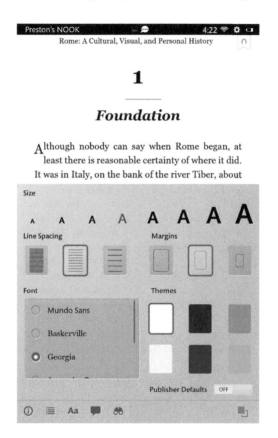

- **Share.** Tap here and you can share information about the book with others—recommend it, review it, "Like" it on Facebook, and more. See page 92 for details.

1

Foundation

Although nobody can say when Rome began, at
least there is reasonable certainty of where it did.
It was in Italy, on the bank of the river Tiber, about
twenty-two kilometers inland from its mouth, a
delta which was to become the seaport of Ostia.

The reason no one can pinpoint when the
foundation took place is that it never ascertainably
did. There was no primal moment when a loose scatter of Iron and Bronze Age villages perched on hills
agr   tself a city. The older a
city   Recommend   t its origins, and Rome
is c   ot prevent the Romans
fro   Post Reading Status   c.e. onward coming up
wit   ng dates for its origins:
Ro   Rate and Review   l, began not just in the
eig   y in 753 b.c.e., and its
fou   Like on Facebook   brother of Remus. Here
a t   many variants, which

- **Find.** Pops up a search box and keyboard so you can search the book you're
reading.

taneous but differently scaled aging of Michelangelo's architectural frame for the horse and rider—the crisper contours of the pedestal, the bloom and discoloration of the mellowed surface of the Palazzo del Senatore.

One's interest in the past is, at a young age, minimal —it seems so distant and irrelevant and, in so many ways, imbued with failure. The future is equally inconceivable; one is overwhelmed by the romance of possibility. But that was the magic of Rome for my younger self. The city was my guide backward as well as forward. It provided insight into beauty as well as destruction, triumph as well as tragedy. Most of all, it gave physical form to the idea of art, not simply as something ethereal for the elite but as something inspiring, even utilitarian. For me, that first time, Rome turned art and history into reality.

Look at the top-right corner of the screen when you bring up the Reading Tools menu, and you see a colorless NOOK icon. That's for creating a bookmark. Tap the icon: It turns blue and elongates. You've just added a bookmark, and it stays there even when the Reading Tools menu disappears. Tap it again and it disappears—you've just deleted a bookmark.

NOTE You can create a bookmark without having to bring up the Reading Tools menu. Just tap the upper-right corner of the screen.

stify to imperial control. Marcus Aurelius' hair stands energetically up, a nimbus of corkscrewing locks, not a bit like the conventional signs for hair that plaster so many Roman marble crania. The extended right hand, in its gesture of calming power, is majestic (as befits the hand of an emperor) but benign (as a Stoic's well might be; this was the hand that wrote Marcus' *Meditations*). The different thrusts and directions of the statue's limbs are adjusted to play off one another, the raised left foreleg of the horse against the splayed legs of the man astride it, with an uncanny appreciation of movement. And then there is the color. The bronze carries the patina of nearly two thousand years. It is something which cannot be replicated by applied chemicals. It speaks of long exposure, running out beyond the scale of dozens of human generations, each contributing its small freight of patches, gold blotches, green streaks, and pinhole discolorations to the venerable surface. When I first saw the Marcus Aurelius, this process had been going on uninterruptedly, like some extremely slow maturation of wine, for a very long time and was part of the simul-

In the Reading Tools menu, you'll find some handy tools for navigating through the book. Tap the "Go to Page" button, and a screen appears that lets you type in a page number to head to. Tap in the page number, tap the Enter key, and off you go.

stify to imperial control. Marcus Aurelius' hair stands energetically up, a nimbus of corkscrewing locks, not a bit like the conventional signs for hair that plaster so many Roman marble crania. The extended right hand, in its gesture of calming power, is majestic (as befits the hand of an emperor) but benign (as a Stoic's well might be; this was the hand that wrote Marcus' *Meditations*). The different thrusts and directions of the statue's limbs are adjusted to play off one another, the raised left foreleg of the horse against the splayed legs of the man astride it, with an uncanny appreciation of movement. And then there is the color. The bronze carries the patina of nearly two thousand years. It is

After you do that, to get to the page you were just reading, tap the "Go Back to Page" link and you head back to where you were.

There's also a nifty slider that shows you your current location in the book, including the chapter number and title, and how many pages remain in the chapter. Drag the slider to move forward or back in the book. As you drag the slider, the page number, chapter number, and title appear to show the location you're moving through.

contained. And so the significance of the churches was bo... ...ich, in turn, c... ...e martyrs' relics they housed. The holy martyr had become, as it were, portable, and a part of the body could signify the entire saint. Reliquaria replaced actual burial spots, which meant that a saint could be efficaciously prayed to wherever his remains could be put.

The first man to become the subject of an extensive relic cult was the first Christian deacon and the first Christian martyr: Saint Stephen. Having incurred the wrath of established Judaism, he had been brought before the court of the high priest and elders in Jerusalem, sentenced, and stoned to death. One of the witnesses to his lapidation was Saul, the future Apostle Paul, whose acute feelings of guilt at assenting to it is said to have helped in his later adherence to Christ.

Bits and pieces of Stephen would be revered in

p. 186   4. Pagans Versus Christians

Go Back to Page 206   Go to Page

Using the Table of Contents

A book's table of contents does a lot more than just let you navigate by chapter title. It's also your gateway into three great NOOK features—Notes, Highlights, and Bookmarks. (You learned how to create a bookmark on page 85; for help on creating notes and highlights, turn to page 97.)

ble afresh. In November, having gathered an army,
Cola went to battle with the nobles' forces outside
the Porta Tiburtina, and succeeded in killing their
ringleader, Stefano Colonna. But he had underes-
timated Pope Clement, who issued a bull of depo-

| Table of Contents | Highlights and Notes | Bookmarks |

5. Medieval Rome and Avignon

6. Renaissance

7. Rome in the Seventeenth Century

8. High Baroque (Bernini, Borromini, Etc.)

9. Eighteenth-Century Rome, Neoclassicism, and the Grand Tour

10. The Nineteenth Century: Orthodoxy Versus Modernism

11. Futurism and Fascism

12. Rome Recaptured

Tap Contents on the Reader Tools menu, and you come to a page with three
tabs: Contents, Highlights and Notes, and Bookmarks.

Tap the Highlights and Notes tab, and you'll see the list of all the notes and highlights you've added to your book. To jump to any, tap it.

Tap a listing, and you go to the page with the note or highlight. The text that you
highlighted or attached a note to is highlighted in green. If there's a note, you
see a yellow note icon in the right margin. Tap the icon to read the note. After
the note appears, you can edit it by tapping the Edit button.

million in modern money, every year, and much of this was funneled directly to Rome for its building plans. Thirty-three churches in the *abitato* are mentioned prior to 1050, of which twelve still exist today. Many more would come later.

| Table of Contents | **Highlights and Notes** | Bookmarks |

Show Notes & Highlights   ON   Clear all

Fritigern...   p. 191
   get more details...
   last edited: 12/13/2012 4:43pm

Theophilos...   p. 191
   ask jim about hin...
   last edited: 12/13/2012 4:44pm

Medieval ...   p. 193
   Can't wait to visiy...
   last edited: 12/13/2012 4:42pm

---

slaves. Much to the amazement of imperial officialdom, the rebels forced a Roman retreat.

Valens could hardly believe this, but he resolved to crush the Visigothic rising. And so, on the eastern frontier, near the modern city of Edirne, Turkey, then known as Adrianople, battle was joined. By now the Roman army, once so unified, homogeneous, and dreaded, consisted largely of mercenaries who were not fighting for their homelands. It did not have the *esprit de corps* of former days, and presently an incredulous Roman citizenry would learn that the barbarians had overwhelmed it at Adrianople—the Visigothic victory was so complete that the corpse of Valens could not even be found beneath the heaps of the Roman dead, containing two-thirds of the Roman army and some thirty-five of its senior officers. Fritigern, the Visigothic leader, could not have dared to expect so total a triumph.

The catastrophe at Adrianople shook Roman self-confidence so badly that it has been regarded, ever since, as comparable to Rome's stupefying loss to Hannibal at Cannae, six centuries before.

This did nothing to ease the transition from

Note 12/13/2012 4:43pm

get more details

Cancel   Edit

Tap the Bookmarks tab, and you see a list of your bookmarks. Tap any to go to one. If you'd like to delete all your bookmarks, tap "Clear all" and they all vamoose. The same holds true for the Highlights and Notes tab—tap "Clear all" to make them vanish.

If you're looking at the table of contents and decide not to use it, tap the page behind it. The table of contents vanishes.

If you read a book on a device other than your NOOK, such as a computer, tablet, or smartphone, the next time you open the book on your NOOK, you'll jump to the page you were reading on that device, even if you haven't yet read the page on the NOOK. This magic only happens, though, if both the device you're reading the book on and the NOOK have Internet access while you're reading.

Sharing Your Reading

For many people, reading is more than a solitary pleasure; it's one they enjoy sharing with others as well. That's where the Share icon on the Reading Tools menu comes in. Tap it, and a menu pops up that lets you share your thoughts about the book you're reading with others. You can even write book reviews. Think of it as your own personalized book club.

> **NOTE** If you download a book to your PC or Mac, and then transfer it to your NOOK, the Share feature may not be available; in that case, the icon will appear faint instead of bright.

Rome: A Cultural, Visual, and Personal History

the apostle and first pope was allegedly buried after his martyrdom. The others are the Basilica of Saint Paul Outside the Walls, San Giovanni in Laterano (the actual cathedral of Rome), Saint Sebastian Outside the Walls, Santa Maria Maggiore (the greatest church dedicated specifically to the cult of Jesus' mother, Mary), Santa Croce in Gerusalemme, and Saint Lawrence Outside the Walls. The "walls" in each case are the Aurelian wall, erected around 271–75 C.E. to girdle the city. Only one of them, Saint Sebastian Outside the Walls, has no works of art of special interest; its attraction—now much diminished, because of the general loss of interest in the cult of relics as distinct from the drawing-power of famous works of art—lay in its relics, among which is a stone

- Recommend
- Post Reading Status
- Rate and Review
- Like on Facebook

us, an arrow which once ular third-century martyrdom of the column to fellow soldiers, having version, shot at him. Of urches do contain art—t the emphasis had always associations than on

195 of 596

If you already hang out on Facebook or Twitter, you may find that the easiest way to share what you're reading. You can link your NOOK account to your existing Facebook or Twitter account; to learn how, flip to page 364. You can also share by email with your NOOK Contacts.

Once you've linked your accounts, you're ready to start sharing. Tap the Share button, and here's what you can do:

- **Recommend.** Tap to launch and you'll be able to recommend your book to others using Facebook or Twitter, or to your contacts. The exact form you fill out depends on which sharing method you choose.

  When you select Contacts, for example, a screen appears that lets you pick the contact or contacts with whom you want to share. Then an email-like screen appears that lets you select the contacts to whom you want to recommend the book. The NOOK thoughtfully enters all the basic information for you about the book—title, description, author, and so on—so that you don't have to do it yourself. There's a place on the form to add a message of your own, but there's a 420-character limit.

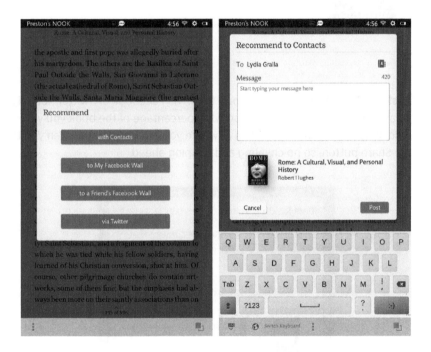

When you send a recommendation, there's also a link to the book so people can buy it, and a photo of the cover. In addition, if the person to whom you've sent the recommendation uses a NOOK, she gets a small notification in the shape of a medal or ribbon on his Notification bar. Tapping that icon and then tapping the screen that appears opens up the full recommendation, book cover and all. She can then download a sample of the book, view all the details about it, or remove the recommendation.

- **Post Reading Status.** Lets the world know via Facebook or Twitter not only what book you're reading, but also what percentage of the book you've read. It calculates that by looking at where you are in the book when you tap the Share button, so no cheating and jumping ahead.

- **Rate and Review.** How good or bad is the book you're reading on a one-to-five star scale? What do you have to say about it? Tap here to share your views. Your review is posted on BN.com and appears when people browse the book; it also shows up when people view the book on their NOOK. You can also post the review to Facebook or Twitter.

- **Like on Facebook.** Tap here, and you instantly add a "Like" to the book on your Facebook account.

Changing the Text and Display

Want to make the text of the book larger or smaller, change its font, spacing, and more? Simply tap the Text icon in the Reading Tools menu. Here's what you can customize:

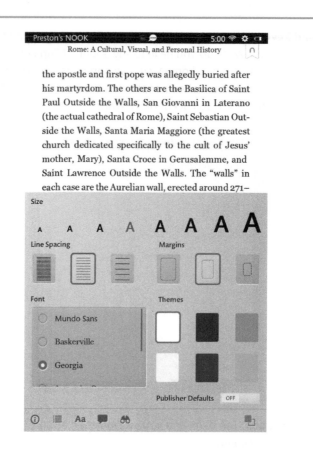

- **Size.** When it comes to reading, size does matter. Just tap any one of the eight font sizes. The text behind the menu changes so you can see a preview.

- **Font.** Scroll through the list and make your choice. As with all other selections, the text behind the menu changes so you can see how the font you chose will look.

- **Line spacing.** Changes how much space there is between lines of text. The leftmost choice puts the least amount of space between the lines, the rightmost choice puts the most, and the one in the middle is somewhere between the two. With this choice, you want to seek a balance between more lines on a page (so you do less page turning) and the potential eyestrain of having lines too close together.

- **Theme.** Changes the background and text color combination. Out of the box, the NOOK uses the Day theme, which has black text against a white background; Night has white text against a black background. Other choices include different colored text, such as black text on a sepia background.

- **Margins.** Do you like wide margins? Narrow ones? Somewhere in the middle? Make your choice here.

As you can see in the nearby figures, the changes you can make are quite dramatic—one figure shows the text and display as out of the box, the other after it's been customized.

Rome: A Cultural, Visual, and Personal History

the apostle and first pope was allegedly buried after his martyrdom. The others are the Basilica of Saint Paul Outside the Walls, San Giovanni in Laterano (the actual cathedral of Rome), Saint Sebastian Outside the Walls, Santa Maria Maggiore (the greatest church dedicated specifically to the cult of Jesus' mother, Mary), Santa Croce in Gerusalemme, and Saint Lawrence Outside the Walls. The "walls" in each case are the Aurelian wall, erected around 271–75 C.E. to girdle the city. Only one of them, Saint Sebastian Outside the Walls, has no works of art of special interest; its attraction—now much diminished, because of the general loss of interest in the cult of relics as distinct from the drawing-power of famous works of art—lay in its relics, among which is a stone carrying the footprints of Jesus, an arrow which once pierced the body of that popular third-century martyr Saint Sebastian, and a fragment of the column to which he was tied while his fellow soldiers, having learned of his Christian conversion, shot at him. Of course, other pilgrimage churches do contain artworks, some of them fine; but the emphasis had always been more on their saintly associations than on

195 of 596

Rome: A Cultural, Visual, and Personal History

purple curtains, it reminds us of that glowing heaven, bathed in whose glories Dante saw SS. Bernard, Francis, Dominic, and Bonaventura. Then the spell of the work seizes us with its radiance like the music of some majestic anthem."

This is one of the few mosaic works in Rome that one may compare, in grandeur and intensity, to the Byzantine mosaics in Ravenna. Another is to be found in one of the ancient Roman churches, that of Saints Cosmas and Damian. Its history is actually much older than Christianity, since it was built, in the early sixth century C.E., into and on top of two Roman structures whose remains stood in the Forum of Ves-

194 of 596

Selecting Text, Taking Notes, Highlighting Text, and More

One of the niftiest things about the NOOK HD—and what sets it apart from reading a paper book—are the extras it gives you: notes, text highlighting, and the ability to select text and then do something with it—look up a word in a dictionary, say, or share it with others via email or social networking sites like Facebook.

It all starts with selecting text. Press and hold your finger on a word. As you hold your finger on it, the word gets highlighted and appears magnified inside a balloon so you can more easily read it.

2

Augustus

Until the advent of photography and then of TV, which effectively replaced them, propaganda statues were indispensable when it came to perpetuating the iconography of leadership. They were produced in mass numbers all over the world to celebrate the virtues and achievements of military heroes, political figures, wielders of every sort of power over all kinds of people. Most of them are wretched kitsch, but not all, and one of history's more successful icons of power is a marble statue exhumed in a villa that once belonged to the Empress Livia, wife of Octavian and mother of the future Emperor Tiber Octavius site of the Prima Porta, one of the ma......o ancient Rome. It is a portrait of her husband, by that time known as Gaius Julius Caesar Octavius, but known to the world and to history as the first of the Roman emperors, Augustus (63 B.C.–14 C.E.).

Rome: A Cultural, Visual, and Personal History

2

Augustus

Until the advent of photography and then of TV, which effectively replaced them, propaganda statues were indispensable when it came to perpetuating the iconography of leadership. They were produced in mass numbers all over the world to celebrate the virtues and achievements of military heroes, political figures, wielders of every sort of power over all kinds of people. Most of them are wretched kitsch, but not all, and one of history's more successful icons of power is a marble statue exhumed in a villa that once belonged to the Empress Livia, wife of Octavian and mother of the fu-

| Highlight | Add Note | Share Quote | Look Up | Find in Book |

It is a portrait of her husband, by that time known as Gaius Julius Caesar Octavius, but known to the world and to history as the first of the Roman emperors, Augustus (63 B.C.–14 C.E.).

71 of 596

When you release your finger, two vertical bars appear at each end of the word, and the Text Selection toolbar pops up as well. If you want to select more than the single word you just highlighted, drag one or both of the bars to highlight more text. The Text Selection toolbar stays above the highlighted section.

Now tap a button on the toolbar to do one of the following:

- **Highlight.** Does what the name says. After you highlight the text, as explained earlier, you can see a list of all your highlights by tapping Reading Tools→Contents.

- **Add Note.** Highlights the text and adds a note, as explained on page 97. As you read a book, you see a yellow note icon where you've added a note. Tap a note to read and edit it. As with highlights, you can see a list of all your notes by tapping Reading Tools→Contents.

- **Share Quote.** Tap and you can share the highlighted text (what the NOOK calls a quote) with your contacts, or with others on Facebook or Twitter. You'll have to first link your NOOK account to your Facebook and Twitter accounts if you want to share on those services. When you share via Contacts, a window opens where you can choose a contact or multiple contacts with whom to share the highlighted text via email; tap the Add Contacts button to select them. When you select either option for sharing with Facebook (either to your wall or a friend's wall), a window pops up that lets you post the highlighted text along with a note to your (or a friend's) Facebook wall. When you select Twitter, a window pops up letting you post it to your Twitter account.

NOTE When you share the quote, there's also a link to the book on the BN.com website. Keep in mind that Twitter only lets you post messages of 140 characters or less, so your quote and any comment have to be shorter than that. In fact, they'll have to be even shorter, since the link included in the Tweet uses some characters. Check the number in the lower-right corner of your Twitter window, which tells you how many characters you have left. If you see a negative number, you've gone over the limit, so you'll have to delete some text.

If you've copied the book you're reading from your computer to your NOOK, you may not be able to share the highlighted text with other people, and the button may be grayed out.

- **Look Up.** Searches the Merriam-Webster Collegiate Dictionary built into the NOOK, and shows you the results. But it does more than that as well. Your search term appears at the top of the screen, and next to it are two icons that may look familiar—they're for Google (the colorful letter g in the middle) and the online encyclopedia Wikipedia. Tap either icon and you'll go to Google or Wikipedia in the NOOK's browser and see the results of your search there. You can also change your search term in the search box to launch a new search.

- **Find in Book.** Tap this to search the book for other mentions of the term. See page 103 for more details about how to search inside the book.

If you decide to call the whole thing off and don't want to do anything with the text you just highlighted, tap anywhere on the screen; the Text Selection toolbar vanishes.

Handling Notes

When you tap the Add Note button on the Text Selection toolbar, a note-writing screen appears. You've got up 512 characters, so you can be more expansive than when using Twitter, with its 140-character limit. You can't write the Great American Novel in the text box, though—or even the Great American Short Story.

When you're done writing the note, tap Save. The Text Selection toolbar vanishes, and you're sent back to the book. The text you've just highlighted is in green, and there's a yellow note icon in the right margin of the page next to it.

To read the note, tap it. If you then want to edit it, tap Edit. You go back to the note-writing screen.

Want to do more with the note, such as changing its color, removing it, removing its color, and more? There's a simple way to do it. Tap the highlighted text (not the note icon), and a screen appears with these options:

2

Augustus

Until the advent of photography and then of TV, which effectively replaced them, propaganda statues were indispensable when it came to perpetuating the iconography of leadership. They were produced in mass numbers all over the world to celebrate the vir View Note ements of military heroes, political   rs of every sort of power over all l Edit Note Most of them are wretched kitsch   d one of history's more successful Remove Note is a marble statue exhumed in a vi   longed to the Empress Livia, wife Remove Highlight l mother of the future Emperor T   e site of the Prima Porta, one of the Change Color s to ancient Rome. It is a portrait of   y that time known as Gaius Julius C   but known to the world and to his   of the Roman emperors, Augustu   ).

71 of 596

- **View Note.** Does the same thing as tapping the note icon—you read the note.

- **Edit Note.** Takes you to the now-familiar note-editing screen.

NOTE Make sure that you just *tap* the note—don't hold your finger on it. If you press too long, you'll either see the text enlarged in a bubble or bring up the Text Selection toolbar.

- **Remove Note.** Deletes the note but keeps the text highlighted.

- **Remove Highlight.** Deletes both the note and the highlight.

- **Change Color.** Tap the color you want your notes to be, and that's what they'll use from now on.

TIP Want to remove all notes in one fell swoop? Use the Reader Tools menu to go to the table of contents, and then tap the Highlights and Notes tab and tap "Clear all."

To see all your notes, go to the book's table of contents from the Reader Tools menu, and then tap the Highlights and Notes tab. You'll see them all listed by the highlighted text associated with them. To jump to the note itself, tap the listing.

When you're on the Highlights and Notes tab, you can also hide all of your notes and highlights for a clutter-free reading experience. Turn off the Show Notes & Highlights button at the top of the screen. You can still see your notes and highlights on the Highlights and Notes tab; they just don't show up in the text itself.

TIP When you hide your notes and highlights, you can still create them in the normal way. As soon as you create a note or highlight, though, all your notes and highlights reappear again. You must return to the table of contents to turn them off again.

Handling Highlights

You handle highlights in the same way you handle notes. Create them by using the Text Selection toolbar, and view the list by going to the Highlights and Notes tab of the table of contents. Tap any highlight to see a menu of options similar to the one you get when you tap a note, although it's more limited. You can add a note to the highlight, remove the highlight, or change its color. If you add a note to the highlight, it then acts like any other note.

The statue is perhaps not, in itself, a great work of art; but it is competent, effective, and memorable, a marble copy of what was probably a Greek portrait in bronze, showing the hero in military dress, in the act of giving a speech either to the state as a whole or, more probably, to his army, on the eve of battle. As an image of calm, self-sufficient power projecting itself upon the world, it has few equals in the domain of sculpture. It does not ask of the viewer any particular knowledge of Roman history. But little is wholly self-explanatory. Take the design on the cuirass he is wearing, which shows—as most l   would have known, though we   pected to—the recovery by August   rmy's military standards, capture   y by the Parthians on the Eastern   .E.: the cancellation, therefore, of   lisgrace. It also helps to know that   f the love god Eros next to August   here to remind us that his family, t   ed to have descended from the g   so its presence reinforces the belief that Augustus was a living

Add Note

Remove Highlight

Change Color

Searching in Books

One of the most useful things you can do on your NOOK HD is search for a word or phrase in it. Try that with a printed book! You have two convenient ways to do it—the Reading Tools menu or the Text Selection toolbar.

To search using the Reading Tools menu, bring up the menu by tapping anywhere in the center of the screen; then tap Find. A search box and the keyboard appear. Type your search word or term, and then tap the Search button.

TIP When the search box appears, you see two X's at its right—one inside the box, and one to the far right outside the box. Tap the X *inside* the box to delete the search term already in the box. Tap the X *outside* the box to make the search box and keyboard disappear.

After a little while, a screen pops up showing you the results. You'll see the chapter and page number, the text surrounding your search term, and the search term itself. Scroll through the results and tap any of them; you jump to that spot in the book with the search term highlighted.

in stone all told."

Augustus (the name is a title bestowed by the
Senate, meaning "worthy of veneration," and it
carried the implication of numinousness, of semi-
divinity) was the son of Julius Caesar's niece,

Find

1. Foundation, p.69

grand-nephew, a weedy eighteen-year-old named Gaius **Octavius**. But it
turned out that in his will Caesar

1. Foundation, p.70

Meanwhile, barred from access to Caesar's fortune, Gaius **Octavius** used
his own lesser but still-considerable funds to raise

1. Foundation, p.70

Caesar was still magical to these old campaigners, and **Octavius** had
inherited its mana. And although he was no

1. Foundation, p.70

the dead Caesar's friend.   **Octavius** now marched his army of
hardened professionals on Rome.

2. Augustus, p.71

husband, by that time known as Gaius Julius Caesar **Octavius**, but known
to the world and to history as

Octavius

Underneath the results screen, you see a Search toolbar. You can type a new
search in its search box, or tap the double forward arrow to jump to the next
search result, or tap the double back arrow to jump to the previous search result.
Tap the small Table of Contents icon to the right of the search box to make the
search results screen disappear or to make it appear again if you've made it go
away. In both cases, though, the Search toolbar still stays in place.

When you select text and choose Find from the Text Selection toolbar, that does
the exact same thing as choosing Find from the Reading Tools menu. The NOOK
searches the book for the term you highlighted, and it shows the results in the
same way.

Reading Mode and Zooming in on Images

Most of the time, you'll probably read books with the NOOK HD held vertically—the standard reading mode. But there may come a time when you'd prefer to read in landscape mode—with the NOOK held horizontally. For example, you may come across a photo that's best viewed horizontally, or a table that looks best that way. Or you may just be in the mood for some widescreen reading—you renegade! No matter the reason, all you have to do is turn your NOOK so the longest side is at the bottom, and your NOOK automatically orients the book that way.

When you're viewing graphics or photos, the NOOK gives you an awesome power—the power to zoom. Tap the picture twice to zoom in. Tap the Close button at upper right to return to the normal view.

If you want to make sure your NOOK *never* changes orientation, tap the gear icon on the Notification bar so the Quick Settings screen appears. Then turn on the "Lock Rotation" toggle. That way, the NOOK always stays in landscape mode if that's where it was when you locked it. If it was in portrait mode, it will lock to that. To let it change its orientation, toggle it off.

Video Inside Books

Reading a book on the NOOK HD is more than a text-based experience; you can enjoy videos embedded in books, too. When you come across a video, tap its triangle to play it. Control the video using the usual controls at bottom for stopping and resuming, and dragging the bar to go forward or backward.

The Good H[Buy Now]Cookbook

CHOCOLATE GARNISHES

CHOCOLATE CURLS

Use these curls to garnish ice cream, cakes, and pies.

Prep: 15 minutes plus chilling

1 package (6 ounces) semisweet chocolate chips
2 tablespoons vegetable shortening

1. In heavy 1-quart saucepan, combine chocolate chips and shortening; heat over low heat, stirring frequently, until melted and smooth.

2. Pour chocolate mixture into foil-lined or disposable $5\frac{1}{2}$" by $3\frac{1}{4}$" loaf pan. Refrigerate until chocolate is set, about 2 hours.

3 of 8

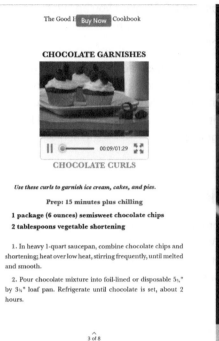

If you'd like to see the video taking up the full screen, tap the icon that has four outward-pointing arrows. You'll see video controls for a few seconds, but then they vanish. To make them reappear, tap the screen. To get back to the page you were just reading, tap the Back button at upper left.

Tapping Links

Some books include links in them, for example, from text to footnotes or endnotes. Links aren't underlined as they often are on the Web. Instead, they're in blue. Tap to follow the link. Generally, when you tap a link and go to its destination, there's also a link you can tap to get you back to where you were before you followed the link.

Reading PDFs

When you buy books for your NOOK HD, they're in a format called EPUB. NOOK books you borrow and lend are in that format as well. But your NOOK is a do-everything device when it comes to e-reading, and it can handle more than EPUB books—it can read PDF files as well.

You typically get PDF files by copying them to your NOOK from your computer, as described on page 277.

NOTE When you tap a PDF to read it, you'll be asked whether you want to open it in OfficeSuite or the Reader. The Reader has more reading features than OfficeSuite, so it's your best bet. If you want PDFs to always open in the Reader (or OfficeSuite), turn on the checkbox next to "Use by default for this option" before making your choice.

Reading a PDF is much like reading a book, with some important differences:

- At the top of the Reading Tools menu there's a thumbnail viewer that shows thumbnails of every page in the PDF. Swipe through the thumbnails, and when you find a page you want to read, tap it. Tapping it also closes the Reading Tools menu.

- Zoom in on a page by double-tapping it; zoom out by double-tapping it again.

- Most of the tools on the Reading Tools menu aren't available for PDFs. You can't share quotes or reviews of the PDF, highlight text, create highlights, or change the display of the pages.

Reading Magazines

The NOOK HD is great for reading magazines as well as newspapers, with plenty of features designed specifically for magazines. Some tools are similar to reading books—like the way you turn the pages—but others are entirely new, like ArticleView, where you see only the text of an article, without illustrations.

NOTE Magazines come in a variety of formats, and so the features in each magazine may vary somewhat. This section covers the format used by most popular magazines.

You can read a magazine in two different views:

- **Magazine View.** In this view, the magazine looks exactly like the printed version of the magazine, including the page layout, photos and graphics, and advertising.

- **ArticleView.** In this view, you see only the text of articles, with no layout, photographs, graphics, or advertising to get in your way.

Using Magazine View

Just as with a book, you get around a magazine in Magazine View by swiping your fingers or tapping on the right or left edges of the screen to go forward one page or back one page.

NOTE The Text Selection tools don't work in all magazines.

You can use regular (portrait) or landscape mode when reading a magazine. Depending on the magazine's layout, one or the other may look better. Photo spreads or the beginning of highly designed articles often look better in landscape than portrait mode, as do certain photographs.

In Magazine View, text may be small and difficult to read. If that's the case, spread your thumb and forefinger outward to zoom in; pinch them in to zoom back out. You can also double-tap to zoom in and then zoom out, but pinching gives you finer control over the level of zoom. (For a refresher on gestures, see page 35.)

Magazines also have their own specialized Reading Tools menu. Tap the center of the screen to make it appear. It doesn't have the full complement of tools you'll find in the Reading Tools menu for books—no sharing, no changing the display. But it does the job, and it also has a feature that you won't find in books: a row of small thumbnails of every page in the magazine. Swipe through the pages, tap the one you want to read, and you're there.

But the Reading Tools menu has more features than just the thumbnails. Here's what you'll find:

- **Information button.** This button on the lower left brings you back to the description of the magazine you get when you tap it in the NOOK Shop.

- **Table of Contents.** Lists the magazine's table of contents, including small thumbnails of the front page of each article, the title of the article, and a short description. Tap any to go there. In the table of contents, tap the Bookmarks icon to see any bookmarks you've placed in the magazine. Adding a bookmark is simple: There's a very small plus sign at the top right of each magazine page. Tap that plus sign, and it turns into a dog-ear— you've just bookmarked the page. To remove the bookmark, tap the dog-ear and it turns back into a plus sign.

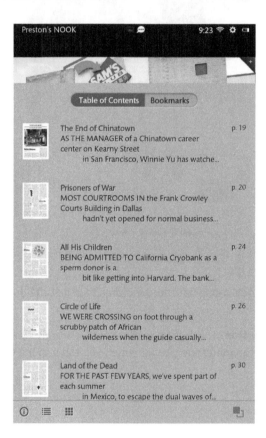

- **Grid button.** Shows the magazine pages laid out in a grid of two-page spreads. Tap the button again to return to the normal view.

- **Clip to Scrapbook.** This lets you save the current page as a clip to the NOOK HD's nifty Scrapbook feature, which lets you keep copies of pages from magazines and catalogs in separate scrapbooks. See page 122 for details.

Clip this page to...

New Scrapbook

Cancel

- **ArticleView.** In this view, you see only the text of articles, with no layout, photographs, graphics, or advertising to get in your way. How does it work? Glad you asked. That's what we'll cover in the next section.

NOTE Not all of these features are available in all magazines.

Using ArticleView

When you're getting down to serious article reading, you may want to use ArticleView. Although you won't see the layout or pictures, the text is larger and appears in a long, scrollable window—no distractions. You can also adjust the text size and font in ArticleView, something you can't do in Magazine View.

Siberian Paradise

AT PLAY IN RUSSIA'S "SACRED SEA"

By Nicholas Schmidle

Russia's Lake Baikal, the world's oldest and deepest lake, has lured shamans, explorers, and adventurers for centuries.

PER-ANDRE HOFFMANN/AURORA PHOTOS

ONE RECENT AUTUMN evening, in the bosom of Siberia, I stood outside a modest log cabin perched on the shore of Lake Baikal and prepared to lose my clothes. The mercury hovered in the low 40s, and a chill, foreboding breeze kicked up off the lake. Aspens, Siberian firs, and yellowing birches cloaked the surrounding hills. My friend Sergey Bikkinaev and I leaned against the railing on the cabin's front porch and peered, through the dusk, across an inlet of the world's deepest lake.

From where we stood, at Lake Baikal's southernmost end, the distance to the northern tip was roughly the same as the distance between Baltimore and Boston. Containing about a fifth of the world's unfrozen fresh water, the banana-shaped lake covers a

Magazine View

NOTE Not all magazines let you use ArticleView.

To use ArticleView, when you're in Magazine View, tap the ArticleView button at the top of the screen to open the scrollable text window. The entire article is in that window, so you don't have to turn pages. Sometimes there'll be a photo or graphic at the very beginning of the article, but apart from that, there are no pictures.

To read the article, just scroll. To close ArticleView and return to Magazine View, tap the Magazine View button at the bottom of the page.

ArticleView has its own Reading Tools menu. Tap the center of the screen, and it appears. You'll find the information button, table of contents button, and grid view button. And you'll also find a Text button that lets you change the size of text, font, line spacing, margins, and so on (black on white, white on black, black on gray, and so on), in the same way you can do it in books.

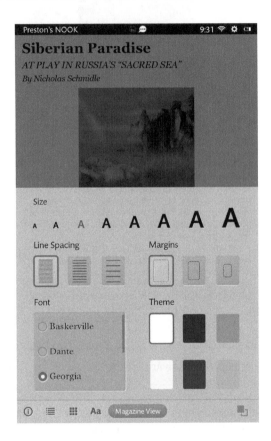

Navigating isn't as easy in ArticleView as in Magazine View, because each article is its own self-enclosed world and there's no thumbnail display. So to get around in ArticleView, tap the middle of the page to open the Reading Tools menu, tap the Content icon to get to the table of contents, and then tap the next article you want to read. When you get there, though, you'll be in Magazine View, so if you want to read in ArticleView, tap the ArticleView icon again.

Reading Newspapers

Bruce Springsteen Releases New Sci-Fi Concept Album About Struggles Of Poor Miners Working On Mars

RUMSON, NJ—After more than a year of writing and recording, Bruce Springsteen released his 18th studio album Tuesday, a concept record titled Red Dust that explores the everyday lives and struggles of immigrant workers scraping by in the 23rd-century carbonate mines on Mars.

According to the 61-year-old songwriter, the new

Reading newspapers is much like reading books, and even includes the same Reading Tools menu. You open a newspaper in the same way you do a book or a magazine—by tapping its cover. The NOOK newspaper won't look like its print counterpart. Instead of laid-out newspaper pages, you'll see scrollable lists of stories.

NOTE The NOOK version of a newspaper may not include *everything* that's in the paper-based version. It may not have all the photos, comics, or puzzles, for example.

The Onion Inc

Previous Article Next Article

News

Bruce Springsteen Releases New Sci-Fi Concept Album About Struggles Of Poor Miners Working On Mars

RUMSON, NJ—After more than a year of writing and recording, Bruce Springsteen released his 18th studio album Tuesday, a concept record titled Red Dust that explores the everyday lives and struggles of immigrant workers scraping by in the 23rd-century carbon-

A.V. Club Film   272 of 3663

Go to Page

ⓘ ≣ Aa 💬 👓

Tap any story to read it. Navigate through the story just as you do in a book, by swiping your finger or tapping the page edges. Tap anywhere in the center of the page to bring up the Reading Tools menu, which works just as it does in books. To bookmark a page, tap in the upper-right corner. The Text Selection toolbar works the same way as well, but it may be a bit tricky to manage when you're reading the newspaper on the subway.

Reading Comic Books

The NOOK HD also lets you read comic books. You navigate the same way as with magazines. The text tool may or may not work, depending on the comic book you're reading.

Reading Catalogs

Are you a fan of catalogs? If so you're in luck, because the NOOK Shop has plenty for you, and they're easy to read—they use the same reading tools as magazines.

Using Scrapbooks

Scrapbooks are a nifty way to save pages from books and magazines. You create individual scrapbooks and keep pages in them. So, for example, you might have one scrapbook devoted to food, another to sports, another to opera, and so on.

Saving pages in a Scrapbook is easy. You can do it in two different ways:

- Tap the center of the screen in a magazine or catalog to open the Reading Tools menu, and then tap the scissors icon.

- In a magazine or catalog, swipe down from the center of the screen with two fingers.

Either way, you come to a screen that shows a thumbnail of the current page at the top, and at the bottom lets you save the page to any existing Scrapbook or to a new Scrapbook. Tap the Scrapbook you want to save it to. You'll get a notification that page has been saved to the Scrapbook.

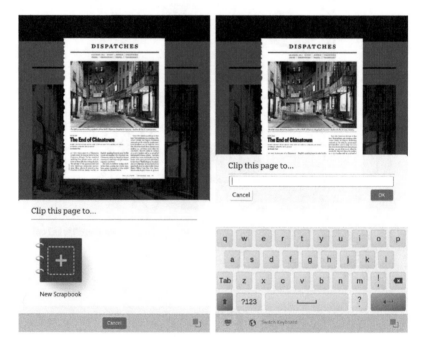

To create a new Scrapbook to save the page to, tap "New Scrapbook." A screen appears that lets you type in the name of the Scrapbook. Type in the name, tap OK, and the new Scrapbook gets saved, with the page in it. You'll get a notification that the page has been saved to the new scrapbook.

Reading Scrapbooks

To read a Scrapbook, tap the Library on the Home screen, and then scroll to the My Scrapbooks section. Tap any you want to open. You'll come to the first page of the Scrapbook if it's the first time you're opening it, or else to the last page of the Scrapbook you read.

Navigate through the Scrapbook in the same way you do through magazines, by swiping left or right. As with magazines, bookmark a page in it by tapping the upper right-corner part of the screen, and zoom in and out as you do with magazines.

Scrapbooks have their own Reading Tools menu; tap the center of the screen to display it. They have a table of contents that lists every page, and also shows any notes you've put into the scrapbook (more on that in a minute), and any bookmarks you've created.

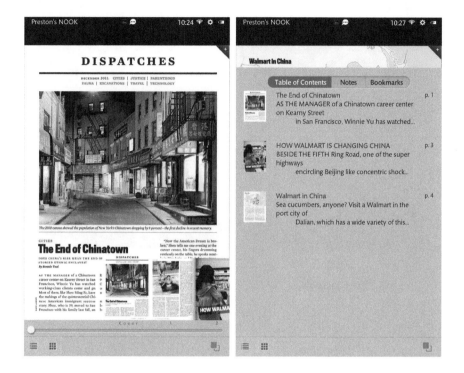

To add a note to a page, hold your finger on the page, and a small menu pops up. Tap Note, type in your note from the screen that appears, and then tap Save. As with notes in books, you'll see a small yellow icon indicating there's a note on the page. Tap it to read it. When you're reading it, tap Delete to delete it, or Edit to edit it. You can also see all your notes in the table of contents and jump to them.

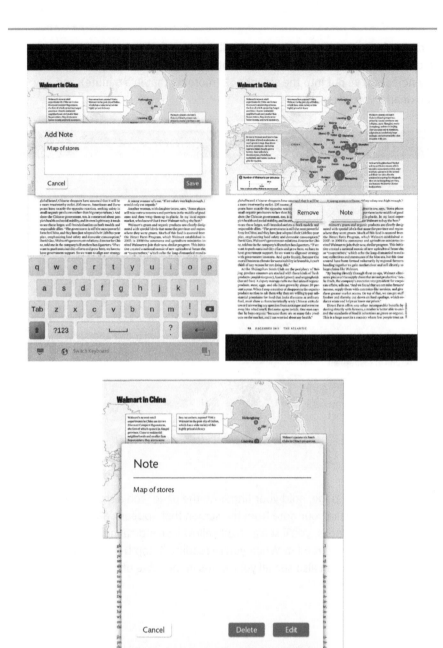

To remove a page from the Scrapbook, hold your finger on the page and tap Remove. A popup asks if you want to remove the page. Tap OK to remove the page, or Cancel to keep it.

Nearby the Elephant's uncle, the hairy Baboon, was busy eating a juicy melon. "What makes melons taste just so, Uncle Baboon?"

"SHUSH!" the Baboon bellowed. "So many questions! Take your nosy-nose somewhere else!"

So the Elephant did exactly that.

CHAPTER 6

Reading NOOK Kids Books

KIDS' BOOKS TRULY COME alive on the NOOK, with interactive activities and features—you can even record yourself reading the book, so your child can listen to you reading even when you can't be there. You'll learn how to do all that and more in this chapter.

What Can NOOK Kids Books Do?

Kids aren't like adults, and the books they read aren't the same as adult books, either. NOOK Kids books are different from NOOK books for adults, with plenty of additional features. They're specifically formatted for high-resolution touch-screen displays, and they're designed to be read in landscape mode (horizontally) rather than most books' vertical orientation. That way, you can see an entire two-page spread at a time—the way children's books are designed to be read.

A NOOK Kids book can also read itself aloud, or, as mentioned earlier, you can record your own voice doing the reading. What could be more comforting to your child when you're not around?

Beyond all that, many NOOK books for kids also have interactive features, including games and educational play.

Buying a NOOK Kids Book

A NOOK Kids book can have any number of features, such as interactivity or the ability to record your voice reading the book to your child. Not all kids' books have all the available features. When you open a book, you can see its capabilities, which may include the following:

- **Read by Myself.** The child can read the book to herself onscreen. Every children's book falls into this category.

- **Read to Me.** The book includes narration so the child can hear the book read aloud.

- **Read and Play.** The book includes narration as well as interactive features, such as playing games or drawing on the screen.

- **Read and Record.** You can record your voice reading the book aloud, so your kid can listen to it whenever he wants.

Before buying a kids' book, carefully read its description to make sure you're getting the features that are most important to you and your children. "Read and Play" means that the book is interactive, and "Read to Me" means that the book will read itself to your kids. Many "Read and Play" books frequently have the "Read to Me" feature as well.

The book description may also have more details, including what types of interactive features are included.

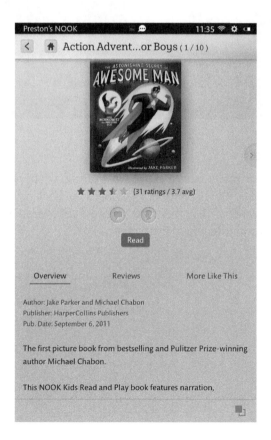

Reading a NOOK Kids Book

Open a NOOK Kids book as you do any other book—tap its cover. The book opens to landscape mode, so turn the NOOK to match its orientation. On the righthand side of the screen you see the book cover, and on the left you find square buttons, letting you choose in which mode to open the book—"Read by Myself," "Read and Play," "Read to Me," and "Read and Record." The exact buttons that appear depend upon the capabilities built into the book.

Read by Myself

If you and your child (or your child alone) want to read the book without narration, tap the "Read by Myself" button. That opens the book without using the audio track or narration, although the activities are still available—tap the white star when it appears at the top of the screen.

Go forward or back as you would normally in a book: Swipe to the left or right to move forward or back a page, or tap the right (forward) or left (back) side of the screen.

If the text in a book is too small to read, double-tap on the text and you zoom in on it. Double-tap again or tap anywhere on the page or pinch your fingers to zoom out. If the book has an audio track, when you enlarge the text, you see a Play button in the shape of an orange triangle in the top-left corner. Tap that button to play the audio—and, yes, you can play it even if you've opened the book in "Read by Myself" mode. If there are any animations associated with the audio, they'll play as well.

NOTE When you turn the page after you've enlarged text, you see normal-size text on the next page, not the enlarged size. And if you've played audio on the page, the next page won't automatically play audio.

You can also zoom in on pictures by pinching out, as you normally do on the NOOK. When you're zoomed in you can also move the page around to get a better look at the picture you've zoomed in on, for example, moving it toward the center of the screen. Double-tap anywhere on the screen to zoom out and to return the page to its normal position.

NOTE You can also enlarge text by pinching out, but when you enlarge text in this way, you don't get to play the audio track. You can play the audio track only if you double-tap the text to enlarge it. Strange but true.

When you come across a page with a star on it, that means you can play an activity, which can be just about anything—changing the colors on the page, drawing on the page, and more. Tap the star to run the activity. Arrows appear at either side of the page, the star turns into a square, and a narrator tells you about the activity and how you can play it—for example, tapping anywhere on a page to add mutant alien slime (thankfully it's onscreen only; no cleanup required).

NOTE   Even on pages without stars on them, try tapping pictures. In some cases, when you tap they'll animate or play music.

To move to the next or previous page, tap either arrow. That's right, when you're playing, you tap arrows, rather than the screen margins. That's because, when you do an activity, the screen becomes active, so touching it spurs an action of some kind, like adding color instead of turning pages. If you want to stay on the same page but would like the activity to end, tap the square, and you go back to normal reading mode.

Listening to "Read to Me" and "Read and Play" Books

If you'd prefer to have the book read aloud to your child, tap the "Read to Me" or "Read and Play" button when you open the book. (Not all books have activities; if you open one that doesn't, there's no "Read and Play" button.)

At this point, nothing could be simpler: The book opens, and a narrator starts reading. The narration plays only for that page, and stops when the full page is read. To go on to the next page or back to the previous page, use your favorite page-turning gesture. When you get to the new page, the narration starts. If you want to go to the next or previous page in the middle of a page being read, just turn the page; the narration stops, and then begins reading the page to which you've turned.

Everything in the books works just like "Read by Myself" mode—you can zoom in and out of text and graphics, do activities when you see a star, and so on. When you do activities, the narration stops, but it continues if you zoom in and out of graphics and text.

Navigating Kids Books

When you're reading a NOOK Kids book, the Reading Tools menu doesn't work as it does in typical NOOK books. Tapping the center of the page does nothing. But if you tap the small up arrow at the bottom of the screen, you see a navigation toolbar with thumbnails of every page in the book. Swipe through the thumbnails, tap the page you want to read (or have read to you), and there you go. If you decide you don't want to go to another page, tap the down arrow or anywhere on the page to make the thumbnail navigation disappear.

NOTE   Because there's no Reading Tools menu in Kids books, there's no way to get to a table of contents, no way to change the text display or brightness, and so on.

He then saw his tall uncle. "Uncle Giraffe!" the Elephant called out. "How many spots do you have?"

"SHOO!" his uncle muttered. "So many questions! Take your nosy-nose somewhere else!"

//0 library

The Elephant's Child: How the Eleph...

NOTE The thumbnails don't display the star that tells you whether pages have activities on them. So the only way to know whether there's an activity on a page is to go to it.

Record Reading a NOOK Kids Book for Your Kids

It's an unfortunate fact of parenting that you can't always be there to read to your kids when you want to be there. The NOOK offers the next best thing—the ability to record yourself reading a NOOK Kids book, so that you child can listen to you reading the book to her when you're not there. When she listens to you reading the book, it works just like listening to the normal reading of the book, except it's your voice. And, of course, you don't need to stick to the text of the page; you can add inside jokes, asides, and anything else you want to your recording. (We won't tell.)

TIP As a way to encourage your child to read, you might want to record him reading the book. That way, he can listen to himself read the book afterward, and even read along with himself if he wants.

To record yourself reading a book, open the book and tap the "Read and Record" button. The first page of the book opens. Tap the green Record button to start recording your voice; the green button turns red, and an indicator appears, showing that you're reading. Tap the red Stop button to finish your recording.

The buttons on the bottom of the screen change. Tap Play to listen to your recording. While it's playing, you can pause it by tapping the Pause button. If after you listen to it you're not satisfied, tap Re-record and try again. When you're finished, move on to the next page using the normal way of moving through NOOK books.

Sometimes as you're trying to record yourself reading the book, the Record and other buttons may cover up the text. If that happens, put your finger on the Move button and drag the set of buttons somewhere else.

NOTE   If you're recording yourself reading a book and for some reason you switch away from the book, (for example, to read another book), the NOOK automatically saves your recording. For details about editing a recording, see the next page.

Keep recording yourself until you've finished recording the entire book, or until you want to stop recording for now. As you'll see in the next section, you can always come back later and finish the book or re-record what you've already read.

When you're ready, tap Done. A window appears that lets you name the recording and choose a picture associated with it. This name and picture will appear when your child opens the book, so choose words that mean something to her. Keep it short and easy for your child to read.

The next time your child (or you) opens the book, your recording will be listed on a button at the bottom left of the screen. All he'll need to do is tap it. If he'd prefer to hear the original recording rather than you (no dessert for him if he does!), he can tap the "Read to Me" button instead.

You can have more than one recording for each book. After you've recorded one, when you open the book, tap "Read and Record" and record a second one, giving it a different name and picture. So you might record one, your spouse another, and your kids yet others.

TIP Unlike the audio track that comes with a NOOK Kids book, your recording is not saved as part of the book itself. Instead, it's saved as a separate audio file in the device's My Files section. For details about how to handle that recording, and even listen to it separately from the book itself, see page 144.

Editing or Deleting a Recording

It's easy to edit or delete a recording. After all, even professional voice artists rarely get it perfect in the first take. When you open the book, tap the Edit link, and Edit buttons appear above the names of all of your recordings. Tap the Edit button next to the recording you want to edit or record, and here's what you can do:

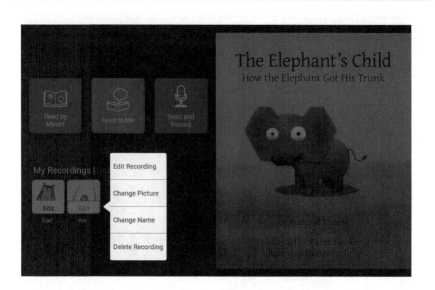

- **Edit Recording.** Sends you to the first page of the book with the Re-record, Play, and Done buttons visible.

- **Change Picture.** Takes you to a window where you can choose a new picture for the recording.

- **Change Name.** Takes you to a window where you can choose a new name for the recording.

- **Delete Recording.** Deletes the recording, but not immediately. Instead, you'll be asked whether you really, truly do want to delete it.

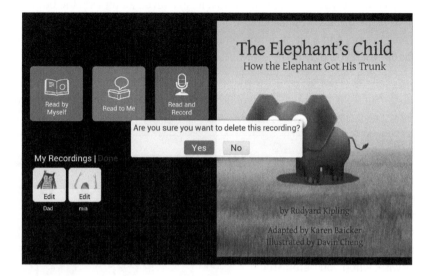

Tips for Better Recording

When your kids hear you reading to them, you obviously want them to hear your voice as clearly as possible, instead of sounding as if you were talking into a tin can. So follow these tips, and they should hear you loud and clear:

- **Speak slowly and distinctly.** Most people talk too quickly when they record audio. Remember, this isn't a race; it's something you want your kids to enjoy.

- **Practice reading each page a few times before recording it.** That way, you'll learn what words and syllables to emphasize, and what kind of emotion you want to put into your voice.

- **Make sure there's as little background noise as possible.** Car horns and emergency sirens don't make for the most pleasant listening experience.

- **Hold your NOOK between a foot and a foot and a half from your face.** That's the optimum distance so that your voice will be recorded clearly with no distortion.

- **Don't cover the microphone with your fingers.** The microphone is a small hole on the upper-right side of the NOOK, to the left of the sound jack. If you cover it up, your voice won't be heard.

Backing Up Your Recordings

When you record yourself reading a book, it isn't saved along with the book itself, as is the book's original audio track. Instead, it's saved on your NOOK's internal storage, and a bit of programming magic merges the audio track with the book when you play it.

NOTE Your NOOK HD stores your recordings on its internal storage, not on an SD card if you've installed one.

Why should you care? If you ever erase all of your NOOK's content and deregister it (see page 407), you can copy the files to your computer so that you'll always have them. Otherwise, when you deregister your device, the recordings will be lost forever. You can also listen to them in the NOOK's Media Player, rather than in the book itself. (Is this a useful or practical thing to do? Not really. Then why do it? Because you can.)

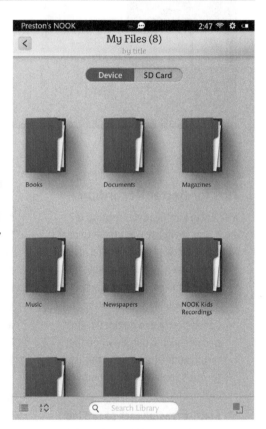

To do it, first browse to see the audio files themselves. In the Library, scroll to "My Files" and tap it. From the screen that appears, tap Device at the top of the screen. Then tap NOOK Kids Recordings. You'll come to a folder named something really useful and enlightening, like 2940000920596. Tap it and you'll come to more folders with even longer and more confusing names. Each of those folders contains all of your recordings for an individual NOOK Kids book.

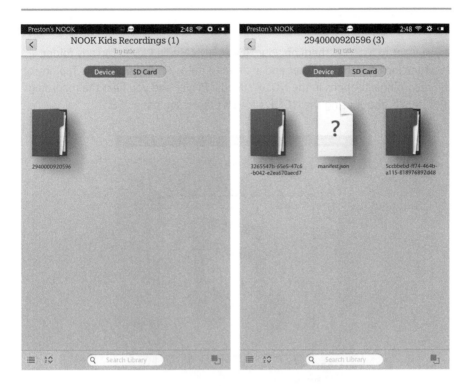

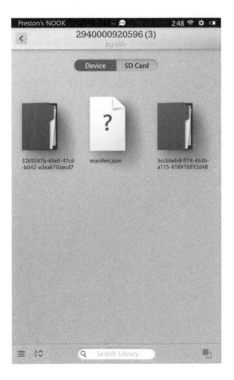

Back these up to a personal computer if you want to preserve them.

If you want to listen to them on your NOOK HD's Media Player, tap any folder, and then look for any files that end in .m4a—1.m4a, 2.m4a, and so on. Tap any of the recordings. It opens in the NOOK's Media Player and you hear the recording. (For details about using the NOOK's Media Player, see page 258.)

Managing Your Library

CHAPTER 7:

Buying Books, Magazines, and Newspapers and Managing Your Library

CHAPTER 8:

Borrowing and Lending Books with LendMe and Your Local Library

Buying Books, Magazines, and Newspapers and Managing Your Library

THE NOOK HD IS your entrée into the world of books, magazines, newspapers, and apps—literally millions of them. And you get them all through the NOOK Shop. Once you've downloaded books, they live in your NOOK's Library. In this chapter you'll learn how to buy books and periodicals in the NOOK Shop and how to manage your Library.

NOTE When you buy a book, newspaper, or magazine, it's available not just on your NOOK, but also to a NOOK app if you have one on another smartphone or tablet, as well as on a personal computer. See "Managing your NOOK Account" on page 187 for details.

Browsing and Searching for Books in the NOOK Shop

To get to the NOOK Shop, from the Home screen tap the Shop icon. You go straight to the NOOK Shop.

NOTE You can get to the NOOK Shop only when you're connected to a WiFi network.

At the upper left of the page are scrollable, changing lists of books and more, such as B&N Top 100, Cool NOOK Books, Picked Just For You (based on your previous purchases), and more. To the right of it are categories—Books, Magazines, Movies & TV, Kids, Apps, Newspapers, and so on.

The bottom half of the screen is taken up by even more lists, such as Innovative Thinking, Read and Play, and so on. Flick through the lists and tap any app, book, movie, or publication that catches your eye.

At the very bottom of the page, there's a search box so you can look for specific books. To the left of the search box are two icons. The heart brings you to your Wish List (more about that on page 181). The small shopping bag icon brings you to items that you've recently viewed.

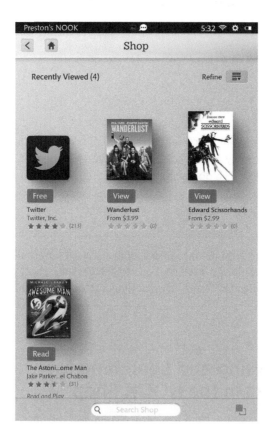

The NOOK Shop also has catalogs you can download for free. Unlike the ones sent to you in the mail, though, the environment isn't harmed in their creation and distribution. Tap the Catalogs button in the NOOK Shop to browse them. You browse through them and download them in essentially the same way as you do books.

Tap Books, and you come to a page that looks a lot like the NOOK Shop's home page, except everything here is about books. There are constantly changing lists of books on the top left, and a list of categories to browse on the upper right, such as New Releases, NYT (New York Times) Bestsellers, NOOK Recommends, and so on. Down in the bottom half of the page are more scrollable lists (of books, of course). And at the very bottom you'll find search as well as the Wish List and Recently Viewed icons.

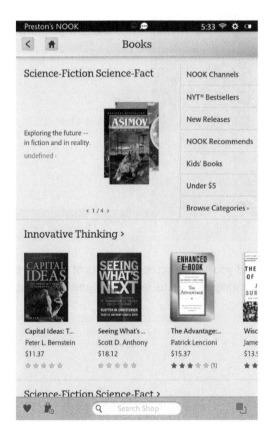

You might overlook one of the most important buttons on the page—Browse Categories. Tap it and a category list pops up. It's a very long list, longer than can fit on a single screen, so scroll through it.

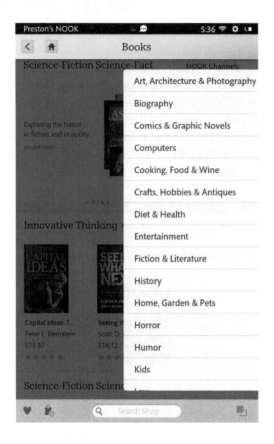

Tap any category and you'll see a screen with lists of books in that category you can scroll horizontally—Books to Talk About and Jane Austen & Heirs, for example.

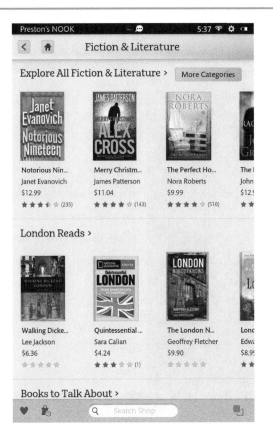

On the upper right of the screen, there's a More Categories button. Tap it, and a scrollable subcategory list appears. From that screen you'll see books in that subcategory, and possibly another More Categories list. Tap it and come to yet another subcategory list, and so on, until you've finally gotten to the precise sub-sub-sub...(you get the idea)...category of book you're interested in. For example, you may start off with Books, then get to the Fiction & Literature category, then to the historical Fiction subcategory, then to the Medieval Europe sub-sub-subcategory.

If a book has a banner (which the NOOK calls a *badge*) with LendMe across it, it means that after you buy the book, you can lend it to your NOOK Friends. See page 191 for details.

When you get there, you see various scrollable lists of books in that subcategory. Tap "Explore All..." to see a list of every book in that category, for example, "Explore All Medieval Europe." Tap any book to see more information about it.

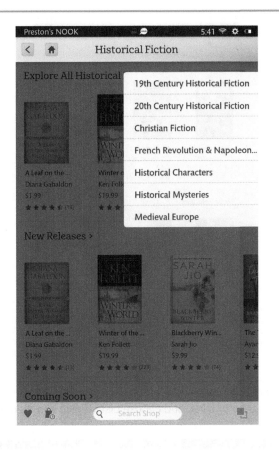

No matter where you are in the NOOK Shop, you can get to the shop's opening screen, its front door. Tap the icon of the house at the top left of the screen. And to move up a single level, tap the back arrow to the left of the house.

What if you want to look at a list of titles in a different order? Up at the top of the screen, tap the icon next to Refine drop-down arrow next to Best Selling, and you can choose to see the books in a different order—the newest first, oldest first, in alphabetical order, reverse alphabetical order, by best-selling, and so on.

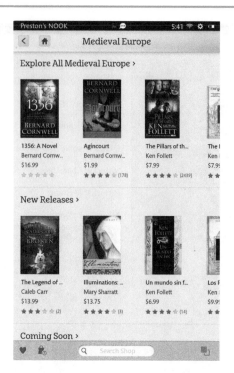

You can even change the way the list looks. Choose Grid View to display the books in a grid instead of a list, and choose List view to see them in a list.

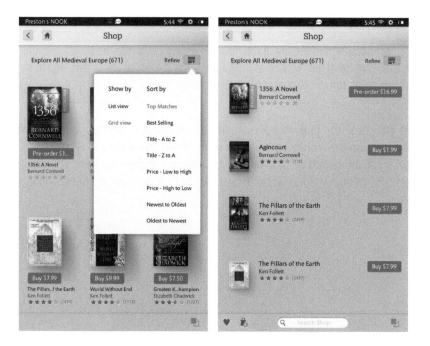

Searching for Books

If you're on a more targeted mission than leisurely browsing—if there's a particular book, author, or topic you're interested in—tap the search box at the bottom of the screen. The box pops up to the top of the screen, and displays your most recent searches. Tap any to launch it again.

If you want to do a new search, type in a search term (or a few terms) into the search box. As you type, the search results narrow down. Tap a result to launch that search, or finish typing your search terms and then tap the Search button on the keyboard.

TIP The NOOK Shop has many, many books you can download and read for free, rang-ing from the classics from authors like Charles Dickens and Jane Austen to reference books and contemporary novels. You won't find them in any one category, though. So if you're looking for free books, search for "free books for nook" in the shop and you'll pull up a massive list.

After you do a search, your results appear in a moment or two. Handle the results list just like any subcategory list—reorder the results and change the way they're displayed to your heart's content.

Sampling and Buying Books

Now that you're done searching and browsing, it's time to take the plunge and buy a book.

NOTE You can also preorder a book that hasn't yet been released. If the book hasn't been released yet, the word "Preorder" appears.

Tap a book's cover. You can buy the book by tapping the blue button with the price on it anytime—but you don't have to commit yet. Say you want more information before you're ready to buy. It's laid right there in front of you. You'll see three links below the price:

- **Overview.** Provides a good deal of information about the book, including customer ratings on a five-star scale (and the total number of people who have reviewed it), a lengthy description of the book, and similar information.
- **Customer Reviews.** Here's where you can read the reviews. You can also rate each review as to how helpful it was, and report the review if you think something is fishy about it—the author rating his own book, perhaps, or if it contains material that violates B&N terms of conduct.

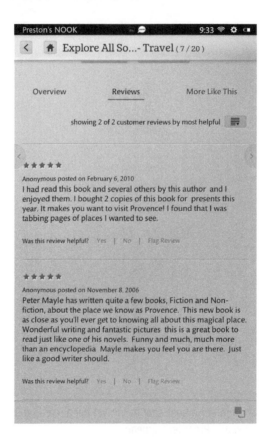

It can be tough sifting through the useful and useless reviews, so the NOOK has thoughtfully given you a tool to help find the useful ones. At the top-right of the reviews there's a button with vertical lines that lets you sort the reviews by customer reviews, editorial reviews, most recent reviews, and so on.

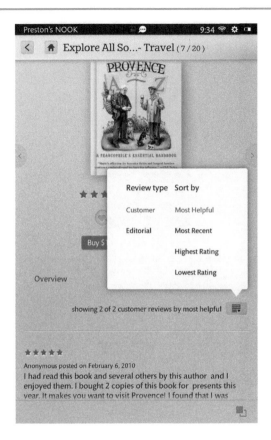

- **More Like This.** Shows a list of books that people who have bought the current book have also bought.

TIP If you think you may want to buy the book at some point but not just yet, add it to your NOOK wish list by tapping "Add to Wishlist" Tab. Keep in mind, though, that your NOOK's wish list is separate from your wish list on the BN.com website. The BN.com wish list contains items that you can't buy on your NOOK (paper-only books and paper-only newspapers and magazines), while the NOOK contains only items you can buy on the NOOK, which includes apps, not just books and periodicals.

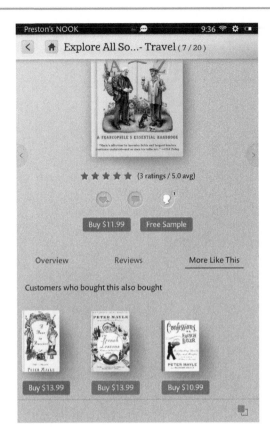

Just below the price and rating of the book are three useful icons:

- **Wish List.** This button is in the shape of a heart. Tap it and it gets added to your Wish List (page 181).

- **Rate and Review.** Tap this and a pop-up menu lets you rate, review, and recommend the book to others. Tap Recommend, and another screen appears, where you can recommend the book to your Facebook wall, on a friend's Facebook wall, via Twitter, or to a contact via email. Tap "Rate and Review" to write a review and rate the book. Tap "Like on Facebook" if all you want to do is give the book a Like on your wall.

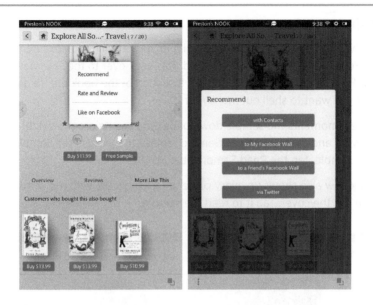

- **Buy for a Profile.** Tap this and you'll see a pop-up menu that lists all of the profiles you've created on your NOOK (page 61). Tap any or all profiles in which you want the purchased book to so a checkmark appears, and then tap Save. You only pay for the book once, and it appears in any or all profiles.

Sampling Books

Say you've gone through all this material and you're still not quite sure you want to buy. You're interested but not yet sold. Tap back over to the Overview tab and tap Free Sample. You can then read a section of the book before deciding whether you want to shell out money for it.

After a few moments the sample downloads (you see its progress right on the book cover), and the words Read Sample replace the words Free Sample. To read the sample, tap the Read Sample button.

The book now also shows up every place books show up, with the word "Sample" on the cover. Tap it to read the sample.

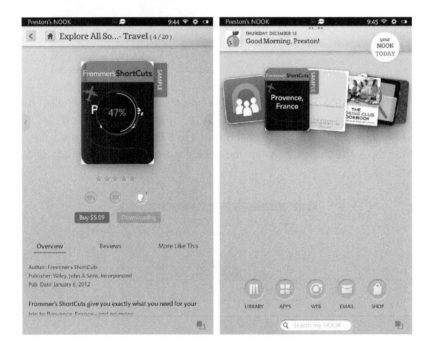

You can now read the book as you would normally. The difference, of course, is that you won't be able to read the entire book. The other difference is that a Buy Now button appears on all the pages.

> **TIP** What if the sample you've downloaded isn't sufficient for you to make a buying decision, and you want to read even more? Head over to your closest Barnes & Noble store. When you're in a B&N store, you get an hour of reading any NOOK book for free (Appendix C).

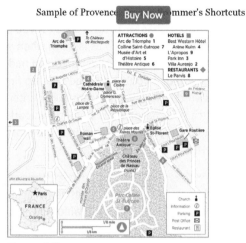

Essentials

Getting There Trains to Orange arrive from Avignon and Marseille, among other places. From the Gare de Lyon Paris, you can catch a TGV train to Orange. For rail information, call *☏* **36-35,** or visit [link:www.-voyages-sncf.com]. For information on bus routes, contact the **gare routière** (*☏* **04-90-34-15-59**), cours Pourtoules, behind the Théâtre Antique. If you're **driving** from Paris, take A6 south to Lyon, then A7 to Orange.

Visitor Information The **Office de Tourisme** is at 5 cours Aristide-Briand (*☏* **04-90-34-70-88;** fax 04-90-34-99-62; www.otorange.fr).

Special Events From early July to early August, a drama, dance, and music festival called **Les Chorégies d'Orange** takes place at the Théâtre Antique, one of the most evocative ancient theaters in Europe. For information or tickets, contact the office, 18 place Silvain, adjacent to the theater (*☏* **04-90-34-24-24;** fax 04-90-11-04-04; www.chore-

Buying Books

Time to buy the book. It's simple to do. If you're reading the sample, tap the Buy Now button. You get sent back to the description of the book in the Shop. If you're already in the Shop, or you just got sent there from the sample, tap the Buy button. The Buy button turns to a Confirm button. Tap the Confirm button to buy the book.

> **NOTE** After you buy a book or a magazine, Barnes & Noble will send you an email confirming your purchase.

When you tap to buy, what happens next depends upon whether you've customized the Shop (see page 400 in Chapter 17 for details). If you haven't done any customization, and just left the Shop set up as is, then when you tap the Confirm button, the book downloads, and the credit card you had on file when you registered the NOOK is charged. If you've told the Shop to first ask you to enter your B&N account password before you buy anything, enter your password. Either way, your credit card is charged, the book downloads, and you can start reading. The book shows up in your Library and in your most recently used items throughout the NOOK HD.

NOTE It may take a little while before your book finishes downloading, depending on the size of the book and the speed of the WiFi network to which you are connected.

Browsing and Buying Magazines and Newspapers

You browse, search for, and buy magazines and newspapers from the NOOK Shop the same way you do books. At the top level of the shop, just tap either Magazines or Newspapers instead of Books and start browsing. Same for searching.

There are only a few minor differences between buying magazines and newspapers instead of books:

- You generally can't download samples of magazines.

- When you buy a magazine or newspaper, you can usually buy a single issue (the current one), or else subscribe to the periodical.

- New NOOK customers can get free 14-day subscriptions to magazines and newspapers.

Using the Library to Manage Your Books and Periodicals

When you buy books, magazines, and newspapers, they show up in your Library, Active Shelf, and Recent Drawer and you can read them from there, or drag them to your Home screen so they're always available. But after a while the books and periodicals vanish from the Active Shelf and Recent Drawer because new items are continually added. And you can't put *all* of your books and periodicals on the Home screen, because it will quickly fill up.

That's where the Library comes in. It's the central location for all your books, newspapers, magazines, and more. Get there by tapping the Library icon at the bottom of the Home screen. Here's what you can access from the Library:

- All the books, newspapers, magazines, and other materials you bought from the NOOK Shop.

- Books you've borrowed from NOOK Friends or your local library. (See Chapter 8 for details.)

- Files like music files, Microsoft Office files (Word, Excel, PowerPoint), PDF files, and books in the EPUB format that you've transferred to your NOOK from your PC or Mac (page 277).

- Files (the same ones as mentioned in the previous point) that you've stored on your SD card, if you've installed one. (See Chapter 12 for details.)

The Library is divided into a number of sections, called Shelves, including Books, Magazines, Movies & TV, Apps, and several others. You can swipe sideways through each to see what's there. You can also collapse any section so that pictures of the content (such as book covers) and the listings aren't visible.

To see all the listings in any section, tap its name. If there's more than can fit on a single screen, you can scroll through it.

Changing the Library View and Re-Sorting the Library

When you're in a shelf or section, look down at the bottom of the screen. You'll see two icons: the one on the left a set of horizontal bars, called the Contents button, and one to its right with two arrows and the letters "A" and "Z." Tap the icon with arrows, and a screen pops up that lets you reorder the list you're looking at—viewing it as a grid or list, or sorting by the most recent, by title, or by author.

The screen that pops up lets you change the display in these ways.

- **View as.** Gives you control over how the items are displayed. Out of the box, the NOOK displays them on a grid of shelves, with large pictures and a little detail about each item— the title and author of a book, for example. But you can instead view them as a list, which essentially shows the same content, but with smaller icons for each, and in a longer scrollable list rather than a grid.

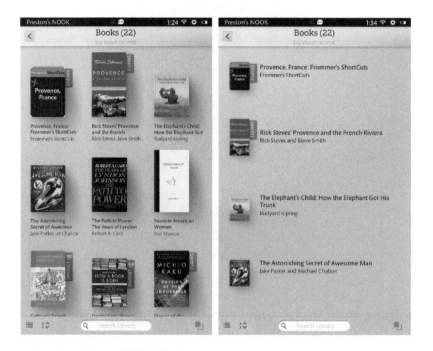

- **Change the sort order.** Tap this button, and you can change the order in which items are displayed. The options available here vary according to what section of the Library you're in. In Books and Kids, you can sort by Most Recent, Title, and Author. In Magazines and Newspapers, you can sort by Most Recent and Title. In Apps, you can sort by Most Recent, App Name, and Category.

Using the Contents Button

Tap the Contents button (the one on the lower left with horizontal lines), and you get these four choices:

- **Create New Shelf.** Lets you create a shelf. See page 177 for details.

- **Manage Content for Profiles.** Lets you add content from the Library to any profile. Tap this, and then select what you want to add to a profile or profiles, tap the profile or profiles you want to add the content to, and then tap Save. (See page 61 for more information about profiles.)

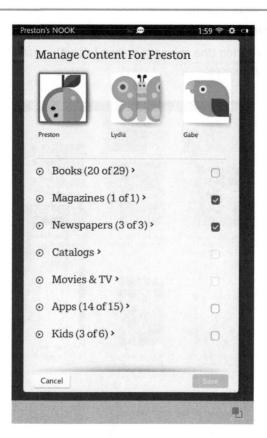

- **View Archive.** Lets you see all the items you've archived to your NOOK Cloud (page 180).

- **Refresh.** Refreshes the library to reflect any new content you've added or taken away.

Contents and Badges

Using the Library is straightforward: Tap a book or periodical you want to read, an app you want to run, and so on, depending upon what area of the Library you're in. That's all there is to it.

When you're in the Books area, you'll see the books' covers, but no further description. In the Magazine area, you'll see the magazines' covers, plus their issue dates. When you're browsing newspapers, you'll see the front page of each newspaper, as well as the headline of the lead story, and its beginning text.

If you buy a book or periodical and it isn't fully downloaded yet, there's a Download banner or sash (which the NOOK calls a *badge*) on it. You also see a bar on the cover that shows how much of the book has been downloaded, and how much is left to go.

There are plenty more badges on book and periodical covers you'll likely come across in the Library, most notably these:

- **Download.** Indicates that the book or periodical hasn't yet been downloaded, or is in the process of downloading. If it hasn't been downloaded, tap to do the deed.

- **New.** The item has recently been downloaded to your NOOK and is anxiously waiting to be read.

- **Sample.** A free excerpt of a book or periodical. These samples generally don't time out and will live forever, but they're only a portion of the book or publication.

- **Recommended.** A NOOK Friend has recommended the item to you. For details, see page 352.

- **LendMe.** You can lend this to a friend. For details, see page 362.

- **Lent.** You've borrowed this item from someone or from a library, or lent to someone.. The badge indicates how many days are left in the borrowing period. Typically you can borrow something for up to 14 days.

- **Pre-order.** The item isn't yet available for sale, but if you want it as soon as it's released, you can order it ahead of time.

> **NOTE** Books that you've copied to your NOOK HD's SD card don't have badges on them. However, they have a small NOOK icon in their lower-right corner to show that they're stored on your SD card.

Nifty Options for Items in Your Library

To read a book or periodical, or to run an app, just tap it. But there's plenty more you can do with your books, magazines, and newspapers (and apps) in the Library. Press and hold your finger on a book, and you get the following choices:

- **View Details.** Shows you details about the book or periodical. It's the same information you saw on the screen before buying.

NOTE When you press and hold on an item, the menu shows you only appropriate choices—for example, Read, Add to Shelf, and other bookish options don't show up when you hold your finger on an app.

- **Share.** Lets you recommend the book or periodical to a friend, or rate and review it.

- **Add to Home.** Puts a shortcut to the item on your Home screen.

- **Add to Shelf.** Lets you add it to a shelf (page 177) that you've created.

- **Remove from Shelf.** Lets you remove it from a shelf.

- **Assign to Profiles.** Lets you assign a book to a profile so that person can read it. (See Chapter 4 for details about profiles.)

- **Move to NOOK Cloud.** Moves it off of your NOOK, but still keeps it accessible whenever you want. See page 180 for details.

- **Delete.** Deletes the item from your NOOK. Be careful when choosing this, because unlike with archiving, you can't retrieve the item if you change your mind later. If you decide at some later point you want to read it again, you'll have to buy it again.

Organizing Your Library by Using Shelves

If you buy enough books or periodicals (which of course you do—why else do you have a NOOK?), you may find that the Library's organization options aren't enough. What if you want to browse your collection of literary novels, mystery novels written by women, or books about footwear in 17th century France? (OK, maybe that last collection isn't big enough to *browse* through, but you get the idea.)

There's a simple solution: Organize your books (or other Library items) into shelves, just as you would on a physical bookshelf. You get to decide which books to keep together so you can find them easily.

NOTE   Unlike real-world shelves, you can have a single item on multiple shelves on your NOOK. So a single book may be on your Books shelf as well as in a Fiction shelf you create, a Dickens shelf you create, and so on.

To organize your books into shelves, tap the Contents icon (the one with horizontal lines in the lower left corner of the screen), and then select Create New Shelf. Here's what to do next:

1. **On the Create New Shelves screen, type the name for your new shelf. Tap Save.** A screen appears that lets you decide what content should go onto the shelf.

NOTE   You're limited to 100 characters when naming a new shelf. In a world in which you're limited to 140 characters for messages in Twitter, that should be no problem.

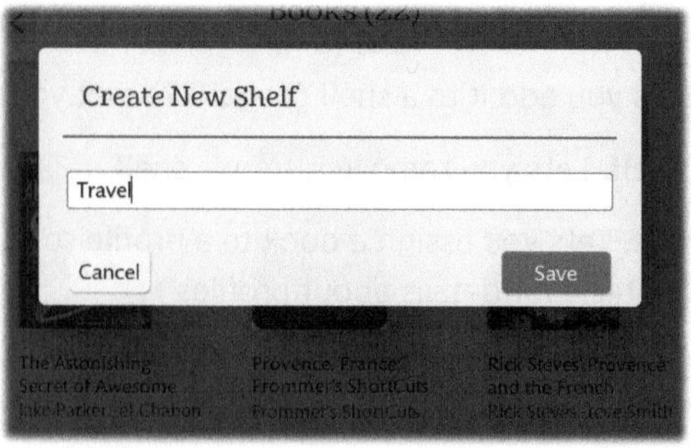

2. **If you want to add all the content for an existing shelf to your new shelf, check the box next to it.**

3. **If you want add only some content from an existing shelf, tap the arrow next to it.** A screen appears with all the items in that shelf. Tap the box next to any item you want to put on the shelf. A checkmark appears next to it. If you've already got items in the shelf, those items also have checkmarks.

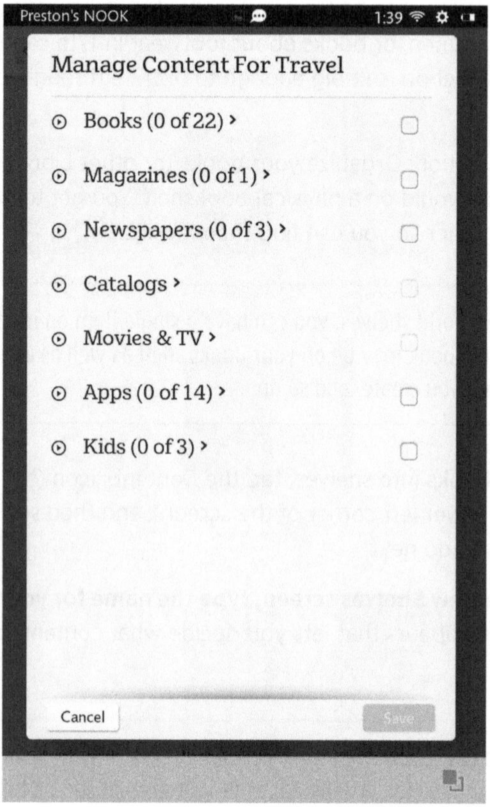

4. **When you're done, tap Save.** You head back to the Library. Scroll down to the My Shelves area and you'll see your new shelf with icons representing some of its contents. Tap the shelf to see the entire contents.

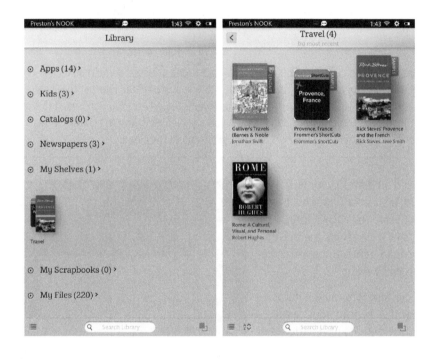

Once you've created a shelf, it's easy to add or remove items from it, or edit its name. To remove an item, hold your finger on the item and select "Remove from Shelf." That removes it from the shelf, but doesn't delete it.

If you want to rename the shelf, delete it, or add new content to it, hold your finger on the shelf. A popup appears letting you do all that. When you remove a shelf, all the items in it remain on your NOOK.

Sending Items to the Cloud

Your NOOK HD has plenty of storage space, and if you add an SD card, you get even more. Still, there may come a time when you begin to run out of space—or feel as if you are. In that case, you can send items to your own personal data cloud called the NOOK Cloud. When you do this, the item is sent over your WiFi network and the Internet to your personal storage area, and it's deleted from the NOOK. The item still shows up on your NOOK, but on its upper-left corner is a small cloud icon with a green arrow on it. That tells you that the item is in your cloud, and needs to be downloaded if you want to use it. Just tap the item and it gets downloaded.

NOTE Have you ever heard the terms *cloud* or *cloud storage*? If you read technology news, you probably have. The cloud refers to storage space on the Internet that you can access whenever you want, from any Internet-connected device. You don't need to store the item on any computer or gadget. When you archive items, you're using your own personal cloud, courtesy of Barnes & Noble. Welcome to the cloud.

To send an item to your NOOK Cloud, hold your finger on it and select Move to NOOK Cloud. That's all it takes. It's there, safe and sound, ready to be retrieved when you want it.

You can also view all the items that you've sent to your cloud. Tap the Contents icon and select View Archive. If you've recently added an item to your NOOK Cloud, it might not yet show up here, because it still might be in the process of being uploaded and processed.

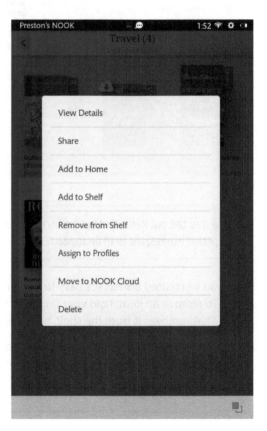

Using the Wish List

When you're browsing and searching for books, magazines, apps, and newspapers, you'll often come across items that you're not quite ready to buy yet, but you might want to later. That's where the NOOK's wish list comes in. When you come across something you think you may want to buy at some point, add it to your wish list.

NOTE The wish list on your NOOK is separate from the wish list on your BN.com account. The wish list on your BN.com account includes printed books and periodicals for your NOOK, and other items you can buy on BN.com, while your NOOK's wish list only has items for your NOOK.

To add a book, newspaper, or magazine to your wish list, when you tap its cover and come to the Details page, simply tap the heart-shaped icon underneath it so the icon turns white. It's been added to your wish list.

To view your wish list, tap the heart-shaped icon at the bottom left of the screen. From here, you can buy books, periodicals, and apps as you would normally.

Accessing Content on Your SD Card and NOOK HD's Built-in Storage

The Library also offers an easy way to view files and content you've transferred to your SD card or to the NOOK's built-in storage—use the Library's My Files feature. (See Chapter 12 for details about how to transfer files to the SD card.)

To get there, tap "My Files" in your Library. You'll come to a screen with two sections: Device, and SD Card. Tap Device to see the files on the NOOK, and SD Card to see files on the SD card.

NOTE If you haven't installed an SD card, the SD Card option doesn't appear.

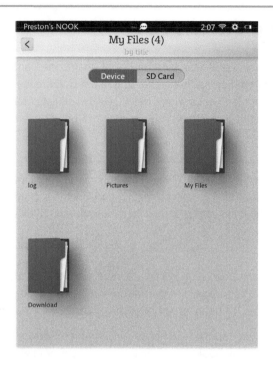

My Files (4)

by title

Device | SD Card

log

Pictures

My Files

Download

Tap Device, and you'll see a variety of folders, including Pictures, My Files, and Download. Tap SD Card and you see the folder structure on your SD card, most likely with four sections: B&N Downloads, LOST.DIR, My Files, and Android. B&N Downloads are for any downloads that you've moved to your SD card, and My Files is the folder you'll use for other files that you move to your SD card from your computer. As for LOST.DIR, you can generally ignore it. If the NOOK determines that you've moved any files that are corrupted or have other kinds of problems, it moves them or copies of them here. Also ignore the Android folder; it contains system files you don't want to muck with.

NOTE Even if you don't have an SD card, you can still transfer files to your NOOK. If you want to see files and books you've transferred to your NOOK, tap the My NOOK button. Go to the My Files folder, just as on the SD card.

Tap the folder you want to browse, such as My Files. You see either the files themselves, or subfolders. Under My Files, for example, you see a variety of folders, including Books, Documents, Magazines, Music, Newspapers, and so on.

Tap the folder that has the files you want to read or view. In the list that appears, tap any to open it. For more details about what files you can view on your NOOK, see Appendix B.

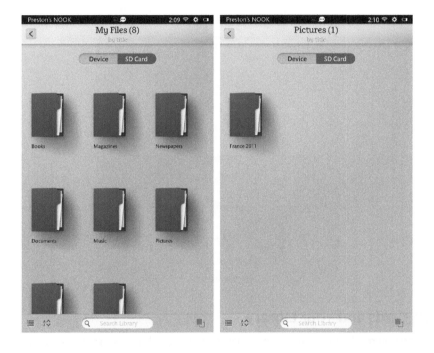

TIP   You can change the folder structure on your SD Card—deleting folders, renaming them, adding them, and so on. You do that not on your NOOK, but by connecting your NOOK to your PC or Mac using the 30-pin USB cable from your PC or Mac. You can then edit the folders just as you can any folder on your computer.

SD Cards and Your Library

When you read a book using your NOOK, you're reading it in a format called EPUB. If you transfer EPUB files to your SD card from your computer, those files show up in your Library. They likely won't have their covers, but they'll show up like other books, with their titles, authors, and so on. The covers are plain gray, and there's a small NOOK icon on the lower right. You can put them in shelves and search for them, just like other books. But you can't archive them or recommend them to others.

The Library on BN.com, PCs, Macs, and Mobile Devices

One of the many great things about the NOOK is that it's not a literary island. When you download a book to your NOOK, you can read it from other places as well—on the Barnes & Noble website, your PC or Mac, as well as on Android phones and tablets, and on iPhones and iPads.

To view your Library and read books on the Web, head to *www.bn.com* and click the My NOOK button at the top of the page. Once you're logged in, click the Library tab, and you'll come to your NOOK Library. From here you can manage books, read them if you've downloaded a NOOK reader, recommend them, and so on.

The site offers additional features, including getting recommendations, interacting with NOOK Friends, and so on.

To read books on your PC or Mac, you need to download Barnes & Noble's free ereader app. The NOOK app does more than just let you read books—it offers a NOOK-like experience, including browsing and searching your Library.

Search in the Apple App Store or in the Android Market for the NOOK app. You can also go directly to the BN.com download page by typing this address into your browser: *http://bit.ly/vBjE2B*. The app looks and works a bit differently for different devices, but on all of them you can browse your Library, and download and read books.

Managing Your NOOK Account

Every NOOK has a NOOK account on it, with important information—your credit card number, any gift cards you've received, and so on. If you want to change your credit card, view your wish list, add a gift card, or look at items you've recently viewed, your NOOK account is the place to go.

NOTE If you want, to manage your settings from the Shop, press the gear icon at the upper right of the Status bar, and then select Shop Settings. That way, all the Shop options will be right in front of you, without having to drill down in the settings screen.

To get there, tap the gear icon at the upper right of the Status bar. From the screen that appears, select All Settings→Applications→Shop. You then have the following five choices:

- **Password-protect purchases for adult profiles.** Turn on this box, and when you buy something in the NOOK Shop, you'll first have to type in a password.

- **Manage Credit Card.** Here's where you find your credit card information, and where you can change it. Tap this option, and from the screen that appears, tap Change Default Credit Card to change the credit card you use when you buy things on the NOOK. You can have only one credit card on your NOOK.

NOTE Your BN.com account can have more than one credit card associated with it, but not your NOOK.

- **Gift Cards.** If you've gotten any NOOK gift cards, here's where you find them. They don't get added to your NOOK automatically; you have to enter them manually. So when you get a NOOK gift card, head here and enter the information. You can also buy a gift card here as well.

- **Clear Recent Shop Searches.** Tap this, and when you next search the Shop, your old searches won't appear.

- **Clear Recently Viewed List.** Tap here, and the list of items you've recently viewed in the Shop won't be visible.

CHAPTER 8

Borrowing and Lending Books with LendMe and Your Local Library

WITH YOUR NOOK HD, you can borrow books from friends and lend them books, and also borrow books from your local library. In fact, in some ways it's even easier to share books with the NOOK HD than with printed books, because you don't need to physically hand off or collect a book. All it takes is a few taps on your NOOK HD.

But how to do it? Which books can and can't you lend? How long can you borrow and lend them for? Read on; this chapter has all you need to know.

Both a Borrower and a Lender Be

You have two ways to lend and borrow books with your NOOK HD: Using the NOOK HD's LendMe features to borrow and lend books with your NOOK Friends, or borrowing books from the library.

Keep in mind that you can't lend out every book you own, or borrow every book your friends own. The same holds true with library books: You can only borrow books that the library assigns for borrowing.

Borrowing and lending may strike you as an odd concept when it comes to NOOK books, because there's no physical object to hand over or take in. In fact, though, an ebook is a physical object of sorts, even though it's made up of bits and bytes rather than paper and print.

When you buy a book using your NOOK, you're downloading an ebook, but that ebook is very different from a physical book in one important way: ebooks are protected with digital rights management (DRM), while physical books aren't.

DRM essentially links a book to your NOOK HD, or any NOOK reader, such as one for a PC, smartphone, or tablet. So you can't simply lend any NOOK book to anyone, or borrow any NOOK book from anyone. The book has to be coded to let it be lent, and not all books have this coding embedded in them.

Why is that coding necessary? Without it, any ebook could literally be given free of charge to millions of people, by someone simply posting it on the Internet, and other people downloading it. If all books were available for free like this, publishers couldn't stay in business, and authors couldn't make a living (including yours truly).

Bottom line: There are certain restrictions and rules about which books can be lent, how they can be lent, and for how long.

With that background out of the way, it's time to take a look at how to borrow and lend books, first between friends, and then from your local library.

Lending and Borrowing Books with LendMe

The NOOK HD's LendMe feature is available directly from the Library as well as through NOOK Friends, so it's always within easy reach. Before getting started with it, here are some things you need to know:

- **Only some books can be lent and borrowed.** Those that can be lent will have a LendMe badge across their cover. That way, you know before buying or downloading a book whether it can be lent out. And when it's in your Library, you can easily see which books you can lend. You'll see the badge when you're browsing in the Library as well as on the detail page you come to when you tap the cover.

You may think that all books you can download for free from the NOOK Shop are lendable. After all, they're free. That's not the case, though; some free books are blocked from lending. So if you're planning to download a free book and want to lend it out, check to see whether there are multiple editions of the book. Sometimes, particularly with classic fiction from authors like Dickens, there are many free editions of a single book, some of which are lendable, and some of which aren't.

- **A book can be lent out only once.** Once you've lent the book, you can't lend it again.

- **You can't read a book while it's lent to someone.** Only one account at a time has access to a book, so during the time you've lent it to someone, you can't read it.

- **Loans last for 14 days.** At the end of that time, it's no longer available to the person to whom you've lent it. If you've borrowed a book, you can only use it for 14 days. As soon as the time expires, it's again available to the lender.

- **You can lend a book only if you've registered your NOOK HD.** The lending feature doesn't work on an unregistered NOOK HD or NOOK Color.

- **Someone borrowing a book must have a Barnes & Noble account with a valid credit card.** No account, no book.

- **Borrowing is free.** No money is charged to either the lender or the borrower.

- **You can lend only one book at a time.** You have to wait until a book is returned to you before you can lend another book.

- **You can't lend a book that someone has lent to you.**

- **You can't copy a borrowed book to your microSD card.**

Seeing Your List of Lendable Books

You have several ways to find which of your books are available for lending. One is to browse around the Library: The LendMe sash appears on any book available for lending.

Depending on whether you've lent and borrowed books before, you'll see the following sashes:

- **LendMe.** As explained on page 362, you can lend this book.

- **Borrowed.** A book you've borrowed from someone. Tap to read it. When you read it, a Buy Now button appears at the top of the screen, in case you decide you want to buy the book at any point while you're reading it.

- **Lent.** A book that's currently lent to someone, or that you've offered to lend, but the potential borrower has yet to accept or decline.

- **Lent to You.** A book that someone has offered to lend to you, but you haven't yet accepted or declined. Tap it to accept or decline.

- **Awaiting Confirmation.** Books someone has offered to lend you. Tap to borrow the book or decline it.

- **Books available for lending.** All your books that can be lent.

NOTE Books you've already lent out don't show up in the Borrowed shelf.

The one last place to go to see what books you can lend is NOOK Friends (Chapter 14). In the NOOK Friends app, tap LendMe. There you'll see four shelves:

- **My lendable books.** All the books you have that can be lent.

NOTE In the My Lendable books section, new books that you can lend have a New badge, rather LendMe. Fear not; you can lend any books in the My Lendable books section, even ones that sport a New badge.

- **Friends' books to borrow.** A great place to go if you're looking to borrow books. It lists all the lendable books from your friends. Tap any to request it. (See page 191 for details.)

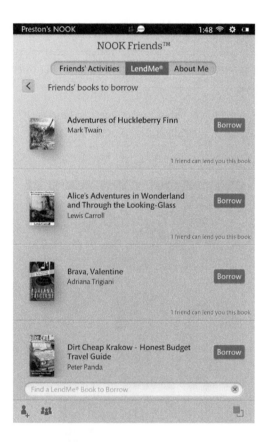

TIP Your friends can see any books you have that are available for lending on their "Friends books to borrow" shelf. If you'd prefer that friends not see certain lendable books or see none at all, tap the Privacy button at the top of the page. See the next page for more details.

- **Offers from friends.** The books that friends have offered to lend you. Tap to accept or decline.

- **Requests.** Requests from friends who've asked to borrow a book. Tap to lend the book or to decline the request.

LendMe Privacy Settings

If for some reason you don't want all of your friends to see all of the books you have available for lending, you can hide some of them from them. At the top LendMe screen in the NOOK Friends app, tap the Privacy button. On the screen that appears, uncheck the boxes next to any books you don't want your friends to see.

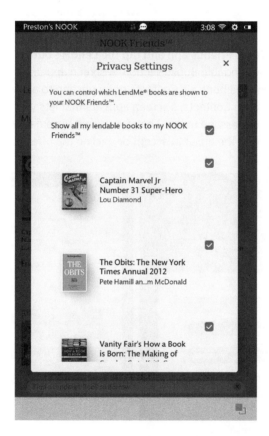

Lending a Book

There are two ways you can lend a book to someone—offering to lend it on your own, because you think someone may want to read it, or by responding to a friend's request to borrow a book. The following sections cover both scenarios.

Making an Offer to Lend a Book

Let's say you've just read Dickens' *Nicholas Nickleby* for the first (or seventh) time and you have a friend who you know will enjoy the book. You'd like to recommend and lend the book to her.

There are three—count 'em, three—ways you can get to a screen that lets you lend a book to a NOOK Friend. Here's how to get to the screen, and what to do once you get there:

- **Launch the NOOK Friends app and tap the LendMe button.** Then tap any book in the My Lendable Books section. A screen appears that lets you send an offer to lend the book via Contacts or by posting to a friend's Facebook wall. If you choose Contacts, a screen appears that lets you select your contact and type a message to her. The offer is sent via email. Your friend can then click a link in the email to accept or decline the offer.

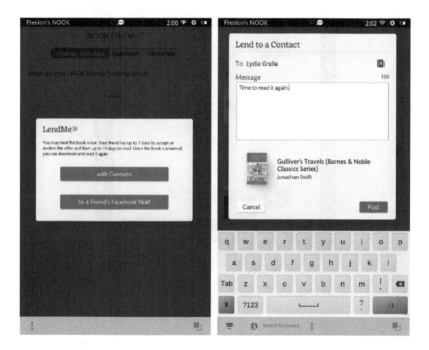

If you choose Facebook, select the Facebook contact to whom you want to lend the book, and then type in a message. The message will be posted on your friend's Facebook wall, and Facebook will also send a notification to her via email about the offer to lend. She can click the message on her wall to accept or decline the offer.

TIP Someone doesn't have to be a NOOK Friend in order for you to send her an invitation to borrow a book. However, if you want to send her an offer to borrow a book via email or Facebook, you must make sure that you can contact her on your NOOK. So before making an offer to lend her a book, put her in your Contacts list, or make sure she's a Facebook friend, and then link your NOOK account to Facebook.

- **In the Library,** or if the book is on your Home Screen or Active Shelf, hold your finger on a book and a pop-up menu appears. Select Share, and then from the screen that appears, select LendMe. After that, the same screen appears as when you make an offer to lend a book from the NOOK Friends app.

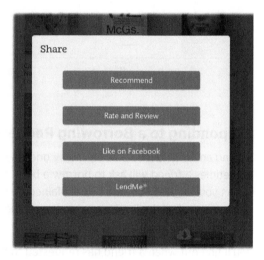

  Whichever way you choose, your NOOK Friend is notified via email or Facebook and has seven days either to accept the offer or decline it.

- **Tap a book's cover** in the Library or on the Active Shelf or Home Screen, and the details page opens. Tap LendMe. You see the now-familiar screen for lending a book via Contacts or Facebook.

As soon as you make the offer to lend the book, the Lent badge appears across the book cover wherever it appears on your NOOK HD. The badge appears even if your friend hasn't yet accepted the offer, because you can't rescind the offer. If your friend accepts the offer, a number appears next to the badge, to show how many days are left in the 14-day lending period. If your friend rejects it, the Lent label disappears and is replaced with the LendMe badge.

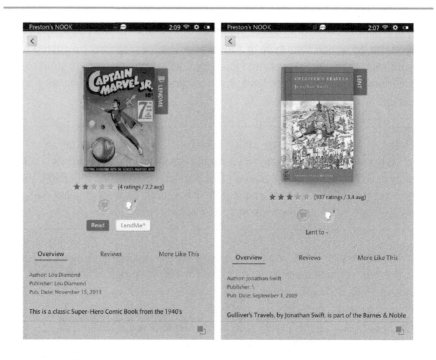

Responding to a Borrowing Request

Making an offer to lend a book is only one way to let a friend borrow a book. Sometimes a friend will ask to borrow a book as well. How does he know what books you've got to borrow? As explained on page 196, the NOOK Friends app shares a list of all the books you have available for lending to your friends (and vice versa).

You'll find out when a friend has requested to borrow a book in any of three ways:

- **You get a notification in the Notification bar.** Tap the Notification bar when you get the request, and you'll see a "Your friend would like to borrow a book" message. Tap that notification, and you come to a screen that shows you who's made the request and which book he wants to borrow.

- **The book shows up on the Requests shelf in the LendMe section of the NOOK Friends app.** It's the bottom shelf, so scroll down to get there. Tap the book and a screen appears with details about who's made the request and which book he wants to borrow.

  When you get to that screen, tap "Yes, Lend the Book" to lend it, "Decline" if you decide you don't want to lend it (feeling selfish, are we?), and Cancel if you simply can't make up your mind and need more time to decide.

Remember, when you lend a book to someone, you can't read it while it's being lent—14 days unless it's returned sooner. So before agreeing to lend the book, make sure you don't need access to it during that time.

- **You get an email with the request.** The email shows you the book's title and who has asked to borrow it. Tap Yes to agree to lend it; or No, Maybe Later to decline the offer for now.

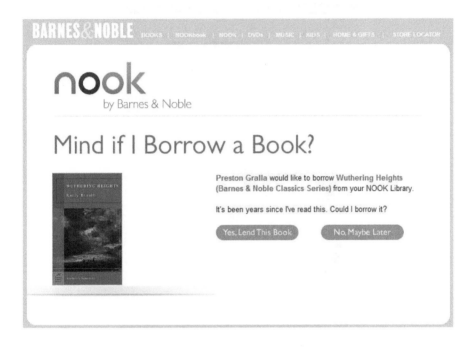

Borrowing a Book

It may be better to give than to receive, but admit it, receiving is pretty nice, too, especially when it comes to borrowing books. So you'll want to take advantage of book borrowing on your NOOK, especially since it's so easy to do.

As with lending a book, there are two ways to borrow a book—ask a friend to borrow a book, and agree to borrow one when a friend recommends a book and offers to lend it to you.

Suppose you want to borrow a book from a friend. NOOK Friends is the way you do it, so make sure anyone from whom you want to borrow a book is a NOOK Friend. Then open the NOOK Friends app by pressing the NOOK button, selecting Apps, and tapping NOOK Friends.

Once you're in the NOOK Friends app, tap LendMe and go to the shelf labeled "Friends' books to borrow." There may be more than are visible, so scroll through the shelf to see them all.

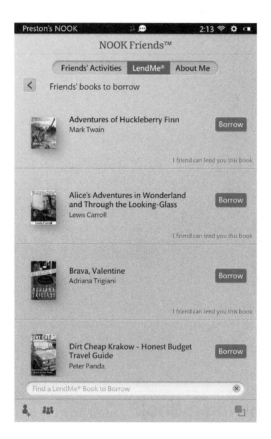

Tap any book you want to request. A screen appears with the book's title and author, and the name of the person who has it available for lending. Tap Request. A screen appears with the person's name in the Recipient field. Type a message ("pretty please" is usually effective) and then tap Send. The request goes off on its merry way via email.

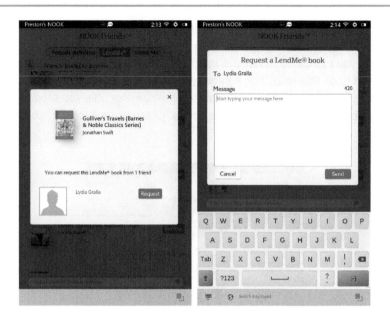

Want to see some details about any of the books on the list? On the bookshelf, tap the cover of the book. You'll see the usual details screen. If you decide you want to borrow it, go back to the list of books your friends have to lend and tap Borrow to request it.

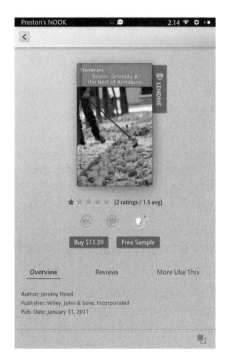

If you've got lots of friends with plenty of lendable books (lucky you!), it may take quite a while to scroll through them all. So if you have a specific book in mind that you're looking to borrow, head to the bottom of the LendMe screen and type a book title or author. As you type, the list of books that matches your search narrows. When you've typed in the name or title, you see a list of matching books. Tap any cover to see details, or tap Borrow to ask to borrow the book.

Your friend now gets the request in any of the three ways outlined on page 200 earlier in this chapter. When he accepts the request, the book shows up in your Library with a Borrowed badge on it, and the number of days still left in the borrowing period next to it. After 14 days, the book disappears from your Library.

> **TIP** You can return a book before the 14-day period is up. For details, see page 206.

Once you develop borrowing-and-lending friendships with people, you'll find that they'll often offer to lend you books they think you might like. So someone may offer to lend you a book, and you'll find out about it in all the ways outlined on page 196.

If you get a notification via email that your request to lend has been accepted, click the View My Offer button and you're sent to your Barnes & Noble account on the Web, where you can accept or decline the offer. (You may need to log into the account first.) Similarly, when you click on the offer on Facebook, you're also sent to your Barnes & Noble account on the Web. Click Accept next to any book you want to borrow, and Reject next to any you don't.

To see all the books that people have offered to lend you, go to the NOOK Friends app, tap LendMe, and go to the "Offers from friends" bookshelf. Tap to accept the offer or decline it.

Returning Books Early

When you've borrowed a book from someone, he can't read it for the 14 days that you have it. But if you finish the book before that time, or decide you don't want to read it anymore before the period is up, you can return it. Why bother? Remember, when you have the book, your friend can't read it, so he gets access to the book sooner if you return it early.

To return a book, log into your Barnes & Noble account, tap NOOK Books, and you see your entire Library, including books that you've borrowed. Tap Return next to any book you want to return early.

Borrowing Books from the Library

Just as you can borrow printed books from libraries, you can borrow NOOK books as well. You don't have to go to your local library to borrow the book; instead you head to the library's Internet site.

Not all libraries have NOOK books available for lending, and the way you borrow may vary from library to library. This section, though, covers the most popular way, and should go a long way to help you borrow whatever is available. Before you borrow, here's what you need to know:

- **You can usually borrow a book for 14 days.** As with books you borrow from friends, at the end of the borrowing period, the book automatically gets returned to the library.

- **Not all books can be borrowed for the NOOK.** Publishers make far fewer books available for lending for the NOOK than they make available in print. They worry that it's easier to borrow a NOOK book than a print book, because it doesn't require going to the library. So don't be surprised if you can't find your favorite book for the NOOK at the library, or if there are fewer copies for the NOOK than there are for the printed version.

- **Only one copy of a library ebook can be borrowed at a time.** Just as with a physical book, only one copy can be out at a time. Libraries typically have far fewer copies of a book in ebook format than in print, so you may have to wait to borrow an ebook you want.

- **You need a library card to borrow books.** Want to borrow a NOOK book from the New York Public Library? You need a New York Public Library card. You can't borrow books from libraries that let only residents borrow books if you're not a resident. Check with your local library for details.

- **There may be limits on how many ebooks you can borrow at one time.** Your local library may limit you to a maximum number of ebooks—five, for example.

- **Look for ebooks in the EPUB or PDF formats.** Those are the common formats your NOOK HD can read, so when browsing or searching, look for them.

How to Borrow and Read NOOK Books

As mentioned previously, libraries may have different methods for lending out ebooks, and for you then to transfer them to your NOOK. Typically, though, you must download the free Adobe Digital Editions software, and then register it. If you don't first do so, you may not be able to borrow books.

Head to *www.adobe.com/products/digitaleditions* and install the software. You must also register for an Adobe ID to use the software and borrow books from a library. If you don't have one, head to *www.adobe.com/account.html* and create one. Then, when you're asked to activate your computer after the Adobe Digital Edition software is installed, enter that ID and password.

Now that you've got the software activated, it's time to borrow a book. Ask your library for the website it uses to lend ebooks, and ask to have a user name and password set up. Also check for any special lending policies, and whether the library offers online help.

Once you do all that, you're ready to go. Head to your library's ebook-lending website. Different libraries organize their ebook collections differently; you may be able to search and browse or only one of the two.

Look for the NOOK section. If there seems to be one, look for books in EPUB and PDF formats. Those are the ones you can borrow.

TIP For excellent all-around help with borrowing ebooks, head to the NOOK ebook Central site run by Google and the New York Public Library (*https://sites.google.com/a/ nypl.org/ebook-central/home/device/nook*). Although much of what's there is specifically for borrowing books from the New York Public Library, it's a good overall resource for advice about how to borrow books from any library using your NOOK HD.

Once you've found a book you want to borrow, follow these steps:

1. **Follow the site's instructions for downloading the book.** Typically, you'll click the book's link, follow a checkout procedure, and then download the book. Make sure you remember where you saved the downloaded book. It will end in .acsm, such as DombeyandSon9781775410713.acsm, or in .pdf.

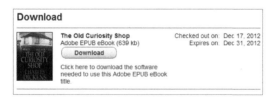

2. **Open the file.** The book opens in Adobe Digital Editions. If you want, you can read the book in that program.

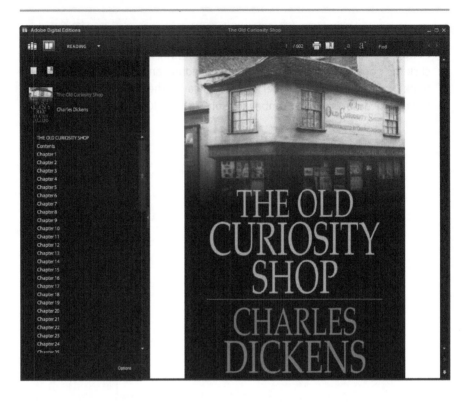

3. **Connect your NOOK HD to your computer.** A screen on your computer appears, telling you that you need to authorize the NOOK to use Adobe Digital Editions. Click Authorize Device. After a moment, your NOOK is authorized.

   A new shelf appears on the Adobe Digital Editions screen titled My NOOK.

4. **Drag the book you just borrowed to this shelf.**

5. **Disconnect your NOOK HD from your computer.** The book won't appear on a shelf in your Library. Instead, you have to open it as a file. In the Library, tap My Files, and in the My NOOK section, you'll see a Digital Editions folder. Tap it.

6. **Look for the file name of the book you just transferred,** for example, Dombey_and_Son.epub. It will end in .epub or .pdf. Tap it.

   The book opens. You can now read it just as you can any other book on your NOOK.

Remember, you can borrow the book for only 14 days. After that, it automatically gets returned to the library.

Even when you have the book on your NOOK HD, you can continue to read it on your computer using Adobe Digital Editions.

Apps, Media, and Files

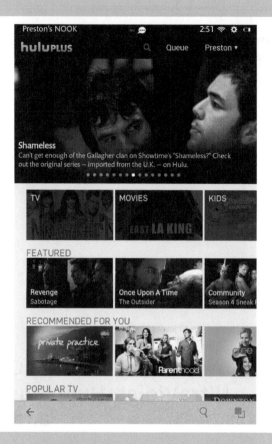

CHAPTER 9

Streaming Media: NOOK Video, UltraViolet, Hulu Plus, Netflix, and Pandora

YOUR NOOK HD IS a superb ereader, of course, but it's also a great enter-tainment machine for watching movies and TV shows and listening to music. Its high-resolution screen gives you crisp, clean video. And using the NOOK HD's headphone jack, you can listen to music or movies in glorious stereo on head-phones or an external speaker. So check out the rest of this chapter to learn how to do all that and more.

Understanding Streaming Media

NOOK Video, Netflix, Hulu Plus, UltraViolet, and Pandora all use a technique called *streaming*, which means the movies, TV shows, and music aren't stored on your NOOK HD or played from there. Instead, they live on big computers called *servers* owned by those services, which send the video wirelessly to your NOOK HD—when it's connected to a WiFi network. So if you're not connected to a WiFi network, you can't use those services or other streaming media services like Grooveshark or Rhapsody.

Furthermore, if your WiFi connection isn't a strong one, you may experience hiccups when watching movies or TV shows and listening to music. So if you find blips and delays, try to find a better WiFi connection. If you're at home, try repositioning your router, or moving to a different seat or room. If you're using a public WiFi service, try moving to a different location.

Using NOOK Video

When B&N rolled out the NOOK HD and HD+, it also introduced a new video service called NOOK Video, which lets you rent movies and buy or rent TV shows. Unlike Hulu Plus and Netflix, with NOOK Video, you can download movies and TV shows to your NOOK and watch them from your NOOK instead of streaming them.

There are pros and cons to each method. Streaming video gives you instant satisfaction—you can start watching the TV or movie immediately, without waiting for it to download. That's a big plus, because a movie can take hours to download. And because you're not downloading the movie, it won't take up any storage space on your NOOK. On the other hand, you may experience lags and timeouts when you stream video, making for a less satisfying experience. So you'll have to balance instant satisfaction versus quality of streaming and storage use. And, of course, if you're going to be somewhere without WiFi access—on a plane flight without WiFi, for example—you'll have to go the download route.

How do you use NOOK Video? Don't go looking for a NOOK Video app, because you won't find one. Instead, just go to the NOOK Shop on your NOOK and start shopping, and then watch the video. Head into the next sections to find out how.

Using the Shop to Find TV Shows and Movies

Head to the NOOK Shop, tap Movies & TV, and you're ready to shop. To find movies and TV shows, you simply browse and search just like you do when you're looking for books, magazines, and so on. (For more details about how to use the NOOK Shop, turn to page 151.)

When you see a movie or TV show that interests you, tap it. You'll find a description of TV show or movie, details about whether you can buy it or rent it, reviews and ratings, and so on. If there's a preview available, you'll see a green arrow inside a filmstrip on the TV show or movie poster. Tap it to watch the preview.

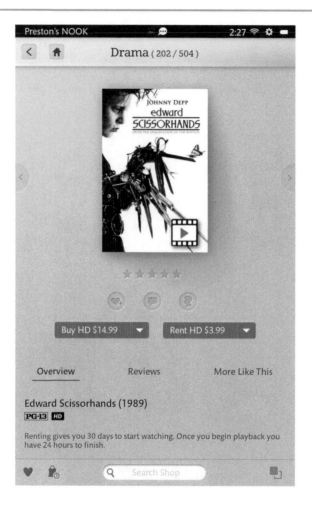

You may have more than one option for buying and renting—a higher price for buying or renting an HD movie than a lower-resolution SD movie, for example. Typically if you have a choice, it will cost you one dollar less to watch the lower-resolution version.

Just underneath the picture of the movie or TV show, you'll see the rating of the movie, if people have rated it. And just below that are three ubiquitous gray NOOK Shop icons (page 164). The leftmost one adds the movie or TV show to your wish list; the middle one lets you rate, review, recommend, and "Like" a movie on Facebook; and the rightmost one lets you create and manage your profiles.

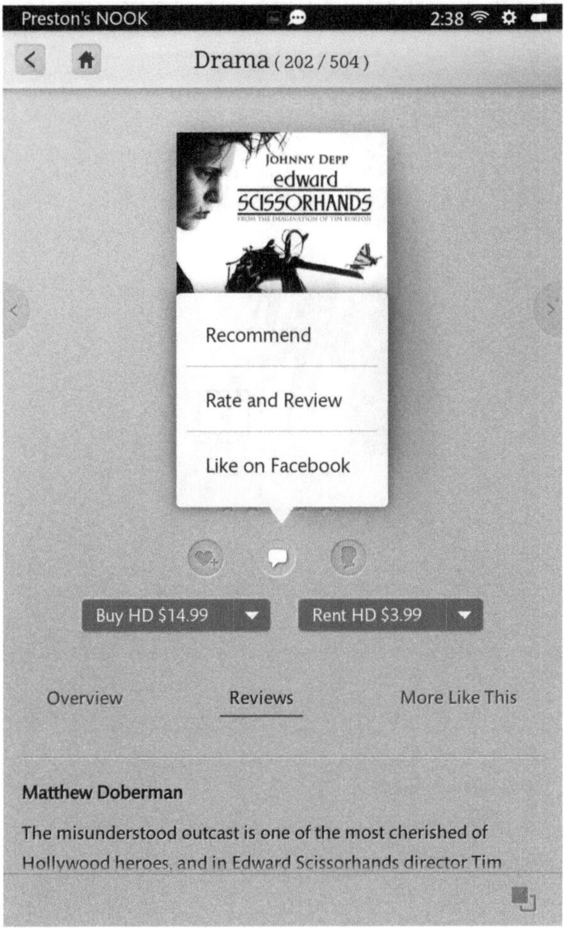

Drama (202 / 504)

JOHNNY DEPP
edward
SCISSORHANDS
FROM THE IMAGINATION OF TIM BURTON

Recommend

Rate and Review

Like on Facebook

Buy HD $14.99 ▼   Rent HD $3.99 ▼

Overview   Reviews   More Like This

Matthew Doberman

The misunderstood outcast is one of the most cherished of
Hollywood heroes, and in Edward Scissorhands director Tim

Tap your choice, and you get a confirmation screen. Tap to say yes, you do want
to buy or rent the movie or video, and after a few moments the screen changes
and you get a choice of either streaming or downloading the video. There's also
a tag added to the picture of the video, telling you how many days you have left
to watch it.

How many days is that? Well, it can get a bit confusing. Here's what you need to know about renting TV and movies:

- You have thirty days from the day and time you bought the video to watch it.

- Once you start watching the video, you have to watch the complete video in 24 hours. After your 24 hours is up, if you want to keep watching or watch again, you have to pay for it again. However, during that 24-hour period you can watch the video as many times as you'd like.

When you're ready to watch, tap either Stream or Download. If you tap Download, go on with what you were doing before you tapped the button, since it will take hours for the movie to download. If you tap Stream, get the popcorn ready—you've got your own private movie theater.

Want to watch a TV or movie on a bigger screen than your NOOK or NOOK HD+? You can do it by connecting your NOOK to your TV, if your TV has an HDMI connection (virtually all newer TVs do). To make the connection, you'll need to buy a NOOK HD HDMI accessory called a *dongle*. You attach the dongle to your NOOK's 30-pin connector, and then run an HDMI cable between the dongle and your TV. Voila! You can now watch on a bigger screen.

When you start watching, you'll first see the usual video controls on the screen.

On the right you'll find volume controls. Up at the top right is a Close button to leave the video. Down at the bottom are the pause, forward, and backward buttons. There's also a slider that shows you the progress of the TV or move, and lets you move forward or backward—just drag the circle. At the bottom right is a control for making the TV show or movie larger, although only slightly larger. Down at the bottom left is a small button for getting information about the movie. Tap it and you're sent back to the Description page for the TV or movie. Tap the Stream button to head back to the movie from there. You'll be asked if you want to start at the point you were when you stopped watching, or instead want to watch from the beginning.

After a moment or two, the controls disappear. If you want to use them again,
tap the screen. They'll appear for a few seconds and then thoughtfully go away
again.

Once you've bought or rented a TV show or movie, it shows up in your Library.
Head to the Movies & TV section of the library, and you'll see it there. It shows
you how many days and minutes you've got to watch it. Tap it to watch it. Again,
you'll get the notice about whether you want to watch from the beginning, or to
watch from where you left off.

Using UltraViolet

There's another built-in way to watch streaming video on your NOOK HD—the UltraViolet video service. If you buy a movie disc (in a retail store or online) that's part of UltraViolet service, not only will you be able to play the movie with the disc, but you can also stream it from the UltraViolet cloud to any UltraViolet-compatible device. The NOOK HD is compatible, so you can watch your UltraViolet videos on it. To connect your UltraViolet account to your NOOK, from the Home screen, tap the settings icon at upper-right (it's in the shape of a gear), and select All Settings→Account Settings and tap UltraViolet to link to your account. You'll then be able to watch UltraViolet videos using your NOOK's video player. For details about UltraViolet, go to *www.uvvu.com*.

Using Hulu Plus

There's yet one more way to watch video on your NOOK HD—use the Hulu Plus app that comes installed on your NOOK. Hulu Plus isn't as well known as Netflix, but it's a great way to watch TV shows, movies, and other video from a wide variety of sources. Current TV shows are well represented, and there are plenty of old favorites as well. Hulu Plus streams video to your NOOK HD.

NOTE Hulu Plus lets you view movies as well as television shows, but it has a very limited selection of them. Netflix is far better for movie watching than Hulu Plus.

Hulu offers both free and paid services, but on the NOOK HD, you can *only* use the for-pay version. At press time, it costs $7.99 per month, and it gives you a wider range of TV and video than the free version, including streaming access to full seasons and past seasons of TV shows. (The non-pay version, which you can watch on the Web, typically offers single episodes or clips.)

To watch TV or video on your NOOK Color using Netflix, go to the Apps screen, and then tap the Hulu Plus icon. You'll come to a login screen. Tap in your login information, or if you haven't yet subscribed to Hulu Plus, tap the icon to sign up. You can also subscribe to Hulu Plus by heading to *www.hulu.com* in a computer's browser.

Once you've signed up and logged in, you come to a screen that lists TV shows, movies, and more. To manage your account, tap your name in the upper-right of the screen. To search, tap the Search button and type in what you're searching for. To see a queue of what you've got lined up to watch, tap the Queue link at the top of the screen.

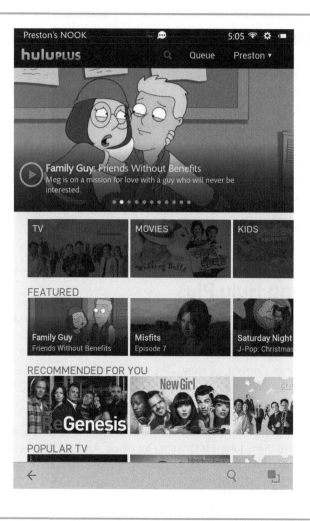

NOTE Hulu Plus on the NOOK syncs your watching with Hulu Plus on the Web. So if you have a queue there, you'll see it on your NOOK and vice versa. Any changes you make in one place will be reflected in the other.

Just beneath the featured TV or movie, you'll see major categories of what you can watch—TV, Movies, Clips, Favorites, and so on. Tap any to see further subcategories. Swipe and flick through the listings until you find something you want to watch.

When you tap a video you want to watch, you come to an information screen. The screen varies according to what you've tapped—for example, if you've tapped a TV show, you'll have options for watching other episodes. The screen gives information about the TV or movie, lets you add it to your favorites, offers links to clips, and more.

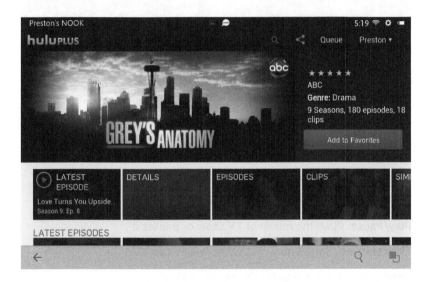

To start watching, tap the play arrow. The movie, TV show, trailer, or other video loads. When you tap a movie or TV show, the NOOK's orientation changes to landscape. If you tap a TV show, you may see an ad or two before it starts, and sometimes while you're watching as well. (Don't try to fast-forward through the ads—you can't do it.) Then the TV or movie starts playing, and you briefly see a series of controls and information onscreen. To make the controls go away, tap the screen. To make them reappear again, tap again. Control the volume using your NOOK's volume control. And if you can't hear even with the sound turned all the way up, use headphones or external speakers.

Here are the controls and information you'll find:

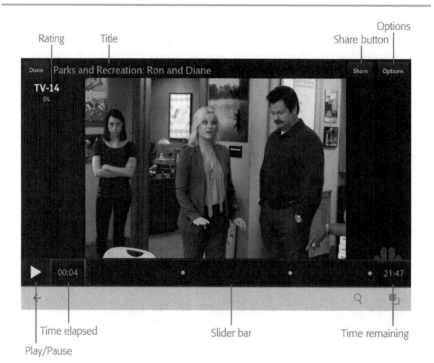

Rating   Title

Options

Share button

Done | Parks and Recreation: Ron and Diane   Share   Options

TV-14

DL

▶   00:04   21:47

Time elapsed   Slider bar   Time remaining

Play/Pause

- **Title.** Displays the title of the movie or TV show.

- **Play/Pause.** Plays the movie or TV show or pauses it.

- **Time elapsed.** Shows how much time has elapsed.

- **Rating.** Shows the rating for the movie or TV show.

- **Slider bar.** Drag the bar and you move forward or back through the show. You can also tap to jump to a different spot in the video.

> **NOTE** When an ad is playing, sadly, you can't use the slider bar to move through it.

- **Time remaining.** Shows how much time is left in the video.

- **Share.** Lets you share information about what you're watching with others.

- **Options.** Brings up a screen that lets you change the video quality of what you're watching. You can choose from High and Low. Generally, you should choose High, but if you're having a problem with hiccups or other streaming glitches, choose Low and see if that solves the problem.

Using Netflix

The well-known Netflix service doesn't have an app that comes with the NOOK, but you can download one. Head over to the NOOK Shop, search for the Netflix app, download it, sign in, and you're ready to go. Netflix is a two-pronged service: You can have DVDs delivered to your home or stream videos straight to your computer, NOOK HD, or any other device that supports the use of Netflix.

Because it's a two-pronged service, you may get confused about exactly what you're buying when you subscribe to Netflix, and what can be streamed versus what can be delivered to you on DVD.

It's really pretty simple, though. You can subscribe to the streaming-only service, the DVD-only service, or a combination of the two. The unlimited streaming service and the DVD-only service are your least expensive options. The combination service charges different rates, depending on whether you want to have one, two, three, or four DVDs out simultaneously.

To use Netflix on your NOOK HD, you need to subscribe to the streaming-only service or one of the combo services.

To watch movies or TV shows on your NOOK Color using Netflix, go to the Apps screen, and then tap the Netflix icon. You'll come to a login screen. Tap in your login information, or if you haven't yet subscribed to Netflix, tap the Netflix.com link to set one up. You can also set up a Netflix account by heading to *www. netflix.com* on a computer's browser.

At the top of the screen, in the Continue Watching area, you'll see any movies or TV shows that you've started watching on your NOOK HD, your PC, or anywhere else. Each will have a red arrow on it. That's one of the niftiest things about the Netflix app—you can start watching on your computer and continue watching on your NOOK HD, and vice versa. To watch something you were previously watching, just tap it. You can also scroll through the Continue Watching area by swiping with your finger.

Once you tap a show to watch, make sure to turn your NOOK HD horizontally, since Netflix always plays in landscape mode. When your TV show or movie begins, the bottom of the screen has a variety of controls for playing it. Those controls vanish after a second or two. To make them appear again, tap the screen.

The Netflix main screen also shows you movies and TV shows in a variety of categories, depending on what you've watched before. So you may see a Top Ten list customized to your taste—French Movies, Crime Movies, or whatever it is you've been watching. Swipe sideways in any category to see more movies and TV shows. Scroll down to see more categories.

NOTE The Netflix app lets you watch streaming movies and TV shows, but it doesn't include ordering DVDs to be delivered to your home.

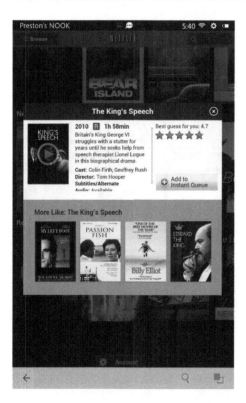

Tap any of the movies or TV shows and you'll come to a screen that tells you its title, release date, cast, director, rating you're likely to give it based on your past ratings, and other movies or TV shows you might want to watch. To watch it now, tap the arrow icon on the shows picture. To add to your instant watching queue, tap "Add to Instant Queue." If you already have it in your queue and want to remove it, tap "Remove from Instant Queue." If you tap a TV series, you'll see a list of multiple episodes at the bottom of the screen. Tap any to play it.

Watching a Movie or TV Show

When you tap a movie or TV show, the NOOK's orientation changes to land-scape, the movie or show starts playing, and you'll briefly see a series of controls and information onscreen. To make the controls go away, tap the screen. To make them appear again, tap the screen again.

Here's what each does:

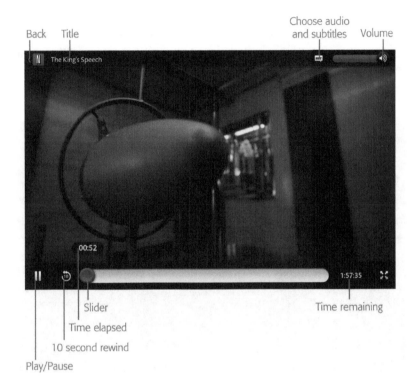

- **Title.** Shows the title of the movie or TV show, including the season and episode number if it's a TV show.
- **Play/Pause.** Plays the movie or TV show or pauses it.
- **Time elapsed.** Shows how much time has elapsed.
- **Slider.** Lets you move forward or back.
- **Time remaining.** Shows how much time is left.
- **Change resolution.** Switches between high and low resolution.
- **Back.** Takes you back to the screen where you were previously.
- **Volume.** Controls the volume.

- **Choose audio and subtitles.** Brings up a screen that lets you choose whether to use subtitles (if any are available) and the language of the audio track (if more than one is available).

- **Enlarge/Shrink.** Either enlarges the image or shrinks it. It won't enlarge much, though, so don't expect a big change.

Browsing and Searching for Movies and TV Shows

Netflix has thousands of movies and TV shows you can watch, not just those that show up on the screen when you log in. To browse all categories, tap the Browse button at the top of the screen, and then tap a category. You come to a variety of subcategories, like Classic Dramas, Courtroom Dramas, Newly Added, "Suggestions for You," and so on. Swipe through each, or scroll through the entire list of subcategories. Tap the movie or TV show in which you're interested, and then tap to watch it or add it to your queue.

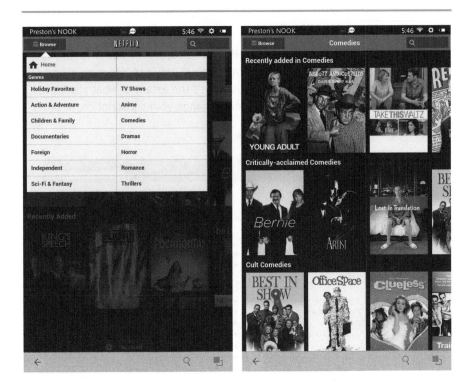

To search for a movie, tap in the search box and type in your search term. As you type, the results narrow. When you find a movie or TV show you want to watch, tap it, and then follow the usual routine for watching or adding to your queue.

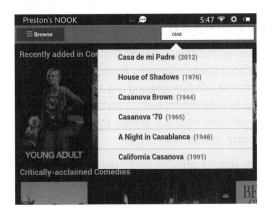

Managing Your Netflix Queue

There's one thing missing in the NOOK HD's Netflix app—the ability to manage your queue or Netflix account. As explained before, you can add movies and TV shows to your queue, or remove them, but that's the extent of what you can do. If you want to reorder what's in your queue, change your subscription, or order DVD rentals, head to the Web.

Using Pandora

Wish you had a personalized music station that would play exactly the kind of music you want, without obnoxious radio announcers and interruptions? How about your own personal jukebox, playing any kind of music you want at the tap of a button—rap for one mood, techno for another, jazz for another, opera for another, and so on? And what if it played you music that you've never heard before, but that fit right in with your tastes?

Stop wishing. You've got Pandora built into the NOOK HD. This free, fabulous music service may forever change the way you think about and listen to music.

You may already know Pandora from the Web; it started life as a web-based music service. But it's expanded into Android as well, and now you can use it on your NOOK HD. Head to Apps and tap the Pandora icon, and then sign up for an account. If you already have an account, just sign in.

Once you've got your account set up, the fun begins. Tap the plus icon at the top of the screen, and then type in the name of an artist, a song title, or a composer that's closest to the kind of music you want to create a station for. As you type, Pandora lists possible matches. Tap a match, or keep typing until you type in the full name. Then Pandora goes about creating the station for you and starts playing the music.

As the music plays, a graphic of the album from which the song is taken is displayed, along with the title of the album, the title of the song, and the name of the artist.

> **NOTE** If you switch to something else on your NOOK HD while you're listening to music on Pandora—reading a book, say—Pandora keeps the music playing. To make it stop, tap the small Pandora icon in the Notification bar, and then tap the Pandora notification that appears. That switches you to Pandora. Tap the pause button to stop the music.

Want to know more information about the current song and artist? At the upper-right of the screen, tap the small icon of four arrows (this only appears in the vertical screen orientation) and you come to a page with information about the artist, and the lyrics of the song. There's also more interesting information as well at the bottom of the screen in the "Features of this track" area. You may or may not understand what it's telling you, but it's well worth checking out. For example, when playing the Grover Washington, Jr. song "Just the Two Of Us,"

Pandora might say it chose the song for you because it features "R'n'B influences," "funky rhythms," "vamping harmony," and other details identified in the Music Genome Project. What "vamping harmony" means is anybody's guess…the point is, Pandora usually succeeds in playing music you're sure to enjoy.

NOTE The Music Genome Project is an attempt to understand music at its most fundamental level, based on its core musical components—its "genome." It's the core of Pandora's technology.

At the bottom of the screen is a set of buttons for controlling Pandora. The buttons are fairly self-explanatory. The thumbs-down button tells Pandora that you don't like the current song. When you tap it, the song stops playing—and Pandora has learned something about your musical tastes. Based on that, it stops playing songs with some of the characteristics of that particular song. The thumbs-up button tells Pandora that you like the current song, and so it plays more songs with its characteristics. The middle button lets you bookmark a song or artist. You can't use these bookmarks on your NOOK HD, though; instead, you have to head to the Web and click Profile. From there, you can see the artists or songs you've bookmarked, and use them in a variety of ways, such as getting lyrics, seeing similar tracks, playing a sample of the song, and more.

The other two buttons are the usual controls for pause/play and skip.

You'll notice that Pandora displays ads as you play music. If you want them to go away, you'll have to pay for it by upgrading to the for-pay Pandora service.

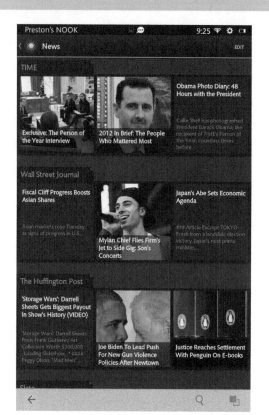

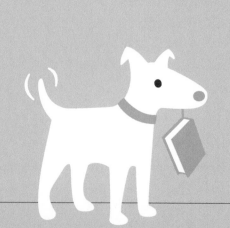

CHAPTER 10

Downloading and Using Apps

THE NOOK HD is more than just an ereader. It's a tablet as well. Just like other tablets, it can do lots of things other than letting you read books—notably running apps. Just as with all tablets and smartphones, the NOOK lets you download apps to do all kinds of nifty things, from playing music to playing games or keeping track of your diet. Bottom line: Anything you can do on a traditional tablet, you can do on your NOOK HD. (And yes, that includes Angry Birds.)

In this chapter, you'll learn all about how to get apps, how to install them, how to manage them, and how to use them—including the built-in apps on your NOOK HD. You'll also get advice on some great apps to download.

Running Apps

The NOOK HD runs on the Android operating system, even though its interface doesn't look like other Android tablets or smartphones you've seen. That's because Barnes & Noble customized the Android operating system for e-reading and other purposes.

NOTE The Android operating system was created by Google, which makes it available free of charge to tablet and smartphone manufacturers.

Because the NOOK HD is built on Android, it runs Android apps. But unlike many tablets and smartphones, it doesn't give you the power to download just *any* Android app. Apps must get the OK from Barnes & Noble to run on the NOOK HD because of the company's operating system customizations. The only apps you can run are those built into the NOOK HD or the ones you can download from the NOOK Shop. You'll find you can't download apps from Google Play, Google's Android app market (*http://play.google.com*).

> **NOTE** People have been able to *root* some of the earlier versions of the NOOK, including the NOOK Tablet and NOOK Color, to make them work like an ordinary Android device and run any Android app. Doing so, however, may damage the NOOK HD, void the warranty, and get you no support from Barnes & Noble. Rooting also removes all of the ereader capabilities described in this book. If you still want to go ahead with rooting, see Chapter 18 for guidance. Keep in mind that rooting can be a difficult, technical process, and if you don't do it correctly, you can *brick* your NOOK HD. Forewarned is forearmed.

Running an app is simple. On the Home screen, tap the Apps button, scroll to the Apps section, tap the Apps button to see the apps in your Library, and then tap the app you want to run. You can also go to the Apps section of your Library and run apps from there.

When you run an app and want to quit it, most the time you don't need to shut it down. Just press the NOOK button and go on your merry way to perform another task.

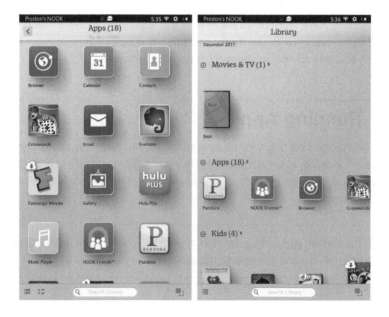

Managing and Deleting Apps

Got an app that you love so much you want it always to be just a tap away? Then put it on your Home screen. You can do that and plenty more, including deleting it, adding it to a library shelf, and other nifty things as well. To do it, hold your finger on an app and from the screen that appears, choose the following:

- **View details.** Shows you details about the app. It's the same information you saw on the screen before buying and downloading it.

- **Share.** Lets you recommend the app to a friend, rate it and review it, or "Like" it on Facebook.

NOTE Not all of these options are available for apps that are built directly into the NOOK HD, such as NOOK Friends, Crosswords, or the E-mail app. When you hold your finger on them, you only have two options: "Add to Home" and "Add to Shelf."

- **Add to Home.** Puts a shortcut to the app on your Home screen.

- **Add to Shelf.** Lets you add it to a shelf that you've created in My Shelf (page 177).

- **Remove from Shelf.** Lets you remove it from a shelf.

- **Move to NOOK Cloud.** Moves it off of your NOOK, but still keeps it accessible whenever you want to use it again, on the NOOK Cloud (page 180).

- **Delete.** Deletes the app from your NOOK. Be very careful when doing this, because unlike with archiving, you can't retrieve the app if you change your mind later. If you decide you want to use it again, you have to buy it again.

Built-in NOOK Apps

The NOOK HD comes with a number of built-in apps, including ones for Pandora; Hulu Plus (Chapter 9); Contacts (Chapter 16); playing music, viewing pictures and videos (Chapter 11); and more. The following pages tell you about two other notable apps built into the NOOK HD.

• **Crossword.** You have a NOOK HD, so no doubt you're a book lover. There's a good chance that you're a crossword lover as well, so try out this app. Fight the urge to tap the Hint button—that's cheating!

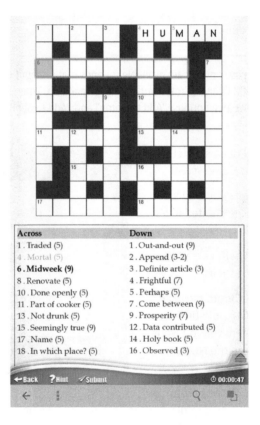

• **Spotify.** This great music service lets you play countless music tracks. There's a free version and a for-pay version. If you're a music lover, or just like to listen every once in a while, you owe it to yourself to give it a try.

Preston's NOOK 5:54

Muddy Waters

OGRAPHY OVERVIEW RELATED ARTIS

Muddy Waters

A postwar Chicago blues scene without the magnificent contributions of Muddy Waters is absolutely unimaginable. From the late '40s on, he eloquently defined the city's aggressive, swaggering, Delta-rooted sound...

TOP HITS

01 Mannish Boy

02 Champagne & Reefer - Live

03 Got My Mojo Working - Live

04 Hoochie Coochie Man

05 Baby Please Don't Go - Live

Mannish Boy
Muddy Waters - Muddy Waters Long Distant Call

Getting Apps in the NOOK Shop

To get more apps, head to the NOOK Shop. Press the NOOK button to get to the Home screen and then tap Shop. On the top left part of the screen, in the promotion area, you'll usually find links to apps or to categories of apps as various promotions scroll by.

Tap the Apps link at upper right, and you arrive at Apps shop's main screen. At the top left are scrolling promotions for individual apps and categories of apps. On the upper right are various lists, such as Staff Picks, Kids Can Learn, Seasonal Apps, Popular Apps, and others. Tap any list to see the apps there.

At the bottom of the lists is a Browse Categories link. Tap it, and then from the pop-up screen that appears, tap any category to see apps in that category. You may see subcategories, and in these subcategories you'll usually see lists of apps.

NOTE On the main screen of the NOOK Shop, you'll also find lists of apps, which change over time—"Top Picks in Apps," "What's New in NOOK Apps," and possibly others.

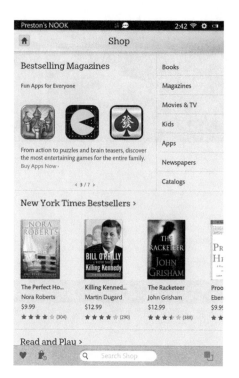

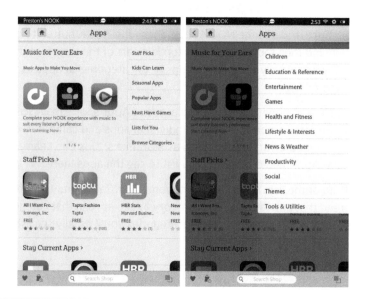

At some point when browsing the subcategories, you'll see a list of all apps in the subcategory. Scroll through them until you see an app you're interested in, and then tap the app for more details.

Tap an app, and you come to a screen that includes the name of the app and overall user rating and price, as well as plenty of other details just a tap away. Just above the screenshots are links to more information—an overview of the app, including screenshots (tap any to see them), a Reviews link to read user reviews, and a "More Like This" link that leads to a list of similar apps.

Just beneath the name and ratings of the app you'll find three small gray buttons. The leftmost one adds the app to your wish list, to which you can return and download any app. The middle button lets you rate and review an app. The rightmost one is the Profile button, which lets you switch profiles or create new ones.

When deciding whether to pay for and download an app, be careful about using the ratings and reviews as your guide. For example, if there are only a handful of reviews and they're all positive, the developers (or their friends) may be doing the rating. If there are dozens of reviews or more, it's less likely that the developers and their friends are behind them all.

When you tap the Reviews link, don't just read the first reviews you come across. You can filter reviews in multiple ways, including those rated most help-ful by others, the most recent reviews, and so on. Just tap the small icon that appears on top of the first review for a drop-down menu.

When you're looking at an app description in a category or list, you can see the next or previous app in the category or list by swiping to the left or right.

If you decide you want to pay for the app and download it, tap the blue price (or Free) button. The button turns into a green Confirm button. Tap the button to download it; if the app was for-pay, the credit card associated with your Barnes & Noble account gets charged. A number and percent sign appear on the app's icon to show its progress. After it downloads, the button displays the word Open. Tap to run it now; later, you can run it the way you'd run any app (page 239).

(page 239).

NOTE To download apps, you need a Barnes & Noble account with a valid credit card.

Once you've got the app on your NOOK HD, look at the details page, and you'll see two buttons just above the Open button. One lets you rate it, review it, and share it on Facebook. The other lets you create and manage profiles.

Back and Menu Buttons in Apps

When you use an app, you may notice two small icons in the Notification bar that you don't normally see. The one shaped like an arrow is a back button; tap it to go to what you were doing before opening the app. The other one, with a series of lines, is a menu button. Tap it for various options specific to the app. For example, in the Fandango movie app, the menu lets you go to your account, or switch to a view that shows movies or a view that shows theaters. Not all apps have these buttons.

Got an app you love so much that you want it always to be just a tap away? Put it on your Home screen—hold your finger on the app, and from the menu that appears, select "Add to home."

Five Great Apps to Download

There are thousands of great apps you can download, and you'll want to spend lots of time browsing for them. The five described in this section are ones you might want to give a whirl, though—they're among the best in class.

Pulse News

Are you a news junkie? Then you'll want the great, free news app Pulse. It grabs articles from newspapers, magazines, and websites. Using Pulse, you grab articles and information from all over the Web and display them in a big tablet-friendly format with lots of photos and graphics. You customize exactly what kinds of stories and publications you want to show.

TIP Geeks will want to know that the underlying technology that allows Pulse to accomplish all this magic is RSS, which stands for Really Simple Syndication, a format that lets websites and blogs publish updates, and apps like Pulse grab them.

Tap any story to read it. To share the story, tap the Share button at the top of the screen and you can share via Facebook, Twitter, or Google+. At the top right of the screen, you get icons for more features as well, including changing the text size, style, and brightness; for opening the page in the browser; and more.

Pulse is already set up to grab a variety of news feeds from around the Web, but it's easy to change that to your own selections. Tap the settings icon at the upper right to add or remove news sources.

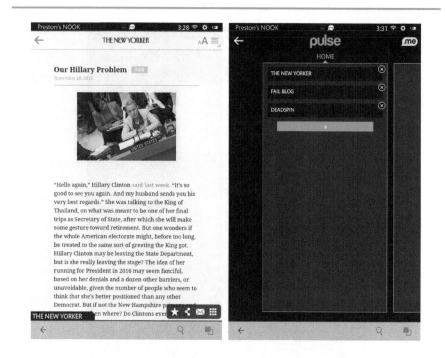

There's a lot more to Pulse as well. It's free and it gives you great sources of information, so if you're a news junkie, or even if you're not, give it a try.

Evernote

If you suffer from information overload, here's your remedy. Evernote does a great job of capturing information from multiple sources, putting them in one location, and then letting you easily find them—whether you're using your computer, your tablet, or another Android device.

Not only that, it's free.

You organize all your information into separate notebooks, and can then browse each notebook, search through it, search through all notebooks, and so on.

No matter where you capture or input information, it's available on every device on which you install Evernote. So if you grab a web page from your PC and put it into a notebook, that information is available on your NOOK HD, and vice versa.

You can capture information from the Web, by taking photos, by speaking, and by pasting in existing documents. And you can also type notes as well.

The upshot of all this? Evernote is the best app you'll find for capturing information and making sense of it all.

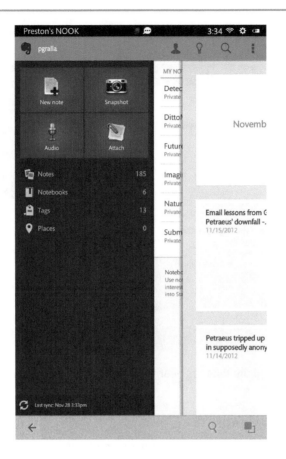

Fandango

Wonder what's on at your local movie theater tonight? Like to find out what other people have thought about the movies? Want to buy tickets before you go?

Fandango does all that, plus more, and it does it for free. Launch the app, and then tap Movies to see a list of currently playing movies. Tap a movie, and you come to a page that lists the name, running time, rating, synopsis, overall rating, trailer, and theater where it's playing. If the theatre lets you, you can buy tickets as well. Tabs at the top of the page lead you to more information, including reviews and director and cast information.

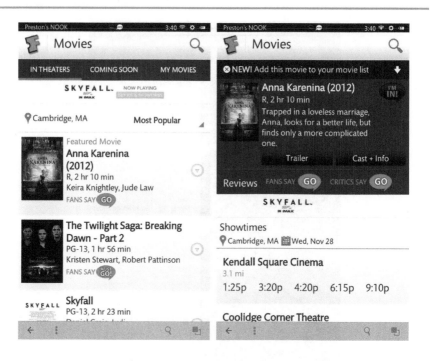

You can also see all the theaters near your home, find out their movie schedules, and buy tickets.

Words With Friends

You've got a NOOK, so you're clearly a word person. If your love extends to word games, and you want to play with other word lovers, then you'll want to get the popular Words With Friends app. (It's a for-pay app, not a free one.)

It's a game similar to Scrabble that you play against friends from Facebook, your Contacts list, Twitter, or other places. The app can even find random opponents for you to play against. One of the many great things about it is that you don't need to play an entire game at once. You can start, play for a few minutes, go off and do something else, pick up the game where you left off...games can last for several days if you like, or you can play straight through. And you can also play multiple games at the same time.

Trip Advisor City Guides

Traveling to a city for business or pleasure? Then you'll want to get the free City Guides from Trip Advisor. There are separate ones for different cities, so in the NOOK Shop, type the name of the city you plan to visit along with the words *City Guide* to find it, like this: *San Francisco City Guide*.

You'll get a great free app that tells you everything you want to know about visiting a city—what restaurants and sites to visit, what hotels are good, information about neighborhoods, local transportation, history, culture, architecture...even an interactive map. You'll find ratings, individual reviews, directions, and more.

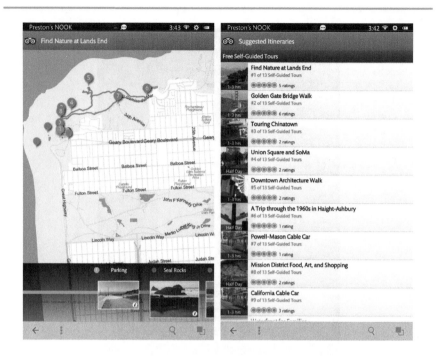

There are guides from around the world. In fact, you may want to download some just to imagine visiting various places. Paris, anyone?

Troubleshooting Apps

In a perfect world, apps would never misbehave. Unfortunately, it's not a perfect world. An app may quit the moment you launch it, or cause your NOOK HD to restart, or do any number of odd things. If that happens, try these steps:

- **Launch the app again.** There's no particular reason why relaunch should work, but it often does. When you launch the app again, it just may work properly.

- **Archive or delete and reinstall.** There may have been an oddball installation problem. So archive or delete the app, and then reinstall it. That action sometimes fixes the problem. When to archive and when to delete? If it's a for-pay app, you'll want to archive rather than delete it, or else you'll have to pay for it again.

- **Restart the NOOK HD.** Just as restarting a computer sometimes fixes problems for no known reason, restarting the NOOK HD may have the same effect.

If none of this works, then it's time to uninstall the app. Don't fret; there are plenty more where it came from.

CHAPTER 11

Music, Pictures, Video, and Documents

YOUR NOOK DOES MORE than work as a great ereader and entertainment player—it's also a great device for listening to music, viewing pictures, playing videos, and even reading work documents such as PDF files and Microsoft Office documents. Everything you need to do all that is built right into the NOOK itself. Read on to learn how to do it all.

Getting Files into Your NOOK

Before you can listen to music, view movies or pictures, or read documents, you have to get them into your NOOK HD. You can get them there in three different ways:

- **Via email.** Someone can send you the files via email, and you can save them on your NOOK HD (page 333).

- **From the Web.** As you browse the Web, you can download files to your NOOK HD.

- **Transferring them from a computer.** Connect your NOOK HD to your computer via the USB cable, and you can drag them to your NOOK's internal storage, or to a microSD card if you've installed one (page 277).

Playing Music and Audio Files

You play music and audio files on your NOOK HD using the built-in Music Player. The Music Player has two modes—Browse mode and Now Playing mode. The first time you launch the app, you launch into Browse mode, which lets you view your music by artists, albums, songs, or playlists. To change the view to any of them, simply tap the appropriate button at the top of the screen.

NOTE Unlike previous versions of the NOOK, the NOOK HD's speakers are stereo rather than monaural.

To play music or a playlist, simply tap it, and the player launches. You switch to Now Playing mode, which has all the familiar controls for pausing, starting, moving forwards and backwards, and so on. Down at the bottom of the screen, just below the controls, you'll see the progress of the song. To switch to Browse mode, tap the arrow icon at the upper-left part of the screen. You can only be in Now Playing mode when you're actually playing music.

NOTE You can also browse the music files on your NOOK HD manually, and then listen to any that you choose. To do that, in the Library, tap My Files and then tap either Device or SD Card, depending on where you've stored the files. Assuming you've stored them on the Music folder in either location, get to them by tapping My Files→Music. Then browse to any file and tap any to play it. The Music Player launches and starts playing the file.

Browse Mode

In Browse mode, across the top of the screen are four buttons for the four different ways you can browse your music:

- **Artist.** Organizes music by artists' names. Next to their names is a small sideways-facing arrow. Tap it, and you'll see each album, including album art (if available) and the number of songs on it. Tap an album to see a list of songs on it. Tap a song to play it.

> **NOTE** When you tap an album to see the list of songs on it, you're switched into Song view.

- **Albums.** Organizes songs by album. It includes artwork (if available), and lists the name and artists. Tap an album to see all the tracks on it. Tap a track to play it.

- **Song.** Lists individual songs, and includes their title, artist, and length. They're organized alphabetically by the name of the file. Scroll through them in the usual way. Tap any track to play it.

- **Playlist.** Shows all your playlists. Even if you haven't created a playlist, one will be there—Recently Added—which shows all the songs you've recently added. Tap any playlist to see all the songs on it and play them. For more details about playlists, see page 265.

The Music app doesn't have its own built-in search feature. To search for music, tap the search icon at the bottom right of the NOOK HD screen (it appears almost anywhere you are on the NOOK). Then type the artist name, album name, or song name. This means that you can search for music even when you're doing something else on your NOOK HD. When you find a song you want to play, tap it. You immediately pop into Now Playing mode, and the music plays. If artwork is available, it takes up most of the screen.

Now Playing Mode

In Now Playing mode, at the bottom of the screen you'll see the usual controls for playing and pausing music, moving to the next and previous track, and scrolling through the track. But you'll notice two curious icons, one on the left side of the playing controls and one on the right. The one on the left is the Repeat button. Tap it to repeat all your songs; double-tap to repeat the song you're currently playing. When you tap twice to repeat the current song, a tiny number 1 appears. The icon on the right is the Shuffle button. Tap it to play your songs in a random order.

At the bottom of the screen, you'll see the progress of the current song via a slider. It shows the total length of the song, as well as your current location in the song.

More Options for Playing Music

When you're browsing for music, press and hold your finger on a song or album, and a menu pops up with these choices:

- **Play.** Plays the song or album.

- **Add to playlist.** Adds it to an existing playlist, or lets you create a new playlist and add it to that one. (See the next section for more details about playlists.)

- **Remove from playlist.** Removes it from its current playlist. (This only appears if the song is on a playlist.)

- **Delete.** Deletes the song.

- **Search.** Searches for the song using Pandora (page 232) in the Music app. Why you would search for a song that you've already located and are holding your finger on is a bit of a mystery, but you can do it if you want.

> **TIP**   What if you don't want to make any of the choices when the menu appears? There appears to be no way to back out and get back to the Music Player. But it's simple to do: Just tap your finger anywhere except on the menu that popped up.

Creating and Managing Playlists

At first glance it's tough to figure out how to create a playlist on your NOOK HD. There seems to be no button to tap to create one. It's simple to do, though. As just detailed, hold your finger on a song or album, and then tap "Add to playlist" from the menu that appears. A screen appears that shows you any playlists you've already created, as well as one that the NOOK HD automatically creates for you—"Current playlist," which contains the songs you've most recently added.

To create a new playlist, tap New, type the name of the playlist you want to create, and then tap Save. The playlist is created, and it'll contain the song you've just added.

NOTE If you hold your finger on an album to create a new playlist, when you create the playlist, it'll contain all the tracks from that album.

Keep adding songs to your playlist this way. To play a playlist, go to Browse mode, and then tap the Playlist icon to see a list of them. Press and hold your finger on any playlist, and from the menu that appears, tap Play. The first song in the Playlist starts up in Now Playing mode. Control music as you would normally. Each song in the playlist plays, one after another.

To see all the tracks in a playlist, tap it (instead of holding your finger on it). But you won't see the playlist's name anywhere. Tap any song to play it; the rest of the songs from that point on in the playlist play in succession.

There's no way to edit the playlist directly by adding or removing songs. Instead, remove a song by pressing and holding your finger on it, and then selecting "Remove from Playlist." To add songs, you have to go to the song or album, as described at the beginning of this section. To delete or rename a playlist, hold your finger on it, and then select either option from the menu that appears.

Listening to Podcasts and Audiobooks

Your NOOK HD can play more than just music; it can also play podcasts and audiobooks, as long as they're in a file format it can recognize. (For a list of audio file formats, see Table 11-1.)

First, subscribe to podcasts as you normally would, using your PC, Mac, iPhone, iPad, iPod, Android tablet or smartphone, or similar device. Then when the podcast is on your computer—for example, in iTunes—copy it to the Music folder of your NOOK HD, just as you would copy music. Make sure that you subscribe to the podcast in MP3 or another NOOK HD-friendly format.

> **TIP** Looking for software for your PC or Mac that will let you subscribe to podcasts so you can transfer them to your NOOK? The free Juice app (*http://juicereceiver.sourceforge.net/*) is a good bet.

As for audiobooks, again, make sure that they're in a format your NOOK HD can play, such as MP3. Then just transfer them to your NOOK HD's Music folder.

> **NOTE** Alas, Audible fans: The audiobooks from Audible.com are in a file format that the NOOK HD can't read.

There are plenty of places on the Internet where you can find audiobooks to download:

- **Barnes & Noble Audio Books** (*http://bit.ly/ycmq2d*). You'll find a big selection here, especially of bestsellers and newly released books.

- **Audiobooks.org** (*www.audiobooks.org*). Nice selection, including free ones.

- **Simply Audiobooks** (*www.simplyaudiobooks.com*) **and Audiobooks.com** (*www.audiobooks.com*). Top-notch services that let you rent audiobooks rather than buy them.

TABLE 11-1 *The NOOK HD can play many, but not all music and audio files. The primary file type that's missing from the list is Windows Media Audio (.wma) files. So if you've got music and audio in those formats, you're out of luck. You'll have to convert them to one of the formats the NOOK can handle if you want to play them.*

AUDIO FILES
.mp4
.m4a
.3gp
.aac
.mp3
.flac
.wav
.ogg
.amr

NOTE Why won't the NOOK play .wma files? It's an Android thing. The NOOK HD and NOOK Color are powered by Google's Android operating system, and Android can't play .wma files. Some Android devices, such as the Droid X2, can play .wma files, but that's not because the capability has been built into Android. The device's manufacturer has added its own special sauce to basic Android to grant it the ability to play .wma files. Unfortunately, Barnes & Noble didn't do that for the NOOK HD.

Using Gallery for Viewing Photos and Playing Video

The NOOK HD has an extremely good high-resolution screen, ideally suited for viewing photos and playing video. As with music and audio files, you'll first have to get them on your NOOK HD via email (page 333), downloading from the Web, or transferring them from your computer (page 277).

Once you've got them on your NOOK HD, you view them using the built-in Gallery app. To launch it, press the NOOK button, tap Apps, and then tap Gallery.

You can also browse the photos and video files on your NOOK HD manually, and then view any that you choose. To do that, in the Library, tap My Files and tap Device or SD Card, depending on where you've stored the files. If you've stored them on your memory card, tap My Files→Pictures. (That's if you've stored them in the Pictures folder; if not, go to whatever folder in which you've stored them.) If you've stored your videos in the Videos folder, tap My Files→Videos. Then browse to any file and tap it to play it. The Gallery app launches and starts playing the file. If the files are instead stored on your device, tap Device, and then tap Pictures or Videos.

The Gallery app opens, which shows you all the folders where your pictures and videos are located. Tap any folder to see individual pictures and videos, or further subfolders if you've stored them in subfolders. Flick through any folder to see them all. The Gallery displays both photos and videos; videos have a small rightward-facing arrow on them.

Tap a photo to view it. For a moment, you'll see not just the photo, but also a row of icons across the bottom of the screen for doing things with the photo—cropping it, setting it as your wallpaper, and more. You'll also see a photo strip along the bottom showing your photos, so you can tap any to go to it, or swipe horizontally to see more photos. After the icons and photo strip go away, you can make them come back by tapping the middle of the photo. When they're onscreen you can make them go away by tapping the middle of the photo again.

Some photos display better horizontally than vertically, so turn your HD 90 degrees, and the orientation changes. Turn it back if you want to view the photo vertically. To view the next photo in the Gallery, swipe to the right; to view the previous one, swipe to the left. To return to the Grid view, tap the middle of the screen to bring up the icons, and then tap Grid at top right. When you're in the Grid view, tap Picture to see the last photo you were viewing.

When you're viewing a picture with the icons visible, here's what you can do by tapping any of the icons across the bottom of the screen:

- **Slideshow.** Plays a photo slideshow, displaying each photo for a few seconds before moving on to the next. Stop the slideshow by tapping the screen.

- **E-Mail.** Launches the E-Mail app and attaches the current photo to an unaddressed recipient. Fill in the recipient, type in any text and send the photo on its merry way. You might have other options when you tap this icon, depending on what apps you have installed. For example, if you've installed Evernote, when you tap this, one of your choices will be to save the photo to Evernote.

- **Delete.** Removes the photo from your NOOK.

- **Rotate.** Rotates the photo ninety degrees to the right. Keep tapping it to keep rotating the photo.

- **Crop.** Tap this option, and a highlighted box appears onscreen. Press the middle of the box to drag it around to the area you want to crop. You can adjust the dimensions of the box by dragging any side in or out. Tap Save to crop the photo to its new dimensions, and tap Cancel to leave your photo in its original uncropped condition.

If you tap a video instead of a photo, it starts running in a video player. You'll see the usual controls for playing, pausing, and moving through the video. Tap the screen to make the controls disappear; tap again to bring them back.

TABLE 11-2 *The NOOK HD can view and play many but not all picture and video formats.*

PICTURE AND PHOTO FILES
.jpg
.gif
.png
.bmp
VIDEO FILES
.3gp
.mp4
.WEBM

Working with Office Documents

Your NOOK HD can do double-duty as a work tablet, letting you view Office documents including Word files (.doc, .docx, .docm, .dotx, .dotm), Excel files, (.xls, .xlsx, .xlsm, .xltx, .xltm), PowerPoint files (.ppt, .pptx, .pptm, .pps, .ppsx, .ppsm, .pot. potx, .potm), and plain text files (.txt).

As with audio files, pictures, and videos, you'll first have to get them on your NOOK HD via email (page 333), by downloading from the Web, or by transferring them from your computer (page 277).

To view the files, you don't first launch an app. Instead, you browse to where you've put them. To do that, in the Library, tap My Files, and then tap Device or SD Card, depending on where you've stored the files. So if you've stored your files in the Documents folder on your SD card, tap Files→SD Card→Documents to get to a list of them.

> **TIP** If you've downloaded files from the Web, you'll find them on the NOOK HD's built-in memory, not on its microSD card. Get to them by tapping My Files→My Download.

Tap any file, and it opens in an app built into the NOOK HD called OfficeSuite. This app lets you view Office files, but not edit them. At the top of the screen you'll find a variety of tools for doing things such as searching, finding the word count, and more.

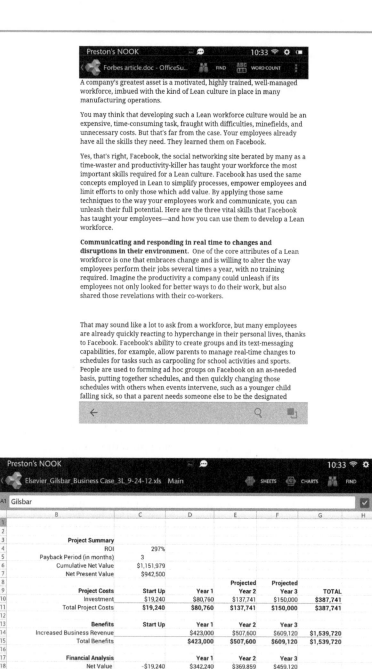

Preston's NOOK · 10:33 · Forbes article.doc - OfficeSu... · FIND · WORD COUNT

A company's greatest asset is a motivated, highly trained, well-managed workforce, imbued with the kind of Lean culture in place in many manufacturing operations.

You may think that developing such a Lean workforce culture would be an expensive, time-consuming task, fraught with difficulties, minefields, and unnecessary costs. But that's far from the case. Your employees already have all the skills they need. They learned them on Facebook.

Yes, that's right, Facebook, the social networking site berated by many as a time-waster and productivity-killer has taught your workforce the most important skills required for a Lean culture. Facebook has used the same concepts employed in Lean to simplify processes, empower employees and limit efforts to only those which add value. By applying those same techniques to the way your employees work and communicate, you can unleash their full potential. Here are the three vital skills that Facebook has taught your employees—and how you can use them to develop a Lean workforce.

Communicating and responding in real time to changes and disruptions in their environment. One of the core attributes of a Lean workforce is one that embraces change and is willing to alter the way employees perform their jobs several times a year, with no training required. Imagine the productivity a company could unleash if its employees not only looked for better ways to do their work, but also shared those revelations with their co-workers.

That may sound like a lot to ask from a workforce, but many employees are already quickly reacting to hyperchange in their personal lives, thanks to Facebook. Facebook's ability to create groups and its text-messaging capabilities, for example, allow parents to manage real-time changes to schedules for tasks such as carpooling for school activities and sports. People are used to forming ad hoc groups on Facebook on an as-needed basis, putting together schedules, and then quickly changing those schedules with others when events intervene, such as a younger child falling sick, so that a parent needs someone else to be the designated

---

Preston's NOOK · 10:33 · Elsevier_Gilsbar_Business Case_3L_9-24-12.xls · Main · SHEETS · CHARTS · FIND

A1 · Gilsbar

	B	C	D	E	F	G	H
1							
2							
3	Project Summary						
4	ROI	297%					
5	Payback Period (in months)	3					
6	Cumulative Net Value	$1,151,979					
7	Net Present Value	$942,500					
8				Projected	Projected		
9	Project Costs	Start Up	Year 1	Year 2	Year 3	TOTAL	
10	Investment	$19,240	$80,760	$137,741	$150,000	$387,741	
11	Total Project Costs	$19,240	$80,760	$137,741	$150,000	$387,741	
12							
13	Benefits	Start Up	Year 1	Year 2	Year 3		
14	Increased Business Revenue		$423,000	$507,600	$609,120	$1,539,720	
15	Total Benefits		$423,000	$507,600	$609,120	$1,539,720	
16							
17	Financial Analysis		Year 1	Year 2	Year 3		
18	Net Value	-$19,240	$342,240	$369,859	$459,120		
19	Cumulative Net Value	-$19,240	$323,000	$692,859	$1,151,979		

Main

If viewing documents isn't enough for you, you can pay to upgrade to the Pro version, which costs $14.99. Download it from the NOOK Shop.

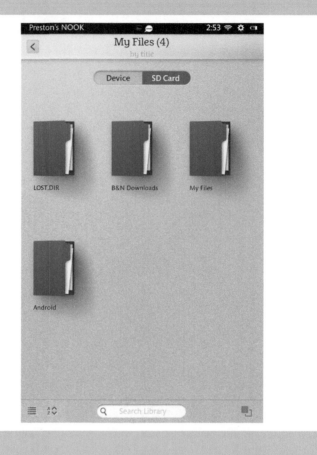

CHAPTER 12

Transferring Files Between Your NOOK HD and Your Computer

YOUR NOOK HD COMES with plenty of storage—either 8 GB or 16 GB for a NOOK HD, or 16 GB or 32 GB for a NOOK HD+. You've got lots of room for books, periodicals, files, videos, and apps. But sometimes that storage GB doesn't go far enough and you want more, because videos, apps, and magazines can take up plenty of space.

Unlike other ereaders, though, your NOOK HD has a built-in slot for a microSD card, which means you can expand its storage, and add lots of it. There's plenty you can do with that storage, adding space for music, Office documents, video, and more. This chapter tells you how to do that, from installing an SD card, to transferring files and then learning how to manage them.

Installing an SD Card

You can add plenty of storage to your NOOK HD—you can put an SD card with up to a whopping 64 GB of memory in it, with room for literally thousands of books, magazines, newspapers, and files.

How many you can actually fit depends on what you put there. Figure that an SD card can store about 1,000 books for every gigabyte of storage space, so a 64 GB SD card can hold an astounding 64,000 books! Even if you're a nonstop reader, that should last you several lifetimes.

Of course, you'll likely store more than books on the SD card. You may store magazines and newspapers as well. And that's where your mileage will vary. Highly interactive magazines with plenty of high-resolution photos can weigh in at an astounding 1 GB each. And if you store music and video files, they can add up as well.

Types of SD Cards You Can Use

When buying an SD card, make sure you buy one of the three formats that work in the NOOK—microSD, microSDHC, and microSDXC. What's the difference? It's right there in the name. The HC in microSDHC stands for *high capacity*. Cards 4 GB or over are called microSDHC, while cards under that capacity are microSD. The XC in microSDXC stands for *extra capacity*. Cards with more than 32 GB of storage are called microSDXC.

MicroSDHC cards can hold more than microSD cards, and microSDXC cards hold more than microSDHC cards. The cost difference generally isn't enormous. You'll find microSDHC cards for $15 and under with 16 GB of storage, and from $20 to $30 for 32 GB of storage. At those prices, there's no reason to spring for the less-expensive microSD cards. As for the microSDXC cards, they typically run about $60 or sometimes a bit more.

NOTE You may hear of UHS (ultra-high speed) file transfer on microSDXC cards. On the NOOK HD, you can use microSDXC cards for their greater capacity, but you won't see the greater UHS speed. Anyway, UHS pertains only to how fast you can transfer files to and from the card, not how quickly you can access your content from it.

Make sure when buying a card that it is formatted with the FAT32 file system or the exFAT file system. As a general rule, most or all are, but it doesn't hurt to check.

NOTE MicroSDHC cards are rated by their class—Class 2, Class 4, and Class 6. Class 2 is the cheapest, and Class 6 is the most expensive. If you don't see a class rating on the packaging, it's a Class 2 card. The higher the class, the more quickly you can transfer files to it, but the class rating has absolutely nothing to do with how quickly you can *display* books from the card. Class 6 cards tend to be significantly more expensive than Class 4 cards, and some people have had problems with them. To be on the safe side, stick with Class 4.

Installing the Card

If you haven't installed a microSD card before, don't fret—it's a piece of cake. Here's how:

1. **Put your NOOK face up on a clean surface.** Make sure you can see the NOOK button...in other words, make sure you haven't put the NOOK HD face-side down.

2. **Locate the small lid to the left of the 30-pin USB port at the NOOK's lower-left edge.** Using your fingertip, pull the lid away from the NOOK's bezel. Pull it straight back, and do it gently. The lid pulls straight back and remains attached to the NOOK by two flexible bands. Push the lid down slightly, and you'll expose a slot.

3. **Holding the card between your thumb and forefinger, with the logo side up, insert it gently into the slot.**

4. **Push the card gently until it clicks into place.**

5. **Push on the gray lid gently to snap it into place.**

If you haven't used the card before, you may see a dialog box telling you that the card needs to be formatted. Tap Format Now. You'll get a warning, telling you that formatting the card will delete all its contents. Tap Format Now again. (If you don't get the alert telling you that the card needs to be formatted, don't worry—that just means it's already formatted and you're ready to go.)

Even if the card has been formatted, you may get a message that you need to erase its contents in order to watch videos on it. So you may need to format it.

Once the card is installed, you'll be able to get to it and its contents in the My Files area of your Library. See page 287 at the end of this chapter for details.

Removing the Card

Removing an SD card is as easy as installing one. Place your NOOK face up and pull out the lid to expose the card slot as described in the previous steps. Push gently against the memory card with your fingertip and then release it; part of the card pops out. You can then slide the card out of the slot and snap the gray lid back into place.

Transferring Files to Your NOOK HD

Before you can enjoy your music, videos, ebooks, and work documents (okay, maybe not enjoy...), you have to get them onto your NOOK HD, and that's what this section is all about. It's a breeze to transfer files between your PC or Mac and your NOOK.

Once you transfer files to your NOOK, you don't need even to know what apps on your NOOK handle each of these file types—the NOOK is smart enough to know. So when you tap one of the files, the right app automatically jumps into action and launches itself, opening the file. But if you're curious about whether a specific file will work on the NOOK HD, see Table 12-1. You don't want to waste your time transferring files that you can't use on your NOOK. This table details what kinds of files work with it.

TABLE 12-1 *You don't want to waste your time transferring files that will merely sit on your NOOK, unloved and unused. This table details what kinds of files work with it.*

NOOK FILES, MICROSOFT OFFICE FILES, AND MULTIMEDIA FILES
EPUB (the main book format for the NOOK)
PDF
DRP
ePIB
FOLIO
OFIP
.rtf
Word (.doc, .docx, .docm, .dotx, .dotm)

NOOK FILES, MICROSOFT OFFICE FILES, AND MULTIMEDIA FILES
Excel (.xls, .xlsx, .xlsm, .xltx, .xltm)
PowerPoint (.ppt, .pptx, .pptm, .pps, .ppsx, .ppsm, .pot. potx, .potm)
Plain text (.txt)
HTML (.htm, .html, .xhtml)
Comic book archive (.cbz)
.zip
.LOG
.csv
.eml

MUSIC FILES
.aac
.amr
.flac
.mp3
.mp4
.mp4a
.ogg
.wav
.3gp

PICTURE AND PHOTO FILES
.jpg
.gif
.png
.bmp

VIDEO FILES
.3gp
.mp4
.webm

As a general rule, EPUB files open in the main NOOK reader; Microsoft Office files open in OfficeSuite; and picture, music, and video files open in the NOOK's built-in media player.

Transferring with a PC

First connect your NOOK to your PC with the 30-pin/micro USB cable that came with the NOOK HD. Don't use any other cable; Barnes & Noble warns that if you use a different cable, you might damage your NOOK. Connect the 30-pin end to your NOOK, and plug the normal-sized USB plug into your computer's USB port.

Depending on your PC and the software installed on it, several things may happen. Sometimes, after a moment or two, you'll get a notice asking how Windows should handle the device (it's the same notice you get when you plug in a USB flash drive). Generally, you can ignore the notice, and it'll go away quickly. If it doesn't, though, click the link that asks whether you want to use the device to transfer files.

Other times, you need to wait a little while as the PC installs driver software that lets your PC talk to your NOOK. In that case, just wait, and soon you'll get the notice asking how you want to handle the device.

Either way, after you've connected it to your PC, launch Windows Explorer. Your NOOK now shows up as a removable disk, just like any USB drive. Its name may vary; for example, it may be called NOOK, or something else. In the nearby illustration, it shows up as a portable device called BNTV400.

You can now use your NOOK as if it were any USB flash device—copying files to and from it, creating folders, and so on. Browse the device and you'll see two folders, one labeled Internal Storage, and one labeled SD Card. (If you haven't installed an SD card, the SD Card folder, naturally, won't show up.)

The folder structure of Internal Storage and SD Card are similar in some ways. Internal Storage has a variety of folders you don't need to worry about, such as B&N Downloads, .profiles, and log, so don't pay any attention to them. Instead, use Windows Explorer to go to the My Files folder. That's where you'll be placing your files.

> **NOTE** Transferring files from your PC or Mac to your NOOK is sometimes called *sideloading*.

Here are the folders you'll find:

- Books

- Documents

- Magazines

- Music

- Newspapers

- NOOK Kids Recordings

- Pictures

- Videos

Unless you're a true nonconformist, you'll put your books in the Books folder, Microsoft Office files in the Documents folder, Music files in the Music folder, and so on. (See Appendix B for details about file types.) Keep in mind that you're not required to use this folder structure; you can put files wherever you want, and you can even create new folders. But for simplicity's sake and overall good housekeeping, you're best off staying with the folder structure that's already there.

NOTE You don't need an SD card in order to transfer files from your computer to your NOOK. You can transfer them directly to internal storage, as outlined here.

The NOOK uses the EPUB file format for books, so when you're borrowing books from a library, or downloading them from the Internet, make sure to look for files in that format. After you've got them on your computer, just drag them over to the Books folder.

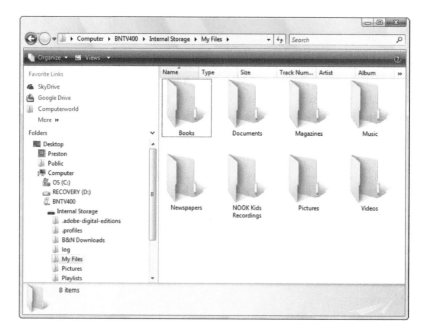

The SD Card folder has a variety of folders as well. But as with the internal storage, the one you're interested in is My Files. Under My Files, you'll find the same subfolders as you do on the NOOK's internal storage. So you can copy files either to your internal storage or to the SD card. Either way, they're usable on your NOOK.

Once you've dragged files from your PC to your NOOK, disconnect the USB cable, and you're ready to start using the files. For details about what you can do with the files once they're on your card and how to see them on the NOOK, turn to page 287 at the end of this chapter.

NOTE Wondering what the LOST.DIR folder is for? If the NOOK determines that you've moved any files to it that are corrupted or have other kinds of problems, it moves them (or copies of them) here.

Transferring with a Mac

Just as with a PC, to transfer files to your NOOK from a Mac, connect your NOOK to your Mac using the micro USB cable that came with the NOOK. You may find that when you connect it, iPhoto immediately launches. Close it down; you won't need it.

Instead, launch Finder. Browse it using the Finder as you would any other USB storage device to transfer files to your NOOK by dragging them.

Troubleshooting Your Connection

There's a chance that you'll run into problems when connecting your NOOK to your PC or Mac—usually, it's a case of the computer not recognizing the NOOK as a USB drive. In that case, there are a few things you can try. First, disconnect the NOOK from your computer. Then on the Home screen, tap the gear-shaped Settings icon in the Status bar. A drop-down screen appears. Tap All Settings→Storage Management→USB Connectivity. From the screen that appears, make sure that there's a check in the box next to "Media device (MTP)."

Connect your NOOK to your computer again. Things should work fine now. If not, disconnect the NOOK from the computer, and on the Home screen, tap Settings again. On the drop-down screen, tap All Settings→Device Information→"Developer options" and turn on the box next to "Enable ADB." That should do the trick.

Finding Books Online to Transfer to Your NOOK HD

Above all, your NOOK is an ereader, so you'll likely want to find books to transfer to it. One of the simplest ways is to check with your local library. Many libraries have programs that lend out books in the EPUB format that the NOOK uses.

> **NOTE** Some websites of local bookstores sell ebooks in the EPUB format. Check with your local store to see if it does.

When you find ebooks online in the EPUB format, you want to make sure that they can legally be distributed for free. The best way to do that is to go to a reputable website known for distributing free books without copyright violations. The best one is Project Gutenberg (*www.gutenberg.org*).

Keep in mind that if you're looking for free ebooks, the NOOK Shop (page 151) is an excellent place to look, because you'll find many high-quality free books there. When you get free ebooks from the NOOK Shop, you won't have to download them to your PC and then transfer them to your NOOK. They're downloaded straight to your Library.

Browsing and Managing
Files on your NOOK HD

To browse the files on your NOOK HD, go to the Library, scroll down and tap My Files. You come to a screen that's divided in two—on the left you find Device, and on the right, SD Card. Tap Device to browse the folders built into the NOOK's main memory, and tap SD Card to browse the memory card. (If you haven't installed a memory card, you'll only see files and folders.)

Tap the folders as described on page 182. So on either the device or SD card, tap My Files to see your subfolders. Then tap the subfolder whose contents you want to see, for example, Music under My Files. You can keep browsing through even more subfolders if there are any. Music, for example, might have a variety of subfolders, one for each of your albums.

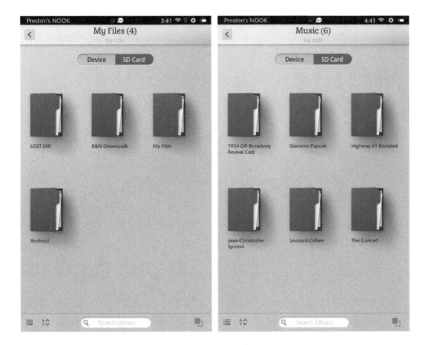

From here, you can delete any files. To delete a file, hold your finger on it, and then select Delete from the menu that appears.

You can also view photos, play music, and so on from here. Tap the photo you want to view, music you want to play, and so on, and it shows up in the correct app; photos in the Gallery for example, and music in the music player.

The Web and Email

CHAPTER 13

Surfing the Web

THE NOOK HD IS more than just the best ereader on the planet. It's also a pro at browsing the Web, with a great built-in browser. You can do anything on it that you can do with big-boy browsers on your PC or Mac—visit anywhere on the Web, bookmarks web pages, use web forms, and so on. The screen may be smaller than your desktop display, but it's big enough and clear enough to give you a satisfying web experience wherever you go. How to do it all? That's what this chapter is for.

A Tour of the NOOK HD's Browser

To access the Web, press the NOOK button, and choose Web from the Quick Nav bar. The NOOK HD's browser launches.

The NOOK's browser has plenty of goodies, much like those in a computer browser, including bookmarks, AutoComplete for web addresses, cookies, password memorization, the ability to save pages...just about the whole nine yards. It's based on Google's Chrome browser, and looks and works like it in quite a few ways. The browser practically bristles with features. You'll find them across the top of the browser window, and down at the bottom.

If you use the Chrome browser on a computer or tablet, those top controls may look familiar. Here are the main controls you need to know about:

NOTE When you're on a web page and scroll down, the controls on top of the page disappear. To make them appear again, drag down on the screen.

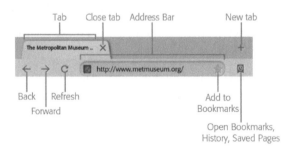

Tab   Close tab   Address Bar   New tab

Back   Refresh

Forward

Add to
Bookmarks

Open Bookmarks,
History, Saved Pages

• **Address bar.** Here's where you enter the URL—the web address—for a page you want to visit.

- **Tab.** The NOOK's browser has multiple tabs so you can visit multiple sites simultaneously. The tab for each shows the title of the page open. Tap the X to close the tab.

- **Open new tab.** Tap here to open a new tab.

- **Forward, back, refresh.** These buttons do exactly what the same buttons do on a computer's browser: send you back or forward in your Web browsing, or refresh the current page.

- **Add bookmark.** Tap the gray star to the right of the URL in the address bar to add the site to your Bookmarks list. (See page 85 for details about how to handle bookmarks.)

- **Open Bookmarks, History, Saved pages.** This opens to a page with three tabs across the top: one for your bookmarks, one to see your browsing history, and one to see your saved pages.

Now it's time to check out the controls at the bottom of the page:

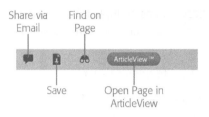

Share via Email   Find on Page

Save   Open Page in ArticleView

- **Share via E-mail.** Tap this and the NOOK's E-Mail app opens with a piece of mail already composed, with the title of the page as the subject, and the URL in the body of the mail. Change or add what you want, choose a recipient, and send it off on its merry way. Depending on the apps you've installed, other options in addition to sharing via email may show up here.

- **Save page.** Tap this to save the page. You can then view it later in your Saved Pages area.

- **Find on page.** Tap this and a search box pops up at the top of the page that lets you search the current page.

TIP The "Find on page" button only searches through your current page. If you want to search the Web, type your search into the address bar, or else tap the Search button on the right bottom side of the screen.

- **Article View.** This displays the current page in a single, long article, without ads or similar material (it does include links, though). It's a great way to read articles on the Web. It's a lot like the ArticleView you can use for magazines on the NOOK (page 116). To go back to the normal view, tap Browser View. When you're in Article View, the controls on the bottom of the screen largely vanish. You can't share via email or search on a page in Article View. However, you can change the text size by tapping the text button that appears.

WARNING If you're reading a long article on the Web and go to Article View, the entire article may not appear. You may have to go back to the Web view to read the entire thing.

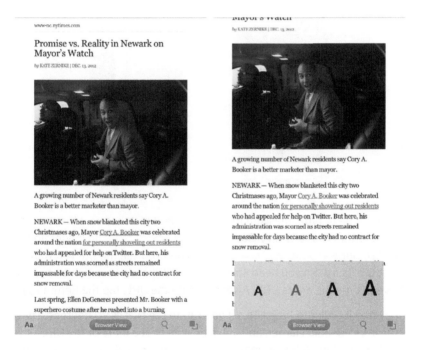

Over to the right of the browser, the controls at the bottom of the page are the controls you normally see just about everywhere on the NOOK: the Search button and the Recent Drawer (see page 46).

The Address Bar

The address bar is the box at the top of the browser where you type the URL of the website you want to visit. To type a URL into the address bar, first tap the text box in the bar. The current URL gets highlighted in blue. To delete the current URL, tap the X that appears on the right side of the screen. However, when the URL is green, you don't really need to do that, since when you start typing, the current URL vanishes and is replaced by what you type.

Then use the keyboard to type an address. As you type, the NOOK displays sites you've visited that match the letters you type. So when you type the letter *C*, for example, it might display *computerworld.com*, *cnn.com*, and so on. It may be a very long list.

As you continue to type, the list narrows down and matches only those sites that match the letters you're typing. So if you type *com*, *cnn.com* no longer appears on your list, but *computerworld.com* does. When you see the site you want to visit, just tap its listing; you head straight there. If there's no match on the list, you have to type the entire URL. After you type the URL, tap the Return key.

You may find it easier to type URLs if you rotate the NOOK 90 degrees. That way, the keys are much larger, and you'll be able to see more of the URL as you type. When you type this way, matching sites and terms show up in boxes just above the keyboard, rather than in a list.

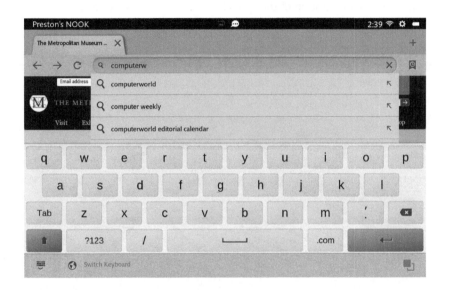

You can also use the address bar to search the Web. Just type your search term, but don't add a .com ending. Your browser searches the Web for the term using Google.

When you head to a page, a small blue progress bar appears just above the address bar, showing you how much of the page has been loaded, and indicating how much is left to go.

Navigating a Web Page

Head to a web page, and most of the time you see an entire page, laid out with the same fonts, links, pictures, and so on, as if you were visiting it using a computer with a larger screen. Move around the page by using the normal NOOK gestures. Of course, looking at an entire web page on the NOOK's screen isn't the same thing as looking at a web page on a 21-inch monitor. The type and photos are small, and the links can be difficult to tap on. But letting you see the entire screen at once makes a good deal of sense, because at a glance, you can see what section of the page you want to view.

That's where the fun begins. You can use the NOOK's zooming and scrolling capabilities to head quickly to the part of the page you want to view, and then zoom in.

You've got three ways to do so:

- **Rotate the NOOK.** Turn it 90 degrees to the left or to the right. The NOOK changes the orientation of the website to fill the wider view, and while doing so, zooms in.

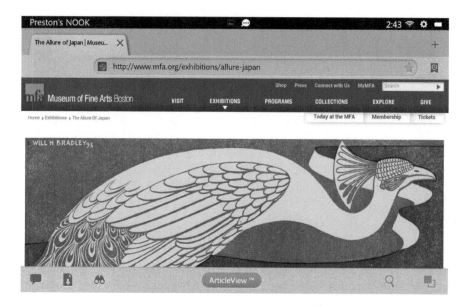

- **Use the two-finger spread.** Put two fingers on the NOOK's screen on the area where you want to zoom in, and move your fingers apart. The web page stretches and zooms in. The more you spread, the greater the zoom. Pinch your fingers together to zoom back out. You may need to do the two-finger spread or pinch several times until you get the exact magnification you want.

- **Double-tap.** Double-tap with a finger on the section of the page where you want to zoom. Double-tap again to zoom out. You can't control the zoom level as finely with the double-tap as you can with the two-finger spread.

Once you've zoomed in, scroll around the web page by dragging or flicking your finger—the same kind of navigation you use for other apps on the NOOK.

Tapping Links

When it comes to links, the NOOK HD's web browser works largely like any computer browser, except that you tap a link rather than click it. Tap the link, and you get sent to a new web page.

But this is the NOOK, so there's a lot more you can do with links than just tapping them. Hold your finger on a link, and a menu appears with these options:

- **Open.** Opens the linked page in the current window.

- **Open in new tab.** Opens the linked page in a new window.

- **Save link.** Puts the link into your Bookmarks list.

- **Copy link URL.** Tap to copy the link's URL to the Clipboard, so you can paste it somewhere else, such as in a document or an email.

```
http://blo.org/wp-content/themes/boston-
lyric/images/bg-hp-glow.png

Open

Open in new tab

Save link

Copy link URL

Save image

View image

Set as wallpaper
```

TIP If you hold your finger on a graphic that's also a link, you get several other options. A "Save image" option appears, which lets you save the graphic (see page 307 for details). There's also a "View image" link, which opens the image in a new browser tab, as well as a "Set as wallpaper" option, which sets the image as your NOOK HD's wallpaper. If you hold your finger on a graphic that's not a link, only the "Save image," "View image," and "Set as wallpaper" options appear.

Using Tabs

The NOOK HD's browser doesn't confine you to a single window—you can use multiple ones and easily switch among them. Just tap the + button on the upper-right side of the screen, and a new tab opens to your Home page. (To change your Home page, see page 316.) To switch between tabs, simply tap the tab to which you want to switch. To close a tab, tap the X on it. If you have more than two tabs open and you're holding the NOOK vertically, you won't be able to see all of your open tabs. Swipe your finger along the tabs to the right and left to see all of your open tabs.

Bookmarks

Just as with computer-based browsers, the NOOK's browser lets you save your favorite sites as bookmarks—sites you can easily visit again without having to retype their URLs.

Whenever you visit a web page you want to add as a bookmark, tap the star-shaped Bookmark button on the right side of the address bar. A screen appears with the name of the page (it's in the label area) and its address. Tap OK, or else edit the screen (for example, to change the title). Here you can edit the name or the actual URL of the bookmark. In the Label box, type a different name if you want, and in the Address box, you can even edit the URL. Then tap OK. Or you can just leave it as is and tap OK. The bookmark is added to your list. You return to the page in the browser, and the Bookmark star has been turned green. Tap it if you want to edit it again.

NOTE If you edit the URL, and the new URL differs from the page you wanted to bookmark, you'll go to the URL you typed in, not the original one you planned to bookmark.

When you're in the browser, to see the bookmarks, tap the Bookmarks, History, and Saved pages button and tap the Bookmarks tab. You see all your bookmarks, including their URLs and thumbnails of them. To head to any, just tap it and you're there.

Managing Bookmarks

The NOOK HD lets you do more than just go to bookmarks. You can delete them, edit them, and more. To get started, head to the Bookmarks screen and then hold your finger on the bookmark you want to edit or manage. A menu appears with the following choices:

- **Open.** Opens the bookmarked site in the current window. Say you're on *www.google.com*, when you go to your bookmarks, and then hold your finger on the *www.bn.com* bookmark. The Barnes & Noble site opens in the window where Google was previously open.

- **Open in new tab.** Opens the bookmarked site in a new tab. So if you're at *www.google.com*, when you open your bookmarks, and then you hold your finger on *www.bn.com*, *www.bn.com* opens in a tab of its own.

- **Edit bookmark.** Brings up a page that lets you edit the name and location of the bookmark. It's the same page for adding a bookmark.

- **Add shortcut to home.** Adds a shortcut to the page to the NOOK HD's Home screen. Just tap the shortcut on the Home screen and you get sent to the page.

- **Share link.** Opens the email app with the title of the page as the subject line, and its URL in the body. Type in a recipient, add text or edit, and send it on its merry way.

- **Copy link URL.** Copies the link to the clipboard so you can later use it.

- **Delete bookmark.** Deletes the bookmark. After you tap it, you get a warning that you're about to delete the bookmark, just in case you want to reconsider, or if you tapped this option by accident.

- **Set as homepage.** Tap this, and from now on whenever you open a new tab, it opens to that site.

History, Most Visited, and Saved Pages Lists

When you go to your bookmarks, you see two ways to browse sites that you've been to before: History and Saved pages. The NOOK HD keeps track of sites you've visited, and puts the History list together based on that. Also on the History screen is the "Most visited" list, which displays the sites you've most frequently visited. The lists are great ways, in addition to bookmarks, to head back to sites you've visited before without having to type—or even remember—the web addresses.

The History list shows all the sites you've visited, in the order you've visited them—today, yesterday, and so on. Just tap the corresponding tab to see the list. On the same screen as the History list is the Most Visited list, which lists the sites you most frequently visited, with the most frequent ones at the top. And the Saved pages list includes all the pages you've saved by tapping the Save page button. The lists are scrollable, so flick through one to see more lists off the bottom of the screen.

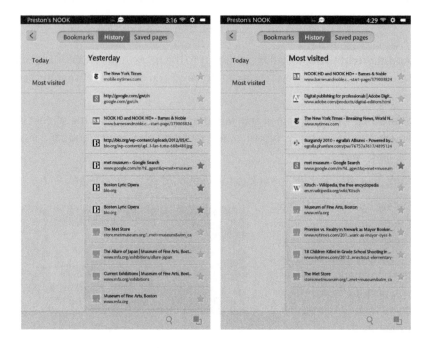

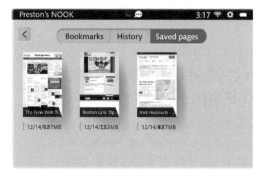

Using the Most Visited List

The "Most visited" list works much like the Bookmarks list—tap the site you want to visit and you immediately get sent there. You'll notice one difference between the Most visited and History lists and the Bookmarks list: The sites all have stars to the right of them, some gray, some green. A green star indicates that the site is on your Bookmarks list. Tapping a gray star adds that site to your Bookmarks (and turns the star green). To remove a site from your Bookmarks list, tap a green star. It turns gray, and the site gets removed from your Bookmarks list. Whenever you add or remove a site from your Bookmarks list in this way, you'll get a brief onscreen notification.

Just as with bookmarks, you can edit and manage the "Most visited" list. Hold your finger on the site you want to edit or manage, and a menu appears, similar to the one you see when you hold your finger on a site in Bookmarks.

The lists are nearly identical, with a few minor differences:

- **Save to bookmarks** is included in the "Most visited" menu so you can add the site to Bookmarks. It's easier to simply tap the gray button to do this, but if you like your NOOK so much that you enjoy holding your finger on it, you can do it this way as well.

- **Remove from history** removes a site from the "Most visited" list as well as from your History list.

If you press and hold a site in your "Most visited" list that's in your Bookmarks list, you'll have the option of removing it from Bookmarks as well.

Using the History List

The History list is organized by day. In it, you can see the sites you've visited in groups—Today, Yesterday, Last Seven Days, Last Month, and so on. Tap any of the groups, and you'll see all the pages in that group.

As with the "Most visited" list, tap a star next to a site to add it to your Bookmarks list, and the star turns green. Tap a green star to remove it from your Bookmarks list, and the star turns gray. Press and hold any site to get the same set of options that you do when you hold your finger on the site in the "Most visited" list.

Using the Saved Pages List

Head to the Saved pages list, and you'll see thumbnails of all the pages you've saved. These are the actual pages themselves, not links to pages that are online. So when you save them, you save their graphics, their video, the HTML that creates the page...the whole shebang. And when you tap the page, you call it up from where it's stored on your NOOK, not by going to the Web.

Saving pages on your NOOK can lead to a bit of confusion. Suppose you visit the home page of a newspaper, like the *New York Times,* and you decide to save it. The next day, you tap it in your Saved pages list. You'll see yesterday's news, the page as it was at the moment you saved it, not as it looks today. To get to the current page, you have to visit it via History, Bookmarks, Most visited, or any of the usual ways.

Hold your finger on a saved page, and there's only one thing you can do with it: Delete it.

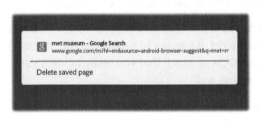

Saving Online Images

When you're browsing the Web, sooner or later you'll come across a picture you'd like to save. For example, if a friend posts a picture from your birthday party on Facebook, you can save it on your NOOK HD and then share it with others.

There's a quick and easy way to save that image. Hold your finger on the picture for a second or two, and a menu appears with the following options:

- **Save image.** Downloads the picture to your NOOK. See the next section to learn how to go back and view all the pictures in this folder.

- **View image.** Opens the image in its own page. As a practical matter, this option doesn't do much, because it doesn't make the image any larger or smaller—you're seeing the same image, just on its own rather than on a web page.

- **Set as wallpaper.** Sets the image as the wallpaper on the NOOK HD's Home screen.

NOTE If the picture is also a link, the menu shows the usual options for bookmarking the link, saving the link, and so on.

Viewing Downloaded Images

When you download an image, a small notification appears in the Status bar telling you that a file has been downloaded. Tap the Notification bar, and you'll see the name of the file you just downloaded and the time it was. (You'll also see the date, depending on how recently it was downloaded.) Tap this message, and you'll open the file in the Gallery. For details about what you can do with a picture once it's in the Gallery, see page 268.

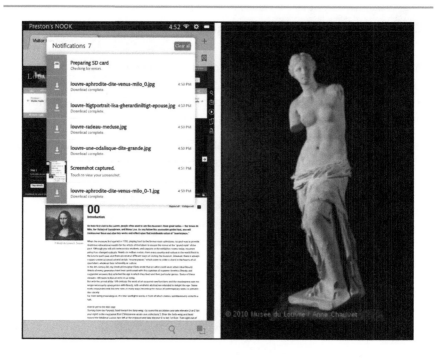

What if you don't want to see the picture right away, or want to see pictures you've previously downloaded? Head to the Library, tap My File at the bottom of the screen, and then tap the Device tab on the screen that appears.

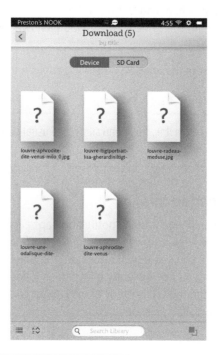

Now tap the Download folder. You'll see all the files you've downloaded. They're listed by file name, which may or may not give you a clue to their contents. If you see something like Serena_Williams.jpg, you'll know it's a photo of the tennis great Serena Williams. But if you see something like Wi231qil.jpg, you won't have a clue what it is.

No matter the name, though, tap any picture to view it in the Gallery. If you want to delete any file, hold your finger on it and tap Delete from the screen that appears. You'll get a warning that you're about to delete the file. Tap Delete to delete it, or Cancel to back out.

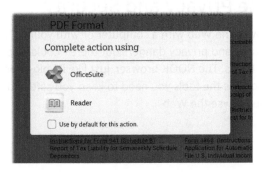

Reading PDF Files

The Web is filled with PDF files, documents that often have complex layouts combined with graphics. These files can't be read directly by your browser. It's easy to read them on your NOOK, though. When you tap a link to a PDF file, it gets downloaded in the same way that a picture does, and you view it the same way as well. So just follow the instructions for viewing pictures, and look, instead, for the PDF file you downloaded. Then tap it, and you get a choice of opening it in OfficeSuite (an app that ships with your NOOK and that lets you read PDF files in addition to Microsoft Office documents such as Word, Excel, and PowerPoint files) or in the PDF Reader built into the NOOK HD. Try both and see which you prefer.

Web Pages Designed for Mobile Devices

As you browse the Web, you may come across sites that differ significantly when viewed on the NOOK HD compared with the exact same sites viewed on a computer. That's because web designers have created pages specifically to be viewed with mobile devices such as smartphones, taking into account that mobile devices have smaller screens than computer screens. And some websites also have pages designed especially for tablets like the NOOK.

ABC News, for example, has sites designed especially for mobile viewing. Head to the same site at the exact same time of day with a smartphone and a computer, and you see very different pages, even though the content of the pages is the same.

Websites know which kind of page to display by detecting what kind of device you're using. Sometimes, though, the websites get confused, and so you may visit the website one day and get delivered a page designed for a mobile device, while on another day, you may see a page designed for a large computer monitor.

Odder still, sometimes the type of page switches depending upon the orientation of your NOOK HD. Visit a page when you're in the vertical orientation, and it displays the page for a mobile device; turn the NOOK horizontally to landscape mode, and the page displays for a full-blown computer monitor. Turn it back to vertical, and it switches to the mobile site again.

As a general rule, though, when you go to websites, they'll display on your NOOK as the sites have been designed for computers, not smartphones.

NOTE The NOOK HD uses Adobe Flash Player, so you can watch the Flash videos you find on websites such as YouTube and many others.

Online Privacy and Security

Whether you browse the Web with a computer or with your NOOK HD, there are potential security and privacy dangers out there—cookies, pop-up ads, and malicious websites. The NOOK browser, just like its big-brother browsers on computers, includes the tools you need to keep you safe and protect your privacy when you browse the Web.

You get at all the privacy and security settings via the browser's Settings menus. When you're in the browser, tap the Settings icon in the Status bar (it's in the shape of a gear), and then tap Browser Settings→Privacy & security.

Out of the box, the NOOK's privacy and security settings are configured to make sure that you're safe and secure. So most likely, you won't need to change any settings. But there are a few options and features you might want to know more about, or that can be used to enhance your privacy, as you'll see in the next sections.

Cookies

Cookies are tiny bits of information that some websites store on the NOOK HD for future use. When you register for a website and create a user name and password, the website can store that information in a cookie so you don't have to retype it every time. Cookies can also remember your habits and preferences when you use a website—your favorite shipping method, or what kinds of news articles you're likely to read.

But not all cookies are innocuous, since they can also track your web browsing from multiple sites and potentially invade your privacy.

The NOOK browser gives you control over how you handle cookies—you can either accept them or tell the browser to reject them. Keep in mind that if you don't allow cookies on your NOOK, you may not be able to take advantage of the features on many sites.

To bar websites from putting cookies on your NOOK in the Privacy settings section of Settings, uncheck the box next to "Accept cookies." The checkmark disappears, and from now on, no cookies will be put on your NOOK. You can always turn this setting back on again if it causes problems with web browsing.

While you're in Privacy settings, you can also delete all the cookies that have been put on your NOOK so far. Tap "Clear all cookie data." You get a warning that you're about to delete your cookies. Tap OK to clear them, or Cancel if you change your mind.

Other Privacy Settings

There's more you can do in the Privacy section of the browser's settings screen to make sure your privacy isn't invaded. For example, you can clear your browsing history so that others who use the browser can't see where you've been.

You can also tap "Clear cache" to clean out website information your browser has stored on your NOOK HD. A *cache* is information the browser stores on your NOOK so it won't have to get that information from the Web the next time you visit that site. The cache speeds up browsing, since it's faster to grab the information—a website image, for example—from your NOOK than from the Web. Tap "Clear cache" if you want to clear all that information out, if you worry that the information there poses a privacy risk.

At many websites, you log in by typing a user name and password, and other information such as your address. The NOOK browser remembers those user names, passwords, and other information, and fills them in for you automatically when you next visit. That's convenient, but it also presents a privacy risk, because someone else using your NOOK HD can log in as you.

If that concerns you, there are two actions you can take. First, in the Privacy section, tap the checkmark next to "Remember form data." When you turn it off, the browser won't remember user names, passwords, and other information you type into forms. You can always turn it on again. To delete all the information already stored on your NOOK, tap "Clear form data." Next, turn off the checkbox next to "Remember passwords." To clear out saved passwords, tap "Clear passwords."

Pop-Up Blocker

What's top on your list of Web annoyances? Most likely at the pinnacle are pop-ups and pop-unders—ugly little windows and ads that either take an in-your-face stance by popping up over your browser so that you have to pay attention, or pop under your browser so that you don't notice they're there until you close the browser window.

Sometimes these pop-ups and pop-unders are malicious, and if you tap them they attempt to install dangerous software or send you to a malicious website. Sometimes they're merely annoying ads. Sometimes, though, they may actually be useful, like a pop-up that shows a seating chart when you're visiting a ticket-buying site. The NOOK browser includes a pop-up blocker, and like all pop-up blockers it can't necessarily distinguish between bad pop-ups and pop-unders and good ones, so it blocks them all.

However, if you're on a website that uses pop-ups that you want to see, you can turn off the pop-up blocker. In the browser settings, tap the Advanced tab, and uncheck the box next to "Block pop-up windows." When you leave the site and want pop-ups blocked again, go back to the setting and tap it to turn it on. The checkmark will reappear next to the setting, and you'll be protected.

NOTE When you turn off the pop-up blocker, it stops blocking pop-ups in all your browser windows, not just on one site. So be careful when you browse other places on the Web when the pop-up blocker is turned off.

Changing Your Home Page, Text Size, and More Settings

There are plenty of other things you can do on the settings page, many of which are too esoteric to bother with. Right out of the box, the NOOK HD has been configured very well.

NOTE If you have a child and you don't want him to be able to use the NOOK's browser, you can set up a child profile that will stop access to the Web. For details, see Chapter 4.

However, there are a few settings worth paying attention to:

- **Text size.** Tap the Accessibility section and you'll be able to change the text size shown on web pages. The choices are somewhat inexact, and range from Tiny to Huge. (Out of the box, the choice is Normal.) People with vision problems will want to make the text larger.

- **Desktop mode.** As explained on page 310, some websites check when people visit them to see what kind of device or computer they're using—a full-sized computer, or a smaller mobile device like a tablet or a smartphone. When you visit a website with your NOOK, the site assumes you're using a tablet, and so when possible displays a page suitable for displaying on the tablet. (At least, that's what happens in theory. In practice, websites tend to show the NOOK pages designed for computer monitors, not tablets.) If you'd like to always see the full-blown computer monitor page, you can trick websites into thinking you're using a monitor. Tap the Advanced section and turn on the checkbox next to Desktop Mode. Come back here again to turn it off if you find it problematic.

- **Set home page.** As explained on page 300, you can change your home page to any website you visit. But you can also change your home page from the Settings area. Tap General, and then tap "Set homepage." A screen appears that lets you change your home page to the current page you're viewing, to a blank page, the default page for the NOOK (a page about the NOOK), or a page from your most visited sites. If you tap Other, you can type in the URL of any page you want to make your home page.

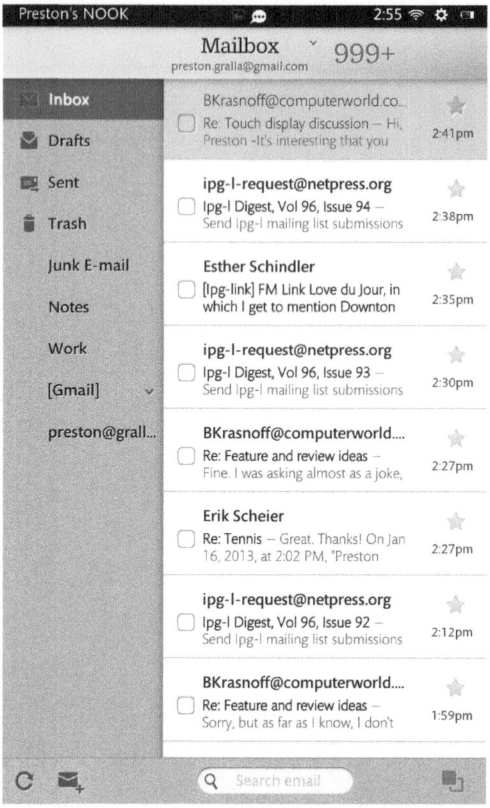

Preston's NOOK
2:55
Mailbox
preston.gralla@gmail.com
999+
Inbox
Drafts
Sent
Trash
Junk E-mail
Notes
Work
[Gmail]
preston@grall...
BKrasnoff@computerworld.co...
Re: Touch display discussion – Hi, Preston -It's interesting that you
2:41pm
ipg-l-request@netpress.org
Ipg-l Digest, Vol 96, Issue 94 – Send Ipg-l mailing list submissions
2:38pm
Esther Schindler
[Ipg-link] FM Link Love du Jour, in which I get to mention Downton
2:35pm
ipg-l-request@netpress.org
Ipg-l Digest, Vol 96, Issue 93 – Send Ipg-l mailing list submissions
2:30pm
BKrasnoff@computerworld....
Re: Feature and review ideas – Fine. I was asking almost as a joke,
2:27pm
Erik Scheier
Re: Tennis – Great. Thanks! On Jan 16, 2013, at 2:02 PM, "Preston
2:27pm
ipg-l-request@netpress.org
Ipg-l Digest, Vol 96, Issue 92 – Send Ipg-l mailing list submissions
2:12pm
BKrasnoff@computerworld....
Re: Feature and review ideas – Sorry, but as far as I know, I don't
1:59pm
Search email

CHAPTER 14

Using Email

YOU WANT EMAIL ON your NOOK HD? You've got it. Your NOOK does a great job of handling email. Want to read attachments like pictures, Microsoft Office documents, and PDFs? The NOOK HD can do that. How about working with just about any email service out there? It can do that, too. You can also manage your mail, sync your mail, and plenty more right on the NOOK. It's a great way to have your email always in your pocket. This chapter shows you how to get the most out of email on the NOOK HD.

Setting Up an Account

To get started, first launch the email app by pressing the NOOK button to get to the Home screen and then tapping the Email icon. You're greeted by an Account setup screen that lets you set up an email account on the NOOK HD. Type your password and email address, and then tap Next.

| Preston's NOOK | 💬 | 2:42 🛜 ⚙ ▬ |

Account setup

Email account

You can set up email for most accounts in just a few steps.

Email address [|]

Password [ ]

[Cancel] [Manual setup] [Next]

```
q   w   e   r   t   y   u   i   o   p
  a   s   d   f   g   h   j   k   l
Tab   z   x   c   v   b   n   m   '   ⌫
 ⇧  ?123  @  [____]  .com  ↵
 ⌨   🌐  Switch Keyboard              🗗
```

What happens next depends upon whether you're setting up a web-based email account such as for Gmail or Microsoft Live Hotmail, or an account that you get through work or an Internet service provider (ISP). If you're setting up a web-based mail account, your NOOK HD will make sure that your settings are correct, then display a screen with a variety of settings for whether to sync contacts, email, and the calendar from the account to the NOOK; whether to notify you when email arrives; whether to make this the default account for sending email, and so on. When you're done, tap Next.

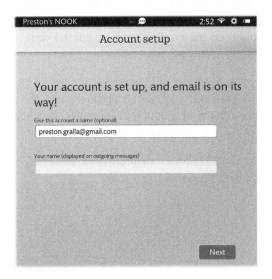

On the next screen, you can give the account a name, and also enter the name as you want it to appear on outgoing mail. Tap Next. When you're done, your email client launches, and you can immediately get your mail.

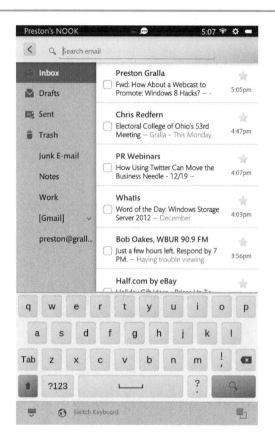

If you're instead setting up an email account through work or an ISP, after you enter your email address and password on the first screen you'll come to a screen that asks you to choose your account type—POP3, IMAP, or Exchange. Not sure what kind of account you have? It's most likely a POP account (also called a POP3 account), so try that first, and if it doesn't work, come back and try IMAP. And if that doesn't work, try Exchange.

TIP if you have an Exchange account, there's a good chance that it's through your place of work, so check with your IT gods at work for details about how to set it up.

You can also turn to page 325 for more information about POP and IMAP accounts, and how best to use them.

After you make your choice, you'll come to a screen full of intimidating-looking techie details. Despair not, though, since there's a very good chance that you won't have to change a thing on it. It has the user name and password you just entered, as well as other information, such as your POP3 or IMAP server name, security type, port number, and whether the NOOK HD should delete email from the server when it checks for email. In the majority of cases, you won't have to change a thing here, so tap Next.

TIP Make sure that Never is selected in the "Delete email from server" section. If you select "When I delete from Inbox" instead, your NOOK HD deletes that email not just from the tablet, but also from the server, and you won't be able to read it on your computer.

Next, you're asked to enter information about your outgoing mail server, which has the techie name SMTP server. As with the previous screen, leave everything as is, and then tap next.

You'll now be asked how often to check for new email, whether to notify you when mail arrives, whether to sync mail from the account, and whether the email account you're setting up should be your default email account. Select your settings and tap Next.

Finally, you come to a screen that lets you give the email account its own name, and also has you fill in how your name should appear when sending email. Tap Next. The NOOK HD takes a moment or two to check your settings and log you in. If life is being good to you, you should be all set—the NOOK HD starts downloading email to your inbox.

If you're already using an email program on your computer, that means you've already set up the account there, and its settings are in the email program. So go to the account settings on the email software on your computer, and grab the settings from there.

However, as you know, life is not always good. The NOOK HD may have trouble logging you in.

At any point during the setup process, the NOOK HD may report it's having a problem setting up your account, so you may encounter problems at several points along the way.

If that's the case, you may have entered your user name and password wrong, so try again. If you're still having problems, some of your ISP's email settings may be different from the ones that the NOOK HD assumes them to be—for example, the name of the POP3 server, the port number, and so on. So take a deep breath and pick up the phone. Then call your ISP's tech support line and read a good book on the NOOK HD while you wait on hold for an hour or three. When a tech comes on the line, explain the problem you're having. Then return to the Welcome screen for setting up an email account, tap "Manual setup," and then select either POP or IMAP; tap OK. That takes you to the screen with all the techie details, including the name of the POP3 or IMAP server, the security type, and port number. Ask the techie for those details, and have her stay on the line while you fill them in and make sure you can connect to your email account.

POP3 and IMAP Accounts

Here's what you need to know about POP3 and IMAP accounts for setting up and using on your NOOK HD:

- With a **POP (Post Office Protocol)** account, the POP server delivers email to your inbox. From then on, the messages live on your NOOK HD—or your home computer, or whichever machine you used to check email. You can't download another copy of that email, because POP servers let you download a message only once. So if you use your account on both a computer and your NOOK HD, you must be careful to set up the account properly, as described in the box on the next page, so you won't accidentally delete email. Despite this caveat, POP accounts remain the most popular type of email accounts, and are generally the easiest to set up and use.

- With an **IMAP (Internet Message Access Protocol)** account, the server doesn't send you the mail and force you to store it on your computer or NOOK HD. Instead, it keeps all your mail on the server, so you can access the exact same mail from your NOOK HD and your computer—or even from multiple devices. The IMAP server always remembers what you've done with your mail—what messages you've read and sent, your folder organization, and so on. So if you read mail and send mail on your NOOK HD, when you then check your mail on a computer, you'll see all those changes, and vice versa.

That's the good news. The bad news is that if you don't remember to regularly clean out your mail, your mailbox can overflow if your account doesn't have enough storage to hold it all. If your IMAP account gets full, then when people send you email, their messages bounce back to them.

WORKAROUND WORKSHOP

Keeping Your POP Mailboxes in Sync

The difference between POP and IMAP accounts is that POP email lives only on whatever machine you download it to. With IMAP, a copy automatically remains on the server so you can download it again on another device. Say you read incoming email on your NOOK HD, delete some of it, keep some of it, and write some new messages. Later that day, you go to your desktop computer and log into the same email account. You won't see those incoming messages you read on your NOOK, nor the ones you sent from it.

When you're using both your NOOK HD and home computer to work with the same POP account, how do you keep them in sync? By making your POP account act more like an IMAP account, so it leaves a copy of all messages on the server when you download them to your home computer. That way, you can

delete messages on the NOOK, and still see them in your inbox at home.

How you set it up depends on which email program you use at home. In Outlook 2010, choose File→Account Settings, and then double-click the account name and select More Settings→Advanced. Turn on "Leave a copy of each message on the server." Also turn on "Delete messages from server after they are deleted from this computer," so you won't fill up the server space allocated to your account.

To get to these settings in earlier versions of Outlook, choose Tools→Email Accounts→Email→View or Change Email Accounts→[your account name]→Change→More Settings→Advanced.

In Entourage, choose Tools→Accounts. Double-click the account name, and then click Options.

Reading Mail

Now that you've got an account, it's time to start reading mail. Launch the email app. You see a list of messages, and the list you see depends on what you were doing the last time you were using the email app. For example, if the last time you used email you were in your Gmail inbox, you see all the mail in your inbox. If you were viewing mail in a different *label* (the term Gmail uses for a folder), you see just the mail in that label.

> **NOTE** This chapter covers how Gmail works on the NOOK HD. POP3-based mail, IMAP mail, and other mail services work similarly, but there might be small differences to what you see here.

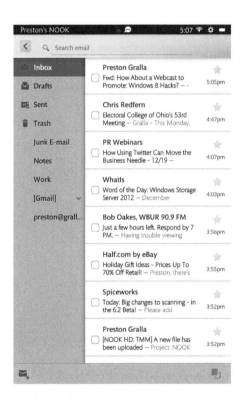

> **NOTE** While most email programs use folders to let you organize your email, Google uses *labels* in its web-based email (page 345), and that's what you use on the NOOK HD.

Most of the time, of course, you'll land in your inbox, which lists all your mail. Mail you haven't read is in black type, and the mail you've already looked at is in gray. The top of your screen displays the total number of new messages in your inbox.

The NOOK HD lets you have multiple email accounts, and you can easily switch among them. (For details, see page 342.) To switch to another account, tap the Mailbox text at the top of the screen, and you'll see all of your accounts, including how many new email messages are in each inbox. Tap the account you want to switch to.

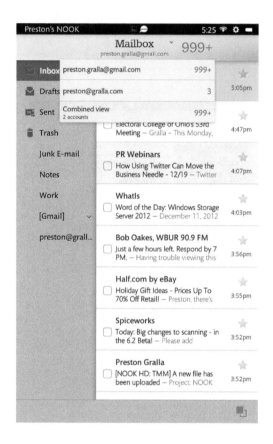

Typically, when you view your email, you're only looking at the latest email that has been downloaded to your NOOK HD. So if you have older mail in Gmail, it won't show up, and if you have downloaded mail to your own computer, it won't show up, either.

When you're viewing mail in a list like this, each piece of mail shows the following:

- The sender

- The subject line

- The date it was sent, or, if it was sent today, the time it was sent

To open a message, tap it. Scroll up, down, and sideways in the message using the usual NOOK HD dragging and flicking gestures. All the links you see in the email message are live—tap one to head to the web page in the NOOK HD's web browser. Tap an email address, and a new email message opens to that address. Tap a YouTube video, and the video plays.

At the top of the screen, you find several important buttons and pieces of information. You'll see the number of messages in your current folder that have been downloaded to your NOOK HD, and where the current email is on that list; for example, 3 out of 25. At the upper left there's a back arrow. Tap it to go back to the enclosing folder. To its right you'll see up and down arrows. Tap the up arrow to read

the previous mail in the folder; tap the down arrow to read the next.

On the right of the screen there's a "read" button. That indicates that the mail will show up as read in its folder—in other words, it shows up as gray. Tap the "read" button and it changes to "unread." Now the message shows up as black and unread in the folder.

Just to the right of the read button there's a star. Tap it and the star turns from gray to green. You've now starred the mail, which means that it will show up in your Starred folder.

Handling Pictures in Mail

You'll often get sent pictures in email. Some are embedded in the content of the message itself—for example, a company logo, or when someone has pasted a picture directly into the message. Other times, the sender attaches the image to the messages, like a family member sending you Thanksgiving photos.

If the graphics are embedded in the content of the message, you see a small button titled Show pictures. In some cases you don't really need to see the graphics (who cares what a company's logo looks like, really?). In that case, do nothing. However, in other cases, the graphic is an integral part of the message, like a graph or a map. If that happens, tap "Show pictures." You see all the graphics on full display, right in the message. After you tap "Show pictures," the text changes to "Always show pictures from this sender." Tap that, and from now on, graphics will always show up right in the email, without you having to tap the button.

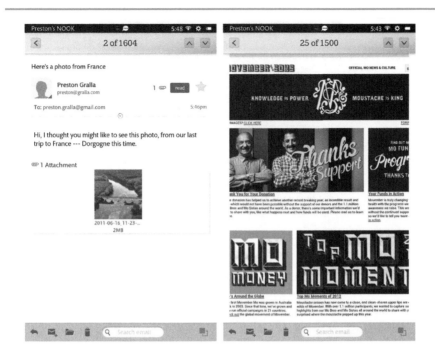

Here's a photo from France

Preston Gralla
preston@gralla.com

To: preston.gralla@gmail.com   5:46pm

Hi, I thought you might like to see this photo, from our last trip to France --- Dorgogne this time.

1 Attachment

2011-06-16_11-23-...
2MB

If someone has attached a graphic instead, you see a paper clip icon along with the file's name and size. If the graphic is large and hasn't been downloaded yet, you'll see an arrow and beneath it a small indicator that the file is downloading. After the file has downloaded, you'll see a tappable thumbnail of the graphic.

When you tap, a screen appears with two choices—View and Save. Tap Save to save the graphic to a folder on your NOOK HD. Tap View to view it in the Gallery (see page 268). When you want to go from the Gallery back to your email software, tap the picture, and then tap the back arrow that appears at the top of the screen.

Here's a photo from France

Preston Gralla
preston@gralla.com

1   read

To: preston.gralla@gmail.com   5:46pm

Hi, I thought you might like to see this photo, from our last trip to France --- Dorgogne this time.

1 Attachment

2011-06-16_11-23-...
2MB

Handling Other Attachments

Your NOOK HD can also let you read and save other files—not just pictures—including Word, Excel and PowerPoint. It lets you preview those files and other file types as well. (For a list of all the file types the NOOK HD can read, see Appendix B.)

The NOOK's email app handles these apps in the same way it does pictures. You'll see an icon of a paper clip, and an icon representing the graphic, along with the file name and its size. Tap it, and you can choose to save it or view it. If you choose to view it and it's a Word, Excel, or PowerPoint file, it opens in an app called OfficeSuite that's built into the NOOK HD. To get back to your email, tap the back arrow at the top left of the screen.

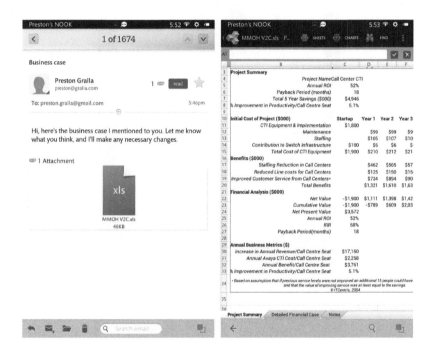

Adding the Sender to Your Contacts

If you're reading an email message from someone and want to add him to your Contacts list, tap the icon next to his name. A screen appears that lets you create a new contact with the sender's name and email address.

Replying to Messages

At the bottom of the screen when you're reading a message, you'll find four icons that do the following:

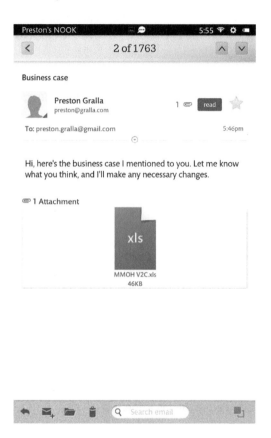

- **Reply.** Tap this and you get three choices: Reply, Reply All, and Forward. Reply sends a message to just the sender, while Reply All sends the message to everyone who has received it. Forward lets you send the message to someone new. In all cases, the original email message is included at the bottom of the message you send.

- **New message.** Tap this to create a new mail message. It has nothing to do with the current mail you're reading; it's just an easy way to put mail creation always within easy reach. (See the next section for details about how to create an email.)

- **Move to.** Tap this and you'll see a list of all folders (or in the case of Gmail, labels) in your account. Tap any folder to move the email to it.

> **NOTE** In POP3 accounts, you can't see your list of folders, so you can't move email to them. You may or may not be able to see folders in web-based mail, but you can in Gmail.

- **Delete.** Tap this to delete the message.

Composing Email

To compose a new piece of email, tap the new message icon that's at the bottom of all your email screens—in your folders, when you're reading mail, and so on. A new, blank message form opens, and the keyboard appears so you can start typing.

Write your message this way:

- **In the To field, type the recipient's address.** As you type, the NOOK HD looks through your Contacts list, as well as the list of people you've sent email to in the past, and displays any matches. (It matches the first few letters of first names as well as last names as you type.) If you find a match, you can tap it instead of typing the rest of the address. You can add as many addresses as you want.

- **Send copies to other recipients.** Tap Cc:/Bcc: and enter names here. Anyone whose email address you put in the Cc and Bcc boxes gets a copy of the email message. The difference is that while everyone can see all the Cc recipients, the Bcc copy is sent in private. None of the other recipients can see the email addresses you enter in the Bcc field.

Cc stands for the term *carbon copy* and Bcc stands for *blind carbon copy*. These are from those long-gone days in the last century when people typed mail, documents, and memos on an ancient device called a typewriter. To make multiple copies, typists added a sheet of carbon paper and another sheet of typing paper. The force of the keys striking the paper would make an imprint on the second sheet, using the ink in the carbon paper.

- **In the Subject field, type the topic of the message.** A clear, concise subject line is a good thing for both you and your recipient, so you can immediately see what the message is about when you scan your inbox.

- **In the text box, type your message.** Type as you would in any other text field.

- **Add any attachments.** If you want to send a photo, document, or other attachment, tap the paper clip icon to the right of the subject line and select what you want to send.

- **Tap Send (or Cancel).** Tap the send icon at the top right of the screen, and the message gets sent immediately. Tap Cancel to cancel it. It then ends up in your Draft folder. To edit the draft message and send it, you'll have to go to your Drafts folder.

Managing and Searching Mail

As explained previously, when you're in a folder (or label in Gmail), you'll see a list of your most recent email. Unread mail appears in boldface, and read mail appears in regular face. There's a lot more you can do from this screen than just scroll through your messages. Here's what you can do:

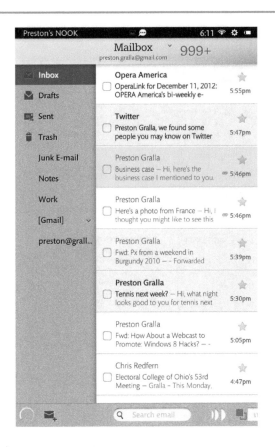

- **Compose mail.** As detailed in the previous section, tap the compose message icon at the bottom of the screen to compose a new email.

- **Switch to a new account.** Tap the name of the folder at the top of the screen to see a listing of your other mail accounts, including how many messages you've got in each. Tap any to go to that account. If you want to see all your email from all your accounts in one place, tap Combined view.

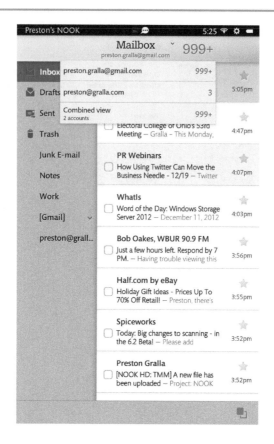

- **Switch to a different folder.** Tap the folder you want to switch to and you head right there.

NOTE You can't create new mail folders or delete old ones using the NOOK HD. You'll have to use your computer, or in the case of web-based mail such as Gmail, you'll have to go to the Web to do it.

- **Delete mail.** You can delete a single email, or an entire group of them. Tap the box to the left of any mail you want to delete, and a checkmark appears. After you've selected all you want to delete, tap the Delete button at the bottom of the screen.

NOTE On POP3 accounts, when you delete email, you're only deleting it from your NOOK HD, not from the server or from any mail stored on your computer. On web-based mail such as Gmail, you'll generally delete it or move it to the Trash.

- **Move mail to a folder.** After you've put a checkmark next to one or more pieces of mail, you can move them to a folder. Tap the "Move to Mail" button at the bottom of the screen.

Move to
All Mail
Junk E-mail
Notes
Spam
Starred
Work
[Gmail]
preston@gralla.com

NOTE The Delete and Move to Folder buttons only show up at the bottom of the screen after you've put a checkmark next to one or more pieces of email.

- **Star mail.** Do you have important emails that you want to highlight so you'll always be able to see them? Tap the star icon to the right of any email, and it turns green. The mail will be put in a special Starred folder. Go to that folder as you would get to any other folder. To unstar a mail, tap the star icon so it turns gray. Note that POP3, IMAP, and many web-based mail accounts won't have a star folder, so you can't use starring with them. You can, however, use it with Gmail.

NOTE The Starred folder doesn't appear until you've put a star next to one or more pieces of email.

- **Get mail.** To check whether you've got new email, tap the small sync icon at the bottom left of the screen. The NOOK checks for new mail, and downloads it if it finds any.

NOTE A Load More Messages button may appear at the bottom of the list of email in a folder. Tap it and you'll get more email—email that's older than the email currently displayed.

- **Search.** Tap in the search box at the bottom of the screen and the box moves to the top and the keyboard appears. Type in your search term, press the Search key, and you'll find a list of mail that matches the term. Tap any piece of mail to read it.

Managing Multiple Accounts and Advanced Email Options

Right out of the box, the NOOK HD's email app is set up just fine. But if you're the kind of person who likes to fiddle and diddle with options, you've got plenty of ways to customize how it works. And if you have more than one email account, you can customize them on an account-by-account basis—for example, have a different signature appended to Gmail than to a personal account, or having the NOOK HD check one account more frequently than others.

To see a list of all your accounts, when you're in the email app, tap the small gear icon at the upper-right portion of the screen in the Status bar and then tap Email Settings. You'll come to a screen that shows all of your accounts. From this screen you can change your global email settings as well as the settings for each individual account—and you can add new accounts.

To add a new account, tap Add Account and follow the instructions as detailed at the beginning of this chapter.

To change the global settings for the email app, tap Email Settings. Here you can change settings such as the size of the text in messages, whether "Reply all" should be the default for replying to emails, and so on. These settings affect every single email account.

To customize the way any account works, tap the name of the account, and a long screenful of settings appears. To change any, fill in the form, and you're done. Here's a list of the most important things you can change, and the effect it will have on your email use:

NOTE The settings available to you vary according to the type of account you're changing. So settings for a Gmail account will be different from settings for a POP3 account.

- **Account name.** Changes the name that shows up in your list of accounts. So if you have a Hotmail account that you would rather have appear as Home, for example, you can change that here.

- **Your name.** Changes the name associated with your account—not the email address, which can't be changed. Think of it as a nickname.

- **Signature.** Changes the signature that's appended to your outgoing email from that account. Tap here, type a new signature, and then tap OK. To go with no signature at all, delete the text and tap OK. You might want to have different signatures for different accounts: one work-related, one family-related, and so on.

- **Default account.** When you compose an email, from which account do you want it to be sent? Turn on the box next to any account, and that becomes the default from now on. If you previously had another account that was the default, the checkmark disappears from its Settings screen.

- **Inbox check frequency.** Changes how often the NOOK HD checks an account for email. Your choices are Automatic (Push), Never, or to check every 5, 10, 15, 30, or 60 minutes.

- **Email notification.** Want to have a notification appear in the System bar every time an email comes in from the account? Make sure this is checked. If you don't want to be bothered, uncheck it.

- **Incoming settings.** Lets you change the settings related to getting mail from the account's server.

- **Outgoing settings.** Lets you change the settings related to sending email via the account's server.

> **NOTE** Incoming settings and Outgoing settings don't show up in Gmail accounts.

- **Sync settings.** Lets you choose whether to sync email, contacts, and Calendar.

- **Default account.** Makes the account the default account for sending email.

- **Remove account.** Deletes the email account.

When you delete an account, you won't delete the email in it. You'll just remove it from the NOOK HD.

Understanding Gmail's Organization

Gmail has its own terminology and worldview when it comes to handling email compared with other mail accounts. So if you're not already a Gmail user, you may need help understanding some new some terms and ideas. Here are the most common Gmail concepts:

- **Labels.** Think of these as email folders. Your regular email program has a folder called Inbox, for example, and lets you create other folders, such as Family, Work, and so on. Gmail calls these email containers *labels*.

  That said, there's a slight underlying difference between how you work with Gmail's labels and how you work with another email program's folders. In your typical email program, you might move mail between folders by dragging them. Not so in Gmail. In Gmail, you affix a label to an email message. When you do that, that email automatically appears when you sort for that label.

  Labels actually give you more flexibility than folders, since you can attach multiple labels to a single email message. For example, if you get an email from your brother about advice for your upcoming trip to France, you can add the labels Family and France to the email. That email then shows up in both your Family label and your France label, making it easier for you to find it when you need it.

The NOOK HD's email app is designed to work in concert with Gmail on the Web, but you can't do everything in the Gmail app that you can do on the Web. The NOOK HD's email app can't create labels, for example, so to create new ones, you must visit your Gmail account on the Web, using either the NOOK's browser or a computer.

- **Overall mail organization.** Because Gmail uses labels rather than folders, you may find mail in more than one location. Also, unlike some email software, Gmail gives you the option of viewing all mail in one single area titled All Mail, even including mail you've archived.

- **Archive.** In some instances, you'll get mail that you want to keep a copy of but don't want cluttering up your inbox. So Gmail lets you *archive* messages. Archiving a message doesn't delete it, but it removes it from your inbox. You can still find the message listed in your All Mail folder. You can also find it by searching.

Gmail's Labels

Labels are an excellent way to organize your email in Gmail, because they're far more flexible than folders, and mail can show up in multiple places. Here are some of the built-in Gmail labels you may see on the NOOK HD:

- **Inbox** contains all your incoming messages.
- **Starred** shows all the messages you've starred (page 341).
- **Sent Mail** lists all messages you've sent.
- **Outbox** shows mail you've created and asked Gmail to send, but that has not yet been sent.
- **Drafts** contains mail you've created but not sent.
- **All Mail** contains all mail, except for Spam and Trash.
- **Spam** contains all mail marked as spam, either by you or by Google.
- **Trash** contains mail you've deleted but that hasn't been removed from the Trash yet because it's not more than 30 days old.

NOTE If you use Gmail's Priority Inbox on the Web, you'll also see a label here called Important, which shows all the messages that Gmail has flagged as being important to you. For details about how Priority Inbox works, and to set it up on the Web, go to *http://mail.google.com/mail/help/priority-inbox.html*.

If you've created any labels other than these using Gmail on the Web, then you see them here as well. You can't create new labels in Gmail on the NOOK HD. To create a new label, visit Gmail on the Web using your NOOK HD's browser or on a computer.

Getting Social

CHAPTER 15:

NOOK Friends, Facebook, Twitter, and Beyond

CHAPTER 16:

Managing Your Contacts

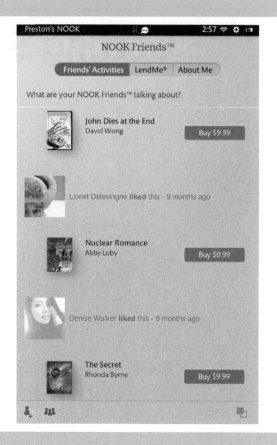

Preston's NOOK 2:57

NOOK Friends™

Friends' Activities | LendMe® | About Me

What are your NOOK Friends™ talking about?

John Dies at the End
David Wong
Buy $9.99

Lionel Delevingne **liked** this - 9 months ago

Nuclear Romance
Abby Luby
Buy $0.99

Denise Walker **liked** this - 9 months ago

The Secret
Rhonda Byrne
Buy $9.99

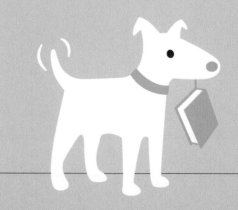

CHAPTER 15

NOOK Friends, Facebook, Twitter, and Beyond

READING, ON THE NOOK, is more than a solitary experience; it's a social one as well. One of the great pleasures of books is sharing your thoughts about them with others, sharing quotes, sharing reading recommendations, and even sharing books. As you know from Chapter 5, the NOOK HD helps you do all that and more, via the NOOK Friends app. Whether you're reading or not, the NOOK HD helps you keep in touch with friends, and offers integration with Facebook and Twitter to boot. This chapter shows you how to do that, and plenty more.

What Can You Do with NOOK Friends?

The best way to do all this sharing is via NOOK Friends, the free app built into the NOOK HD. If you want to share your reading, it's a spectacular app. Here are its nifty features:

- See your friends' activities, such as their book recommendations and favorite quotes from books they're reading.

- Share your own book recommendations and favorite quotes from books you're reading.

- Lend and borrow books on your NOOK.

Getting Started with NOOK Friends

Who exactly is a NOOK Friend? It's someone who has signed up for a Barnes & Noble account, is in your Contacts list with an email address, and who has accepted your invitation to become a NOOK Friend—or whose invitation you have accepted. It's a reciprocal arrangement; once you become someone's NOOK Friend, she's also yours, and vice versa.

You get NOOK Friends another way as well. When you link your NOOK HD to your Facebook account (for details, see page 364), any of your Facebook friends who have a BN.com account automatically get added to your NOOK Friends app. Convenient!

To start, tap the Apps button at the bottom of the Home screen, then tap the NOOK Friends app. That's it; you don't need to do anything else. The NOOK already knows who you are and your email address, and it doesn't need anything else to begin.

When you first launch the app, you may be surprised to see that even though you haven't added any friends yet or accepted any invitations, you've already got friends and are already tracking your friends' activities. That's because, if you've linked your NOOK account to your Facebook account, then any Facebook friend who also has a BN.com account is automatically added to your NOOK Friends, and you are added to his. With convenience comes a bit of presumptuousness.

At the top of the screen are three large buttons:

- **Friends' Activities.** A constantly updated screen that presents a stream of news about your friends' recent activities, such as book recommendations and quotes they want to share.

- **LendMe.** Lets you lend and borrow books.

- **About Me.** Your NOOK Friends profile, which includes your name and photo, how many NOOK books you own, and other information.

Down at the bottom left of the screen you'll find two icons:

- **Add Friend.** As the name says, lets you invite someone to be your NOOK Friend.

- **All Friends.** Displays all your NOOK Friends, and lets you borrow books from them if they have any to lend.

Adding Friends to NOOK Friends

The first thing you'll want to do is invite people to be NOOK Friends with you. After all, you can't throw a party if you haven't invited anyone.

NOTE Even folks who don't have a NOOK can still be your NOOK Friends. They won't be able to participate fully—for example, they obviously won't be able to download NOOK books. But they can still get recommendations, quotes from books, and so on. Friends who don't have NOOKs still need a Barnes & Noble account, though. If they don't already have one, they can sign up, either before you send an invitation, or while accepting your invitation.

To invite a friend:

1. **Tap the Add Friend button.** A screen appears asking whether you want to use the contacts app to invite friends, use Facebook, or instead invite a friend via email.

2. **Tap one of the friend sources.** If you tap "Find friends from my contacts," a screen appears with a list of contacts. At the top of the screen are contacts who are already using NOOK Friends, but aren't one of your NOOK Friends yet. Beneath that is a list of people on your Contacts who aren't using yet NOOK Friends. Tap Invite next to the names of people you want to add, and an invitation gets sent to them.

If you tap "Find friends from Facebook," a screen appears with your Facebook friends who also are NOOK Friends. Tap Add to send an invitation to any to become a NOOK Friend.

If you tap "Invite a friend via email," a screen appears that lets you type in the first name, last name, and email address of someone you want to invite to be your NOOK Friend. Fill in the form, tap Save, and the invitation goes on its merry way.

If you haven't yet imported contacts from Google into your NOOK's Contacts app, you'll see another option on the screen "Find friends from Google." When you tap it, a screen appears that lets you link your NOOK to your Google or Gmail account. After you link the accounts, the NOOK will import your contacts into your Contacts app and will also send you a notification asking if you want to invite any to become NOOK Friends. Tap the notifications, and then tap the name of the person you want to invite to be a friend, and follow the directions for sending an invitation.

When your invitation is accepted, you'll get a notification. Tap it, and you'll see the name of the person who accepted. From there, you can head straight to NOOK Friends and start interacting.

Accepting an Invitation

Other people can invite you to become a NOOK Friend, of course, and how you'll get the invitation varies according to the way it was sent (email, Gmail, Facebook, and so on). But no matter how it was sent, click Confirm Friend, and you'll be connected.

Using and Managing Friends

Once you've invited people to be your NOOK Friend (or you accepted invitations from others), you can see them all by tapping the All Friends button at the bottom left of the screen. You'll see an alphabetical list of all of your NOOK Friends, including photographs if any are available of them (from their Facebook accounts). If you've got more friends than can fit on one screen (lucky you!), you can scroll through them.

Sometimes even good friends have a falling out, so you can remove someone from your NOOK Friends list by tapping the X next to his name. You'll be asked whether you want to remove him from the list before he's deleted, just to make sure it wasn't a passing fancy.

To see a person's most recent NOOK Friends activities, including books he has recommended, quotes he has shared, and so on (for details, see page 352), tap the person's photograph (or generic person icon if there's no photograph available). To see what books he has available for lending, tap LendMe.

To see all the invitations you've sent that have not yet been accepted, tap Pending. The screen is divided into two sections: Awaiting Confirmation and Sent invitations. In the Sent Invitations section, you'll see names and photos of people to whom you've sent invitations, but who haven't accepted yet. To cancel an invitation, tap the Cancel button. When someone accepts an invitation, they vanish from this area, and show up on your NOOK Friend list.

The Awaiting Confirmation section shows all the invitations that have been sent to you that you haven't yet accepted. Tap Accept to become a friend; tap Reject to turn down the invitation.

Using Friends Activities

Once you've got NOOK Friends, you can start sharing with them. One of the key ways is to see what books and periodicals they recommend, and what quotes from books and periodicals they have decided to share with you.

To do that, in the NOOK Friends app, tap the Friends' Activities button at the top left of the screen. You see a scrollable list of the recent activities of your NOOK Friends.

You'll find a variety of activities there:

- Recommendations made directly and privately to you.

- Public recommendations made via Facebook or Twitter.

- Ratings of books, periodicals, and apps.

- Quotes shared publicly via Facebook or Twitter or privately with you.

- Postings of friends' reading status (what book they're currently reading, how far along they are in it, and so on).

- Friends "Liking" a book, periodical, or app on Facebook.

Along with the activity, such as a recommendation, there's also a picture of the book, periodical, or app. Tap its cover or icon to get more details about it. Tap the blue button to buy it (or download it if it's free).

Using About Me

Tap the About Me button at the top of the NOOK Friends app, and you see a summary of all of your activity in NOOK Friends with this information:

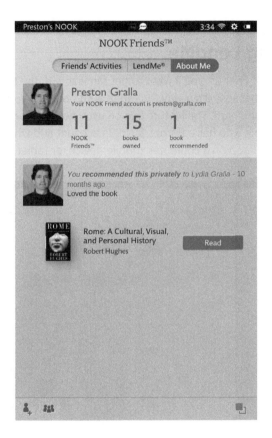

- Your name.
- Your photo, if you've linked the NOOK to your Facebook account (and posted a profile photo on Facebook).

NOTE You can't edit the information on the About Me screen. It merely reflects your NOOK settings and activities.

- Your total number of NOOK Friends
- The number of NOOK books you own.

- The number of books you've recommended.

- A scrollable list of all of your NOOK Friends activities, such as your recommendations and quotes you've shared, either publicly through Facebook or Twitter, or privately.

Using LendMe

If you have NOOK Friends, you'll want to get familiar with the NOOK Friends LendMe feature, because it's a way for you to lend books to your friends and borrow books from them. The feature can be used not only for NOOK Friends, but also for anyone who has a Barnes & Noble account and who uses either a NOOK or a NOOK app on a computer, mobile device, or tablet.

Chapter 8 is entirely devoted lending and borrowing books using your NOOK, but here's a quick recap of what you'll see on the LendMe screen:

NOTE The LendMe feature is available not just in the NOOK Friends app, but in the Library as well.

- Books you own that you can lend to others.

- Books that your NOOK Friends have that are available for lending.

- Offers to lend books to you.

- Requests from NOOK Friends to borrow books from you.

You can lend or borrow only books whose publisher allows lending. The loan lasts for up to 14 days. When the time is up, you don't need to do anything to return it or to ask for it back—it automatically reverts to the owner. When you lend a book to someone, the digital rights for reading it go along with the lending, so if it's a book you've bought, you can't read it while it's lent out. (However, if the book is free from digital rights, you can read it even when you're lending it.)

LendMe Privacy Settings

When you first start using NOOK Friends, every one of your NOOK Friends can see every one of your books available for lending. Whenever you buy a book that can be lent, all your friends know about it.

But what if you don't want them to know what lendable books you have? You can do something about it: Use the LendMe privacy settings to block individual books from being seen, or block the entire list from being seen.

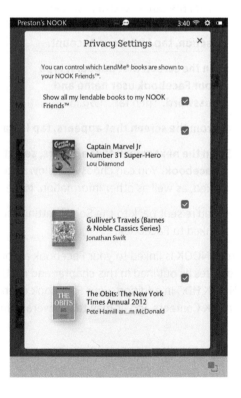

In NOOK Friends, go to the LendMe area, then tap the Privacy button on the upper right of the screen. If you don't want any friends to ever see any of your lendable books, uncheck the box next to "Show all my lendable books to my NOOK Friends."

If you only want *some* lendable books to be hidden from friends' view, tap the check box next to any book. That means that your friends won't see you have it, so won't be able to ask if they can borrow it from you. To let your friends see that the book is available for lending, tap the box so that it's checked.

Linking Your NOOK HD to Facebook

In order to share book quotes, post reviews, lend and borrow books, and so on with your Facebook friends, you need to first link your NOOK HD to your Facebook account. When you link your account, it does more than just let you do all that—you'll also have all your Facebook friend information imported into your Contacts list, so you'll also be able to get in touch via email and more.

It's simple to link to Facebook. First, make sure you're connected to a WiFi network. Then do the following:

1. **Tap the small settings icon (it looks like a gear) on the righthand side of the Status bar and select All Settings→Applications→ "Social Accounts and NOOK Friends"→"Manage your Accounts."**

2. **From the Social settings screen that appears, in the Facebook section, tap Link Your Account.**

3. **On the screen that appears, type your Facebook user name and password.** Then tap "Log In."

4. **From the screen that appears, tap Install.**

5. **On the next screen that appears, select the access you want to give to Facebook.** You can choose to allow Facebook to post information you've liked, as well as other information. Make your choices and log in.

    You're sent back to the Social settings screen, with an indication that you've linked to Facebook.

Your NOOK is linked to your Facebook account, and you can start using all of its features as outlined in this chapter and in "Using Facebook and Twitter on Your NOOK HD." In addition, your Facebook contacts start to be imported into the NOOK Contacts app. It may take several minutes for all of them to be imported.

Unlinking Your Facebook Account

If you decide you want to unlink your NOOK and Facebook accounts, first get back to the Social settings screen by going to the home screen, and pressing the settings icon in the upper right of the screen and selecting All Settings→Applications→Social Accounts and NOOK Friends→Manage your Accounts. Then in the Facebook area, tap Unlink Your Account. When you do so, you'll no longer be able to use the NOOK's Facebook features. In addition, all your Facebook contacts get deleted from your NOOK. You can easily link again.

Linking Your NOOK HD to Twitter

In order to share book quotes, reviews, and do more fun stuff with people on Twitter, you need to link your NOOK HD to your Twitter account, in much the same way you do with Facebook.

First, make sure you're connected to the Internet by WiFi. Then follow these steps:

1. **Tap the small settings icon (it looks like a gear) in the righthand side of the Status bar and select All Settings→Applications→"Social Accounts and NOOK Friends"→"Manage your Accounts."**

2. **From the Social settings screen that appears, in the Twitter section, tap Link Your Account.**

3. **On the screen that appears, type your Twitter user name and password. Then tap "Authorize app."**

   You're sent back to the Social settings screen, with an indication that you've linked to Twitter.

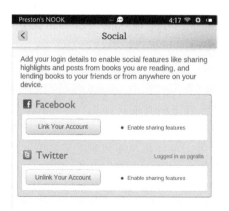

Your NOOK is linked to your Twitter account, and you can start using all of its features as outlined in the next section.

Unlinking Your Twitter Account

If you want to unlink your NOOK and Twitter accounts, first get back to the Social settings screen by Tapping the small settings icon (it looks like a gear) in the righthand side of the Status bar and select All Settings→Applications→ "Social Accounts and NOOK Friends"→"Manage your Accounts." Then in the Twitter area, tap Unlink Your Account. When you do this, you can no longer use all the NOOK's Twitter features. You can easily link again.

Using Facebook and Twitter on Your NOOK HD

At this writing, Facebook doesn't have an app for the NOOK—although you can still link your Facebook and accounts to the NOOK and use them in concert with NOOK Friends, as already described. But that lack of an app could change at any time. So it's worthwhile to head to the NOOK Shop every now and then and search for Facebook to see whether an app become available.

Twitter, though, has a NOOK app, so if you want to use it, download it from the NOOK Shop.

However, there's at least one app that lets you use both Facebook and Twitter on your NOOK HD. It's free, it's available now, and it's worth getting. It's called Seesmic, and you can download it from the NOOK Shop.

After you download it, press the NOOK button, choose Apps, and then look for the Seesmic icon and tap it; the app launches. Tap "Add an account," and you can add accounts not just for Facebook and Twitter, but for other social networking services as well, including Google+. For each account, enter your user name and password, and then tap Sign in.

> **NOTE** Some people have had problems logging into Facebook with Seesmic, so you may not be able to log in.

You can use Seesmic for multiple social networking services, but after you set up your first one, you may think there's no way to set up a second because you seem to be stuck in just that service. Ah, but there's a way: Tap the Menu icon in the Notification bar, and then tap Accounts. You'll come to a list of your existing Seesmic accounts. Tap the + button at the top of the screen to create a new account. Choose the type of account you want to create, enter your user name and password, and then tap "Sign in." Create multiple accounts this way and switch among them by tapping the Menu key and then tapping Accounts.

Using Twitter in Seesmic

When you sign into Twitter, you'll see your usual Twitter stream. At the very top of the screen on the righthand side are icons for tweeting, searching, and refreshing Twitter. The buttons just below show you the most recent posts, replies to your posts, your profile, and so on.

Tap the small menu button in the Notification bar to bring up more options—seeing what topics are trending, changing your settings, and so on. The menu changes according to what you're doing at the time. To the left of the menu button is a Back button.

Seesmic is simple and straightforward—and in some ways easier to use than Twitter on the Web.

Using Facebook in Seesmic

When you sign into Facebook via Seesmic, you can read the news feed from your Facebook friends, see your friends list, view your wall, and so on by tapping the appropriate icons at the bottom of the page.

Create an update by tapping the icon at the upper-right portion of the screen, and refresh by tapping the Refresh icon. As with Twitter, Seesmic gives you a useful menu icon at the bottom of the screen.

Using the Twitter App

If you're interested in only using Twitter, download the Twitter app from the NOOK Shop, run the app, and then log in.

Using it is straightforward. Tap the Home screen icon to see the tweets of everyone you're following; tap the @Connect icon to see mentions of you, your tweets, and notifications that people are following you; tap Discover to see contacts' activities, and recommendations for new people to follow; and tap Me to see your profile and your activity, including your tweets and retweets. To write a new tweet, tap the small feather icon in the upper-right portion of the screen. To search through Twitter, tap the Search button at the top.

CHAPTER 16

Managing Your Contacts

AMONG YOUR NOOK HD'S many tricks is its ability to keep track of all your contacts, including family, friends, and coworkers.

While having your contacts on your NOOK HD is a useful feature, there's a more important reason for having them in your NOOK—your Contacts list integrates with NOOK Friends, Facebook, and email. So even if you don't plan to use your NOOK HD's Contacts app on its own, it pays to know how to use it just for those features. Whatever your reason, this chapter tells you everything you need to know about contacts on the NOOK.

Getting Started with Contacts

First things first: To launch the Contacts app, press the NOOK button, tap Apps, and then tap Contacts. If you've already set up an email account or linked to Facebook, your contacts will already be there waiting for you.

But if you haven't done any of that yet, you'll come to a screen that asks you to either create a contact, sign into an email account, or import or export contacts from storage. (You'll see how to create a new contact later in this chapter, on page 376.) Your best bet is to sign into an email account, because your contacts will then get imported en masse and will be kept in sync. One note of warning, though: If your contacts are in Gmail, this isn't the place to set up your Gmail account on the NOOK HD. Instead, do it through the E-mail app. For details, see page 319.

Tap "Sign into account," and from the screen that appears, enter your email address and password. Then tap Next. The NOOK HD goes about its business, makes a connection, and on the next screen asks you about the various options you want for the account. At this point, you set things up the same as you do when setting up an email account for the first time, as described on page 319.

NOTE Not all email accounts have contacts associated with them. For example, if you use a POP3 or IMAP account, rather than web-based mail such as with Gmail or Outlook.com (once called Hotmail.com or Windows Live Mail), your contacts may not be imported.

Importing and Exporting Contacts

There's another way to get your contacts into your NOOK HD—import them from an SD card. Here's how to do it:

1. **Run whichever app on your PC or other device that has your contacts.** It might be Outlook, Address Book on OS X, or another email program or personal information manager.

2. **Follow the app's directions for exporting contacts.** Not all programs have the ability to do this. Check the help section for guidance on exporting the contacts into.vcf format, which creates digital business cards called *vCards*.

3. **Save the .vcf file to a microSD card.** Some PCs, laptops, and other devices have SD card readers. Not all do, but you can buy a USB microSD card gizmo if your computer doesn't have an SD card reader.

4. **Put the microSD card into your NOOK HD.** See page 277 for details.

5. **If you haven't yet launched the Contacts app and set up contacts, launch it now.** Tap the Import/export contacts button.

6. **If you've already launched the Contacts app, tap the NOOK button, tap the Settings icon, and then select All Settings→Applications→Contacts→ Import/Export.**

7. **Tap "Import from storage."** Follow the prompts to import the .vcf file. Voila! Your contacts are imported.

To export contacts, first put a microSD card into your NOOK HD. Follow the previous steps until you get to the Import/Export screen, and then tap "Export to Storage." Follow the prompts to export your contacts to the SD card. Then put the card in your PC or other device, and follow the instructions of the application into which you want to import contacts.

You'll notice a kind of odd selection on the Import/Export screen—"Share visible contacts." That lets you share the contact that's currently open. Tap the selection, and you create a new email message with an attachment—a .vcf file that includes all the information from your current contact. Send the email to someone with whom you want to share the contact. When she opens the vCard, she'll automatically import its contact information.

Importing Facebook Contacts

If you've got a Facebook account, you can import all your contacts from there as well. To do that, you must link your NOOK HD to your Facebook account. For details, see page 364.

When you import your Facebook contacts, their pictures automatically show up in the Contacts app. As when you import contacts from Google, the only information imported into your NOOK Contacts app is the person's name and email address.

Creating a New Contact

Whether you import contacts into the Contacts app or not, you'll likely want to create a new contact at some point. It's easy to do:

1. **In the Contacts app, tap the Add Contacts icon on the lower-left of the screen.** It looks like a person with a plus sign.

2. **If you've already set up an email account, a screen appears telling you that your new contact will be synchronized with that account.** Tap OK. If you instead want to set up a new email account with contacts, and have this contact appear in that account, click "Add new account" and follow the instructions for adding a new email account (page 319).

3. **Fill in the name phone number email, address, and so on.** There are also additional fields you can add, including the person's phonetic name, instant messenger account, and more. To add any of those fields, tap "Add another field" and choose what you want to add.

4. **Tap Done.** That's it; you've just created a contact.

Searching and Browsing Contacts

Finding a contact by browsing and searching is a breeze. Scroll up and down through the Contacts list in the usual way, and when you see a contact whose information you want to see, tap it. You'll see all the contact information on the right side of the screen.

Notice that there are four small icons in the lower-left portion of the screen. Here's what each does, from left to right:

- **New contact icon.** Tap this to add a new contact.

- **Trash icon.** Deletes the contact.

- **Edit contact icon.** Tap this pencil icon to open the contact so you can edit its information.

5. **Email icon.** Tap this to compose an email. Oddly enough, it won't be addressed to the contact you're currently highlighting, so it really has nothing directly to do with the Contact list.

You may notice something unusual when browsing your Contacts list—the names are alphabetized by first name rather than last name. So if you know a lot of Sams and Sallys, they're all next to one another on the list. Why are they alphabetized that way? It's a Google thing. The operating system running the NOOK HD is Android, created by Google for smartphones, tablets, and other devices, and Android (and Google's Gmail) alphabetizes contacts by first name rather than last name.

NOTE On many Android smartphones and tablets, you can change the way contacts are displayed, and have them show up by last name rather than first name. You can't do that on the NOOK HD, though.

The NOOK HD offers a simple way to make it easier to browse contacts. Tap the down arrow underneath the word Contacts at the top of the screen, and you can display a narrower list of contacts—only NOOK Friends, or only your Favorite contacts (more on that on page 381).

To search for a contact, tap the search icon at lower right and start typing. As you type, the list of matches narrows. It displays contacts that have the letter combination you're typing anywhere in the name. So start searching for *al* and it displays people whose first names are "Alan," "Alvin," and so on, but also "Dale." And it also displays people with last names of "Palmer," "Carvajal," and others. And it also will display contacts whose email addresses have *al* in it, or any contact with *al* in any other field, including notes.

When you search, you search only contacts on the list you're currently displaying. So if you're displaying NOOK Friends, you'll see matches only for NOOK Friends on that list.

Favorites

One of the nifty ways you can browse contacts is by Favorites. You can designate someone as a Favorite so that you can quickly find him by browsing only through Favorites instead of through your entire extensive Contacts list. To make someone a favorite, open the contact and tap the gray star to the right of his name in the righthand pane. The star turns green indicating the person is on your Favorites list. If he later does something to annoy you, tap the green star again and it turns gray. Boom—he's no longer a favorite.

Advanced Topics

CHAPTER 17

Settings

RIGHT OUT OF THE box, your NOOK HD is set up for you and ready to go. But what if you want to change its sounds, customize the way the keyboard works, change the Home screen's settings, and more?

It's simple to do. This chapter tells you all about the NOOK HD's settings, and explains what they do for you. To get to the Settings screen, tap the gear icon in the Status bar, and then tap All Settings from the screen that appears. (If you don't see the Status bar—for example, if you're reading a book—press the NOOK button to get to the Home screen, and then tap the gear icon at the upper right.)

Once you're on the Settings screen, from there, scroll to the setting you want to change or get information from, and tap it.

NOTE When you tap the gear icon, a screen pops up that lets you change a variety of popular NOOK settings, such as screen brightness, Airplane Mode, and so on (page 43). So if you want to change one of those settings, there's no need to tap All Settings.

Wireless & Bluetooth

Here's where you connect to wireless networks, turn WiFi on and off, manage Bluetooth, and more:

- **Airplane Mode.** Turns off your NOOK HD's WiFi and Bluetooth radios, but lets you do everything else with the NOOK, such as reading books.

- **Wi-Fi.** If the ON button is blue, WiFi is turned on. Tap to turn if off. If the OFF button is there, tap to turn WiFi on. When WiFi is on, you'll see the name of the network to which you're connected, its signal strength, and whether it's a secure connection or not. (If it's secure, you'll see a lock icon.)

- **Find other networks.** Tap here and you'll see a list of WiFi networks in range as well as any WiFi networks to which you've connected in the past. It shows you the network to which you're currently connected. (For more details about how to connect to WiFi, turn to page 29.) Tap any network listed here, and you're sent to a connection screen that tells you the type of security used and the signal strength. Type in a password if it's a secure network. Tap the network to which you're currently connected to see more details about it, including whether it uses security and if so what type, signal strength, the speed at which you're connected, and your NOOK HD's IP address. If you want to disconnect from the network, tap Forget. That not only disconnects you, but also means the next time you're in range of the network, your NOOK won't connect to it automatically.

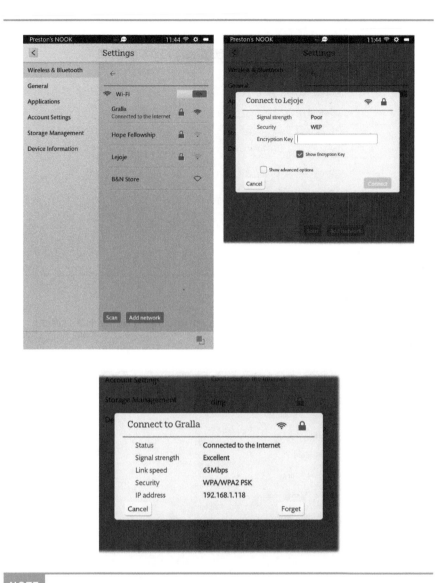

NOTE If you think there are more WiFi networks within range than are shown on the screen, tap Scan to force the NOOK HD to rescan the area for networks.

- **Bluetooth.** Turns Bluetooth on and off. If you want your NOOK to be visible to other Bluetooth devices and able to be connected to them, tap My NOOK when you turn on Bluetooth. It will then be visible to other nearby Bluetooth devices, and you can connect them to one another.

General

Here's where you control a variety of behavior, including NOOK HD's screen, keyboard, volume, and more.

Battery Life

There's only a single, lonely setting here:

- **PowerSave Mode.** Tap to turn this on. It dims your screen and makes a number of minor changes as a way to save power.

Screen

This controls your screen, and has these settings:

- **Lock Rotation.** If you want the NOOK to automatically switch its screen orientation when you rotate it, make sure this box is turned off.

NOTE In some apps and instances, the NOOK won't rotate its screen to match the direction in which you've turned the NOOK. If you're watching a video on Netflix, for example, it plays only in the horizontal (landscape) orientation.

- **Brightness.** Move the slider to change your screen brightness.

- **Screen Timeout.** Shows how long the screen stays on before the NOOK darkens it and puts it to sleep. Tap here, and choose 2 minutes, 5 minutes, 15 minutes, or an hour. The shorter the interval, the longer your battery will last on a charge.

Language

You've got a few settings here:

- **Language.** Tap here to select your language. You may only be able to choose between American English and English spoken in the UK, which will only have a minor effect on some spellings.

- **Spelling correction.** Do you need your spellng corrected when you type? If so, turn on this box.

- **Personal dictionary.** If you use spelling correction, and also often use words that are unique and might be flagged as misspellings, tap here, and then from the screen that appears, tap Add. That way, you can add those words to your dictionary so they don't get flagged as misspelled.

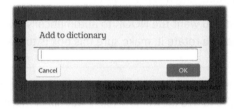

Keyboard

There are two settings for the keyboard:

- **Default.** This selects your default keyboard. Tap it to change it. You may, however, only have one choice, the NOOK keyboard.

- **NOOK keyboard.** Tap the settings icon (a small gear) and you come to a screen that lets you turn auto-capitalization on or off (by default, it's on). It automatically capitalizes the initial words of sentences and names. Oddly, it works only when you're writing recommendations and reviews. Otherwise, like when writing email, you're on your own. The screen also lets you turn on auto correction, which automatically corrects mistyped words.

Speech

Just one setting here:

- **Text-to-speech output.** Tap to configure how the text-to-speech feature works, including changing the speech rate and language.

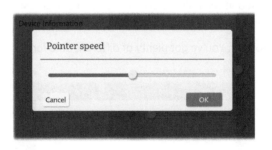

Mouse/Trackpad

Only one setting here as well, and it's an odd one, because the NOOK doesn't have a mouse or trackpad:

- **Pointer speed.** Tap, and a slider appears that lets you change the rate at which the pointer moves, if you ever happen to see a pointer in an app or somewhere else.

Sounds

Head here to customize how sounds work:

- **Set Volume for music and videos.** Move the slider to change the volume.

- **Set Volume for notification.** Here's a slider for setting the volume of your notifications. There's really no need for this setting, though, because you can do the same thing by using the volume control on the top-right side of your NOOK.

- **Alarms.** This slider sets the alarm volume.

- **Screen lock sound.** Do you like the little locking sound the screen lock makes? Then leave this on. Don't like it? Turn it off.

Security

You've got two security settings on your NOOK HD:

- **Security.** Tap here to turn screen lock on and off.

- **Certificate management.** You likely won't need all the settings buried when you tap here, because it's for devices protected by companies who use security certificates.

Date & Time

You can change these settings:

- **Select time zone.** What's your time zone? Select it here.

- **Use 24-hour format.** Turn on this checkbox if you're a fan of 24-hour format, the same as used in the military and many places overseas—14:00 instead of 2 p.m., for example.

- **Select date format.** You've got plenty of different date formats to choose from.

Notifications

- **Notifications.** Turn notifications on and off here.

Applications

Here's where you set all of the options for the apps you've got on your NOOK HD. The precise list that shows up here depends on what you've got installed.

NOTE Turn to the appropriate chapter in this book for more details about settings for individual apps.

Home

Here's where you customize how the Home screen works, and there are plenty of ways to do it:

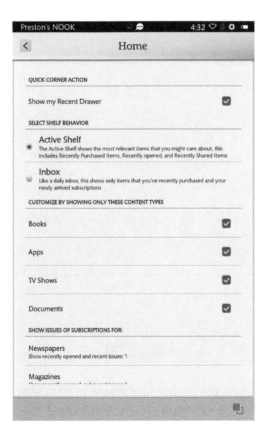

- **Show my Recent Drawer.** Tap here to either display the Recent Drawer of recently used items, apps, and books, or not display it.

- **Active Shelf/Inbox.** Choose one of these to display on your Home screen. (They take up the same real estate, so you can't show both.) The Active Shelf shows items most likely to be relevant to you, such as things you're recently purchased, recently opened, and recently shared. The Inbox only shows things you've bought and your newly arrived subscriptions.

The next section lets you choose what kind of content to show on the Home screen: books, apps, TV shows, and documents. Right underneath that, you can set how many issues of newspapers, catalogs, and magazines to show.

Email

There are a variety of settings here:

- **Auto-advance.** Lets you choose what screen to go to after you delete a message: the next newest message, the next oldest message, or the message list.

- **Message text size.** Tap to choose what size text you want in your email.

- **Reply all.** Check this box and whenever you reply to a message with multiple recipients, your reply goes to everyone by default. If the box isn't checked, you'll instead respond to the sender (but you can of course, add everyone else as well).

- **Ask to show pictures.** This determines whether pictures in messages should be automatically displayed, or instead only shown when you manually ask them to be displayed.

Calendar

There are plenty of settings here, and they're generally self-explanatory, for things such as what day the week should start on, whether events you've declined should be displayed, and details about your notifications such as whether you want pop-up notifications. If you have multiple calendars, make sure to tap "Calendars to display" along the lefthand side of the screen to choose which ones to display.

Contacts

Here, too, most things are straightforward. Three important ones are:

- **Sort list by.** Normally, your contact list is sorted by first name, not last name. If you find that annoying and counterintuitive, you can tap here to change to sorting by last name.

- **View contact names as.** Your contact list normally displays names by first name, not last name. Again, you can change to a last name sort if you like.

- **Import/Export.** Tap here to import and export contacts. See page 375 for details.

Browser

There are countless settings here, most of which you don't need to configure. This section hits the high points. Along the lefthand side are the main categories you can configure. In the General area are these important ones:

- **Set homepage.** Here's where you can set your home page. Out of the box, the NOOK goes to *http://www.nook.com/hd/start*. You'll probably want to change it.

- **Form auto-fill.** With this checked, you'll breeze through filling out forms on the Web, because your NOOK browser will fill in much of the text such as name, address, phone number, and so on.

- **Auto-fill text.** Here's where you enter the text to be auto-filled.

- The **Privacy & security** category has many important settings; see page 310 for the details.

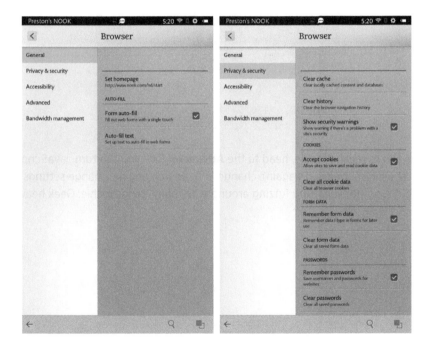

- **Accessibility** covers settings for those who need help seeing what's onscreen. There are options for changing the text size, forcing zoom, and so on.

- If you're feeling techie, head to the **Advanced** tab. You can turn JavaScript off (or turn it back on again), change your search engine, change settings for blocking pop-ups, and futzing around with many things techie. Geek heaven!

- Finally, the **Bandwidth management** section is for when you're on a connection that charges when you use over a certain amount of data. You can change settings for displaying images on web pages (turn them off to save on bandwidth), and for whether to let the browser download pages in the background that you're likely to visit next (turn this setting off to save bandwidth).

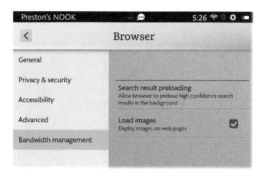

Magazine/Catalog/Comics Reader

These settings control features such as whether to enable live HotSpots on pages, and whether a page should curl or slide when you turn it.

Shop

Here's where to manage your credit card, add a gift card, check your gift card balances, and so on.

Social Accounts and NOOK Friends

Here's where to hop to when you want to link (or unlink) your Facebook and Twitter accounts with your NOOK account.

Reader

This section lets you change a variety of settings, such as how to handle page turns (sliding or curling animation), what dictionary to use, and whether to turn on a two-page display for PDFs when you're reading in landscape mode (holding the NOOK horizontally).

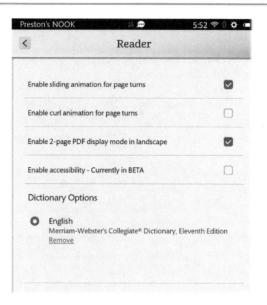

Search

You've got two ways to customize how search works:

- **Searchable items.** Tap here to tell the NOOK what to look for when you perform a search. Choices include the Web, your apps, contacts, your music, your library, and plenty more. If an app is searchable, it shows up here.

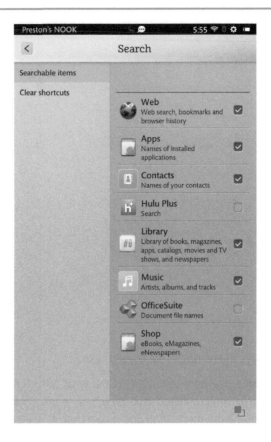

- **Clear shortcuts.** Your NOOK remembers past searches you've performed, and if you start to type the first letters of them in a new search, it will show them so you can choose from them. If you want to clear them out, tap here.

NOOK Video

Not much to set here:

- **Authorized device list.** If you have more than one NOOK that can view NOOK video, you'll see them listed when you tap here. You can unauthorize any when you tap one.

My Apps

This lists all of your apps. Tap any for details about the app, and to manage the app, uninstall it, force it to stop running if it's causing problems, and so on. You'll also see how much data the app is using, and of that data, how much is on the SD card.

Account Settings

This section isn't for the settings on the NOOK itself, but instead for accounts of other services that work with your NOOK. There are two of them:

- **UltraViolet.** UltraViolet is a service that lets you store movies and TV shows in the cloud, and then stream them to multiple devices. The NOOK works with UltraViolet, so if you've got an UltraViolet account, you can stream from it to your NOOK. Tap here to link your account to it.

- **Adobe Digital Editions.** With Adobe Digital Editions, you can borrow books from the library, download them from the Web, and purchase them outside the NOOK Shop, and then copy them to your NOOK. Tap here to do all that.

Storage Management

Do you like charts, graphs, and data? Then you'll love this section. It shows you in great detail your data usage, including how much data you've used and how much you've got free, both on the NOOK's internal storage as well as on its SD card. You can also set whether your default storage should be the NOOK or your SD card. In addition, when the NOOK starts to fill up, it warns you. In the Notification section, tap Internal Storage Capacity, and you can set whether you should get that notification when the NOOK is 75% full, 90% full, or 95% full.

Device Information

Here's where you'll find miscellaneous information about your NOOK HD, ranging from battery life to its model number, to techie details, to legal boilerplate you'll never want to read. There's actually plenty of information here about your NOOK that you may never need to know, although it may sometimes come in handy if you need to get in touch with tech support. It reports on the name and email address of the NOOK's owner, the NOOK's software version, model number, and serial number. There's also something techie called the MAC address. This long, confusing number uniquely identifies the NOOK when it's on the Internet—every Internet-connected device has a unique MAC address. There are a few more things worth calling out.

- **Developer options.** No, you're not a developer. So why would you ever click here? If when you connect your PC to your NOOK, you have problems seeing the NOOK and its files and folders, there may be a fix here. Tap this and from the screen that appears, turn on the checkbox next to "Enable ADB." That might do the trick.

- **Erase & Deregister Device.** Want to nuke your NOOK? Here's where to do
  it. Tap here, and a screen appears that lets you delete all information about
  the NOOK's owner and Barnes & Noble account, and erase all the NOOK's
  content. The books, though, will remain in your Barnes & Noble account, so
  you'll still have access to them. Why would you ever use this feature? If you
  wanted to give your NOOK HD to someone else, you'd erase and deregister
  it, and then the new person can register with her own name.

- **Legal information.** Are you the kind of person who likes to while away the
  hours reading incomprehensible contracts and terms of service? Then Legal
  is the place for you. If you're not a lawyer, you don't want to read this. In
  fact, even if you are a lawyer, you probably don't want to read it.

CHAPTER 18

Rooting Your NOOK

AS YOU'VE FOUND OUT throughout this book, your NOOK HD and NOOK HD+ are much more than just ereaders—they've full-blown tablets that let you browse the Web, read email, keep track of your contacts, watch TV and movies, and download apps that let you do even more.

Both tablets are on Google's Android operating system, which Google gives away for free, letting companies do whatever they want with it. Barnes & Noble used Android 4.0 (also called Ice Cream Sandwich) as the basic operating system for the NOOK HD and NOOK HD+, and then performed some magic and turned them into combination ereaders and Android tablets.

Along the way, Barnes & Noble made so many changes that the NOOK HD and NOOK HD+ don't work like other Android devices in some ways. If you compare the NOOKs to all-purpose Android tablets such as the Motorola XOOM or Samsung Galaxy Tab, you'll notice that the NOOKs simply don't look like other Android tablets. Even though companies like Samsung have made changes to Android, the interface is still recognizable as Android on their tablets. That's not really the case with the NOOKs.

Those changes are more than just skin deep; they're baked into the operating system. Most notably, the only apps you can download onto them are those available through the NOOK Shop. Unlike with other Android tablets, you can't download apps from Google's Android Market or directly from websites. That means there are countless of apps that you can't download.

For those who aren't faint of heart and are willing to get down and dirty with their NOOK, there's a way to turn your NOOK HD or NOOK HD+ into a full-blown Android tablet. It's called *rooting* the device, and essentially it means replacing the NOOK's built-in software with a version that runs Android rather than the software built into the NOOK.

Barnes & Noble frowns on this practice, which is why doing it voids the warranty. And Barnes & Noble does more than frown on it; it also employs ways to make it harder to root the NOOK HD and the NOOK HD+, as you'll see in this chapter. Also, rooting your NOOK could theoretically end up *bricking* it, which is a geeky way of saying it no longer works.

Understanding Rooting

When you root your NOOK, you replace its operating system with a version of Android that lets you install any app you want (via the Android Market), something you can't normally do with the NOOK. When you do that, you give the NOOK the power to do anything that Android can do. On the other hand, you sacrifice the many benefits of the NOOK's operating system, such as the excellent ereader and other built-in apps, although you can always download a version of the NOOK ereading software (see the note on page 186).

The NOOK is based on version 4.0 of the Android operating system. But if you root it, you can install a later version of Android, 4.1, called Jelly Bean.

There are two ways to root your NOOK:

- **Boot your NOOK into Android from a microSD card.** When you use this method, you don't replace the NOOK's operating system with a new one. Instead, you insert a microSD card into the NOOK that has the Android operating system, and run the operating system from there. That way, you don't alter the NOOK in any way. When you want to run the normal NOOK software, just take the microSD card out of the NOOK and restart it.

- **Replace the NOOK's software in its flash memory.** The *flash memory* is the memory built right into the NOOK hardware. When you use this method, you're directly replacing the NOOK's operating system with a version of Android, typically 4.1 Jelly Bean. This voids your warranty. And if you change your mind and want to return your NOOK to its original state, bear in mind that while it's theoretically possible to unroot your NOOK, there's no guarantee that it'll work. As to how you go about unrooting it, at this point your best bet is to search the Web for *unrooting NOOK HD* and hope for the best. In other words, don't count on it.

There are pros and cons to each method of rooting, but most people who want to root their NOOKs are better off using the microSD card method. Here are the facts to consider:

- **Using the microSD method doesn't void your warranty** because you're not altering the NOOK itself. You also don't risk bricking your NOOK.

- **Using the microSD method makes it easy to switch between Android and the NOOK's built-in software.** Boot into Android from a microSD card, and then when you want to use the NOOK's built-in software, take out the card and restart your NOOK.

- **Rooting the NOOK's built-in flash memory makes the NOOK run faster** compared with the microSD method. That's because built-in flash memory is faster than the memory on a microSD card, and so running Android from it is faster.

What You Need to Know about the NOOK Software and Rooting

When the first NOOK came out, it was relatively easy to root. That's because Barnes & Noble didn't notice that people were trying to root the device. By the time the NOOK Tablet and NOOK Color came out, though, Barnes & Noble had taken notice and built anti-rooting technology into the NOOK. No surprise: People found ways to get around it. Anti-rooting features were also built into the NOOK HD and NOOK HD+. Never underestimate the creativity of tinkerers who love mucking around with hardware and software, though, because they soon came up with several different ways to root the NOOK HD and the NOOK HD.

This book doesn't cover in precise detail how to root the NOOK's built-in flash memory. On the Internet, many people have posted ways to root the NOOK's built-in flash memory; however, the instructions are not always clearly explained and don't always work. In addition, they require that you download software and files online, and by the time you read this, those files may no longer exist (and downloading software from a source you don't know is always risky). And every time the NOOK software is updated, the hackers have to start over and find new ways to root it. You can search the Web for *NOOK HD rooting* and see what comes up, but you're taking your chances.

Instead, this chapter focuses on the simpler and safer way of rooting your NOOK HD or NOOK HD—using a microSD card. If you insist on trying to root the NOOK's built-in flash memory, the end of the chapter gives the general steps for rooting your NOOK via this method.

Rooting Your NOOK Temporarily with a microSD Card

As explained at the beginning of this chapter, this method doesn't touch the NOOK's built-in flash memory. Instead, you boot into the Android operating system from a microSD card and run the Android operating from there. When you want to run the NOOK as you would normally, turn the NOOK off, take out the card, and then turn it on again, and you're running the normal NOOK software, with no muss and no fuss.

While it's possible to create your own bootable microSD card to root your NOOK, there's a much simpler solution: Buy a microSD card that already has the software installed on it. You need to buy a microSD card to root your NOOK anyway, and a microSD card with the rooting software already on it doesn't cost much more. The company N2Acards (*www.n2acards.com*) offers a reliable card for the NOOK HD+. The customer service is also exemplary. It's not clear at what point, if ever, a card will be available for the NOOK HD.

The cards range in price from $29.99 to $89.99, depending on the amount of memory. An 8 GB card runs $29.99, a 16 GB card $39.99, a 32 GB card $59.99, and a 64 GB card for $89.99. At some point, there might be separate cards for the NOOK HD and NOOK HD+, so make sure to choose the right one.

TIP When you boot from your microSD card, you also use the card to store your data, so it makes sense to buy a card with plenty of memory up front.

Booting Up from a microSD Card

Once you buy the card, booting up the NOOK from it is a breeze. You follow the same instructions whether you're rooting a NOOK HD or NOOK HD+. Here's what to do:

1. **Turn off your NOOK.**

2. **Insert the microSD card with the rooting software into your NOOK's microSD slot.** For details about how to insert a microSD card into your NOOK, see page 277.

3. **Turn on your NOOK.** After a while, the NOOK boots into Jelly Bean. Voilà—instant Android tablet!

4. **Log into a WiFi network.** To take advantage of your new rooted tablet, you'll want to log into a WiFi network so you can download apps...after all, that's a big part of the reason that you've rooted the NOOK.

Booting into Android, though, is just the start of what you can do. You've got yourself a full-blown Android tablet, and can do pretty much anything you can with a tablet.

Save Money by Downloading and Burning

If you want to save some money, you can buy your own microSD card, and pay for and download a piece of software from N2ACards that will let you burn an image into your microSD card to let it root your NOOK, just as if you bought the whole shebang from N2Acards. You pay $19.99, download the software, and then follow the instructions for burning it into your own microSD card. Then you just follow the previous instructions for booting from an SD card. You won't save a lot of money doing it this way, but you do get that special glow you get from doing something yourself, and a bit of DIY cred.

Using the NOOK as an Android Tablet

After you root your NOOK, you boot into Android. You first see a screen full of apps; tap any to run it. To see more apps, tap an icon to get to a full screen of them. To get more apps, you'll want to go to Google Play, Google's market for apps. Give or take a few, there were more than 600,000 at last count, with many of them free.

TIP For more help using your NOOK as an Android tablet, consider buying *Motorola Xoom: The Missing Manual*. Although that book is specifically for the Motorola Xoom tablet, the Xoom uses a basic Android operating system, similar to what you'll see on the NOOK when you root it, so you may find much of it helpful.

Rooting the Built-in Flash Memory

Rooting the NOOK's built-in flash memory is more problematic than just buying a bootable microSD card. If you plan to do it, head over to *http:// forum.xda-developers.com*, because that's where rooters tend to hang out, and that's where you can search the latest instructions. You can find a specific set of instructions for it at *http://forum.xda-developers.com/showthread. php?t=1981617*. Another good place to check is *http://nookdevs.com/Main_Page*.

Rooting the NOOK's flash memory involves a several-step process. But the devil is in the details, and each of these steps may be a lengthy, several-step process in itself. Make sure when you find instructions that you read any discussions about them, in case people have uncovered problems with them, or have further advice. In general, though, here's what you'll do:

1. **Download software to your PC.**

2. **Use that software to create a disk image on a microSD card.**

3. **Put the microSD card into your NOOK.**

4. **Restart your NOOK and follow the onscreen instructions.**

At that point, you'll have a version of Android running on your NOOK, and you can then use it like an Android tablet, including installing software from the Android Market. Again: Caveat rooter, because you don't know what might happen.

PART VIII

Appendixes

APPENDIX A:
Maintenance and Troubleshooting

APPENDIX B:
File Formats

APPENDIX C:
Visiting B&N with Your NOOK Tablet

Maintenance and Troubleshooting

THEY MAY NOT LOOK like it, but the NOOK HD and NOOK HD+ are at heart computers—computers with a special purpose, but still, computers. And like any computers, they sometimes require special care. This appendix gives you advice on what to do when you run into trouble.

Unfreezing a Frozen NOOK

There may come a time when your NOOK HD may become unresponsive—it may freeze no matter what you do. It's generally easy to fix:

1. **Press the power button, hold it down for 20 seconds, and then release it.** That turns off the NOOK.

2. **Wait a minute and press the power button for 2 seconds.** That turns it back on again. All should be well.

What if your NOOK simply refuses to turn on? It may be that your battery is out of juice, so recharge it. Keep in mind that the battery can be so low that it may take several minutes for it to get enough of a charge to restart. So if you plug it in and it still won't start, go away for several minutes, and then return and restart it.

Fixing SD Card Woes

If you're having trouble with installing the NOOK's SD card, or have had trouble after installation, there are several things you can do.

First, make sure it's the right type of card. The NOOK HD and HD+ handle microSD, microSDHC, and microSDXC cards. MicroSDHC cards are higher capacity than microSD cards, and microSDXC have a higher capacity than microSDHC ones. If you have another type of card, it won't work. The NOOK can handle cards with up to 64 GB capacity.

If you have the right card type, make sure that you've installed it properly and that it isn't loose. (For details about how to install an SD card, see page 277.) Try removing the card and then reinstalling it. After you remove the card, you can reinstall it.

Cleaning Your NOOK's Screen

After all the tapping, touching, and swiping you do, your NOOK's screen will get dirt and grime on it over time. It's a good idea to regularly clean it off, not only so that you can see more clearly, but because if dirt and grime build up, the NOOK might not work properly—it may not respond to taps, or it may think you're tapping it when you're not.

Clean the NOOK's touchscreen with a lint-free, microfiber cleaning cloth. Some cloths for cleaning reading glasses work well on the screen. Make sure that you don't use chemicals, liquids, moisture, or abrasive cloths on the screen, because you could damage the screen or the device itself.

Updating the NOOK's Software

Barnes & Noble regularly updates your NOOK's software without your having to do anything, over your NOOK's WiFi connection. However, it's a good idea to check every once in a while, just to make sure yours has it. From the Home screen, tap the Settings icon in the Status bar and select All Settings→Device Information→ Software version. That shows you the version of the NOOK software you're running. Then tap the "Check for updates" button. Your NOOK checks whether there's an update available, and if there is one, downloads it and installs it.

There's a chance that that won't work, so there's a way for you to manually update it yourself. Also, sometimes Barnes & Noble makes a manual update available before it automatically updates the NOOK via WiFi, so if you absolutely must have the latest update, you can install the update yourself.

First check the version number of your NOOK software, and then see whether Barnes & Noble has a newer version available. To do it:

1. **Check the version number of the software your NOOK is running.** To do it, follow the directions at the beginning of this section to see the version of the NOOK software you have.

2. **Go to the NOOK HD Support page on the Web at** *http://bit.ly/z3rAk7.* If that URL is out of date, go to the Barnes & Noble website, click the NOOK section, and then click the Support link near the top right of the page.

3. **Look for the section of the page that covers your device.** Look for either the NOOK HD or NOOK HD+.

4. **Underneath your device listing, click Software Updates.** You'll see the latest version of the NOOK software listed. If it's the same version as yours, there's no need to do anything else. If it's newer, however, you can manually update your software, as you'll see in the following instructions.

If it turns out that your NOOK software is out of date, you can update the software yourself. Here's what to do:

1. **On the support page for your device, click the + sign next to "Get Version 2.04 Today."** (Of course, the newest version may be more than 2.04 by the time you get there.) Look for the text that says, "Click here for the software update file," and then click it.

2. **Save the file to your computer, and note where you've saved it.** Don't change the name or try to open it. It will be a file in the .zip format.

NOTE Before attempting an update, make sure that your NOOK has a battery charge of at least 20 percent. To check your battery life, tap the Settings icon in the System Tray, and then tap All Settings→Device Information. Towards the bottom of the screen, you'll see how much battery juice you've got left.

---

3. **Connect your NOOK HD to your computer with the 30-pin connector/ USB cable and then drag the .zip file you just downloaded to the main directory of your NOOK's internal storage.** For details about how to connect a NOOK HD to a computer and transfer files, see Chapter 12. Don't create a new folder for it, or rename the file. And don't put it in any other folder or your SD card.

4. **Disconnect your NOOK from your computer.** When your NOOK goes into sleep mode, it will begin the process of installing the update. Make sure not to turn off your NOOK while it's performing the installation.

   When the installation is done, the NOOK will restart, and you're sent to the unlock screen. You'll see an "n" in the Status bar telling you that the update has been successful.

5. **Tap the notification to see the version number of the update, which will match the number you saw on the Web.**

Warranty and Repair

Your NOOK comes with a one-year warranty, for itself as well as for its charger and USB cable. The warranty isn't transferable, so if you give or sell your NOOK to someone, or get it or buy it from someone, the warranty doesn't follow along.

The usual caveats apply to the warranty: If you've misused the device, damaged it by accident, tampered with it, and so on, the warranty is no good any longer.

If the NOOK goes on the blink during the warranty period, and you need Barnes & Noble to take care of it, call 1-800-THE-BOOK (1-800-843-2665) to make your claim. Barnes & Noble will either repair it and send it back to you, or send you a refurbished or new device.

Where to Get Help

If you've got questions about the NOOK, there are several places you can turn. Start off at the Barnes & Noble website, in the Support area for the NOOK HD or NOOK HD+. From the *www.bn.com* website, click NOOK, and from the page you get to, click the Support link toward the top of the page. On the page you come to, underneath the NOOK HD and NOOK HD+, you'll see links to frequently asked questions and video tutorials. Click either of them and see if there are answers to your questions. In the frequently asked questions area, you can also search for answers. There's also a chat link on the page; click it to chat with tech support.

There are also other useful places on the Web to go to:

- **B&N Community (***http://bookclubs.barnesandnoble.com/***)**. This Barnes & Noble community area has discussion forums devoted to the NOOK HD, NOOK Color, and other versions of the NOOK. Check out the discussions, and post any questions you have.

- **nookTalk (***www.nooktalk.net***)**. This site has news, tutorials, and forums where NOOK owners discuss problems and solutions. You can post questions here, as well as look for others who have solved your problem.

- **AndroidTablets.net (***www.androidtablets.net/forum/nook/***)**. This site, devoted to Android tablets, has forums devoted to the NOOK HD and NOOK HD+.

NOOK Accessories

There are plenty of accessories to help you get the most out of your NOOK HD and NOOK Color. In most instances, the same accessory will work with both devices, but it's always a good idea to check before buying, especially because some will work with a NOOK HD, but not a NOOK Color.

A good place to get them is from the NOOK Accessories area of the NOOK section on the Barnes & Noble website; get to it at *http://bit.ly/zv5GeF*. (If that URL doesn't work, go to *www.bn.com*, click the NOOK heading, and then look for the NOOK Shop; click it and head to the Accessories area.) You can also buy many accessories at the NOOK area in any Barnes & Noble store.

The accessory you'll probably want most is a cover to protect the NOOK and its screen. There are plenty of kinds from which to choose. You'll also find chargers, USB cables, reading stands, car-charging kits, and SD cards. For SD cards, you may be better off buying at an online electronics store such as *www.newegg.com*, because the cost and selection can be better than at the Barnes & Noble website. If you want to avoid scratching the NOOK screen, pick up a transparent screen protector.

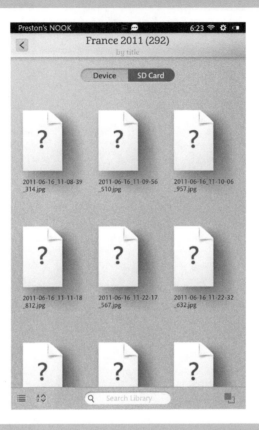

File Formats

THE NOOK IS MORE than just an ereader; it's also a general-purpose tablet that can play media files, let you read Microsoft Office documents, and more. Here's a list of the file types it can handle:

Book Files, Microsoft Office Files, and Multimedia Files

EPUB (the main book format for the NOOK)

PDF

DRP

ePIB

FOLIO

OFIP

.rtf

Word (.doc, .docx, .docm, .dotx, .dotm)

Excel (.xls, .xlsx, .xlsm, .xltx, .xltm)

PowerPoint (.ppt, .pptx, .pptm, .pps, .ppsx, .ppsm, .pot. potx, .potm)

Plain text (.txt)

HTML (.htm, .html, .xhtml)

Comic book archive (.cbz)

.zip

.LOG

.csv

.eml

Music Files

.aac

.amr

.flac

.mp3

.mp4

.mp4a

.ogg

.wav

.3gp

Picture and Photo Files

.jpg

.gif

.png

.bmp

Video Files

.3gp

.mp4

.webm

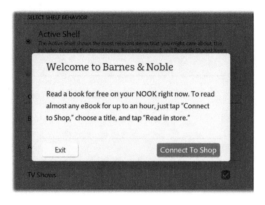

Visiting B&N with Your NOOK Tablet

YOU'LL FIND IT WORTH your while to visit a Barnes & Noble store with your NOOK, because when you do that, you get extras, notably the ability to read many NOOK books for free for an hour.

When you go into a Barnes & Noble store, your NOOK automatically finds the store's WiFi network and connects to it. For this to work, of course, WiFi needs to be turned on; for details, see page 29.

When you're in the store, turn on your NOOK; a screen appears with a Connect to Shop button on it. Click that and then follow the directions for finding any special offers or browsing for books to read for free. From there, you'll be connected right away to the NOOK Shop. If there are no special offers, you'll instead be connected directly to the NOOK Shop.

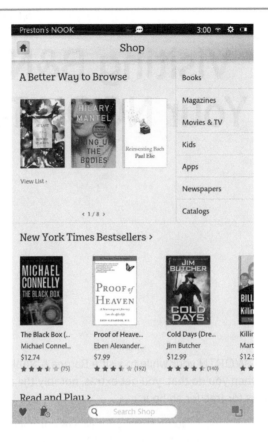

If the screen doesn't appear, or if you move away from the screen and can't get back to it, don't despair; you can still easily find books to read for free. In the NOOK Shop, browse as you would normally. You'll notice a new sash across most if not all of the books you find—Read in Store. Tap the book and you'll see the usual details page, with one addition—a Read In-Store option.

Tap the button, and you'll get a notification that you can read the book for free for an hour. The book downloads to your NOOK; a blue bar shows the download progress. When the blue bar stretches all the way across, the Read button turns blue. Tap it. For the next hour, as long as you stay in the store, you can read the book using all the normal NOOK reading features. After that, you'll no longer be able to read it. You can also buy the book by tapping the Buy Now button at the top of the screen.

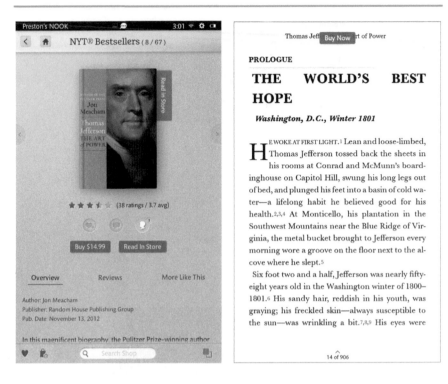

After an hour, a screen appears, telling you that your time is up. At that point, you can buy the book, add it to your wish list, or simply stop reading.

Index

NOOK HD

THE MISSING CD

There's no CD with this book; you just saved $5.00.

Instead, every single Web address, practice file, and piece of downloadable software mentioned in this book is available at *missingmanuals.com* (click the Missing CD icon). There you'll find a tidy list of links, organized by chapter.

Don't miss a thing!
Sign up for the free Missing Manual email announcement list at missingmanuals.com. We'll let you know when we release new titles, make free sample chapters available, and update the features and articles on the Missing Manual website.

Have it your way.

O'Reilly eBooks

- Lifetime access to the book when you buy through oreilly.com
- Provided in up to four DRM-free file formats, for use on the devices of your choice: PDF, .epub, Kindle-compatible .mobi, and Android .apk
- Fully searchable, with copy-and-paste and print functionality
- Alerts when files are updated with corrections and additions

oreilly.com/ebooks/

Safari Books Online

- Access the contents and quickly search over 7000 books on technology, business, and certification guides
- Learn from expert video tutorials, and explore thousands of hours of video on technology and design topics
- Download whole books or chapters in PDF format, at no extra cost, to print or read on the go
- Get early access to books as they're being written
- Interact directly with authors of upcoming books
- Save up to 35% on O'Reilly print books

See the complete Safari Library at safari.oreilly.com

Get even more for your money.

Join the O'Reilly Community, and register the O'Reilly books you own. It's free, and you'll get:

- $4.99 ebook upgrade offer
- 40% upgrade offer on O'Reilly print books
- Membership discounts on books and events
- Free lifetime updates to ebooks and videos
- Multiple ebook formats, DRM FREE
- Participation in the O'Reilly community
- Newsletters
- Account management
- 100% Satisfaction Guarantee

Signing up is easy:

1. **Go to: oreilly.com/go/register**
2. **Create an O'Reilly login.**
3. **Provide your address.**
4. **Register your books.**

Note: English-language books only

To order books online:

oreilly.com/store

For questions about products or an order:

orders@oreilly.com

To sign up to get topic-specific email announcements and/or news about upcoming books, conferences, special offers, and new technologies:

elists@oreilly.com

For technical questions about book content:

booktech@oreilly.com

To submit new book proposals to our editors:

proposals@oreilly.com

O'Reilly books are available in multiple DRM-free ebook formats. For more information:

oreilly.com/ebooks

Spreading the knowledge of innovators   oreilly.com

CPSIA informati
Printed in the US
LVOW01091409

342013LV

31449 359539